Global Mobile Media

With billions of users worldwide, the cell phone is not only a successful communications technology: it is also key to the future of media. *Global Mobile Media* offers an overview of the complex topic of mobile media, looking at the emerging industry structures, new media economies, mobile media cultures and network politics of cell phones as they move centre stage in media industries.

The development, adoption and significance of cell phones for society and culture have been registered in a growing body of work. Where existing books have focused on communication, and on the social and cultural aspects of mobile media, *Global Mobile Media* looks at the media dimensions. Goggin provides a pioneering yet measured evaluation of how cell phone corporations, media interests, users and policy makers are together shaping a new media dispensation.

Global Mobile Media successfully places new mobile media historically, socially and culturally in a wider field of portable media technologies through extensive case studies, including:

- the rise of smartphones, with a detailed discussion of the Apple iPhone and how it has catalysed a new phase in convergent media, audiences and innovation;
- the new agenda in cultural politics and media policy, featuring topics such as iPhone apps and control, mobile commons and open mobile networks;
- a succinct map of the political economy of mobile media, identifying key players, patterns of ownership and control, institutions and issues;
- a critical account of cell phones' involvement in and contribution to much discussed new forms of production and consumption, such as user-generated content, p2p networks, open and free source software networks;
- an anatomy of how cell phones relate to other online media, particularly the internet and wireless technologies.

Global Mobile Media is an engaging, accessible text which will be of immense interest to upper-level undergraduates, postgraduates and researchers in communication studies, cultural studies and media studies, as well as those taking new media courses.

Gerard Goggin is Professor of Digital Communication in the Journalism and Media Research Centre, University of New South Wales, Australia. His research interests focus on mobile media, internet, disability, media history and policy. Previous publications include *Internationalizing Internet Studies* (2009), *Mobile Technologies: From Telecommunications to Media* (with Larissa Hjorth, 2009), *Mobile Phone Cultures* (2008), *Mobile Media* (with Larissa Hjorth, 2007), *Cell Phone Culture* (2006) and *Digital Disability* (2003).

Global Mobile Media

Gerard Goggin

 Routledge
Taylor & Francis Group

LONDON AND NEW YORK

First published 2011
by Routledge
2 Park Square, Milton Park, Abingdon, Oxon, OX14 4RN

Simultaneously published in the USA and Canada
by Routledge
270 Madison Ave, New York, NY 10016

Routledge is an imprint of the Taylor & Francis Group, an informa business

© 2011 Gerard Goggin

Typeset in Baskerville by Taylor & Francis Books
Printed and bound in Great Britain by TJ International Ltd, Padstow, Cornwall

British Library Cataloguing in Publication Data
A catalogue record for this book is available from the British Library

Library of Congress Cataloging in Publication Data
Goggin, Gerard, 1964–
 Global mobile media / Gerard Goggin.
  p. cm.
 Includes bibliographical references and index.
 1. Multimedia communications. 2. Mobile communication systems.
3. Mobile computing. I. Title.
 TK5105.15.G64 2011
 303.48'33–dc22
                2010012111

ISBN13: 978-0-415-46917-3 (hbk)
ISBN13: 978-0-415-46918-0 (pbk)
ISBN13: 978-0-203-84280-5 (ebk)

For Jacqueline

Contents

Tables and figures

Tables

Figures

Acknowledgements

The debts incurred in the writing of this book are many. Firstly, I wish to thank the Australian Research Council for the Australian Research Fellowship, 2004–9, that funded the research and writing of this book (*Mobile Culture: A Biography of the Mobile Phone*, DP 0453023). Secondly, I gratefully acknowledge the support of the University of New South Wales; the Dean of the Faculty of Arts and Social Sciences, Professor James Donald; and my colleagues in the Journalism and Media Research Centre, especially my colleague in things mobile, Kate Crawford. Alice Crawford and Ryan Sengara provided excellent research assistance. Thirdly, I would like to thank Natalie Foster, my gracious and thoughtful editor at Routledge, and her colleagues for their patience and improvements to the manuscript.

The context for this work has very much been a collaborative, social, cosmopolitan experience shaped by formative encounters with many inspiring scholars around the world, especially Leopoldina Fortunati, Rich Ling, James Katz, Juan Miguel Aguado, Inmaculada J. Martínez, Jack Qiu, Kristof Nyíri, Jonathan Donner, Shin Dong Kim, Genevieve Bell, Mark McLelland, Claudio Feijóo and Leslie Haddon. Larissa Hjorth deserves a special mention, as a brilliant, generous and tolerant collaborator and friend, with our jointly organized *Mobile Media* conference at the University of Sydney, July 2006, being a highpoint, not least for allowing us to meet so many colleagues from around the world. The many other projects Larissa and I have worked upon, especially our 2009 collection *Mobile Technologies*, as well as her own outstanding work, have been especially influential upon me.

I have gained a great deal from feedback from presentations on this work at various conferences and seminars in many places including: Hungarian Academy of Sciences, Budapest; Universidad de Murcia; Monash University; the International Association of Media and Communication Research conference, Universidad Nacional Autónoma de México, 2009; the annual conferences of the Australian and New Zealand Communications Association; Rutgers University. My thanks to Dr Susan Ballyn and the Centre d'Estudis Australians, Universidad de Barcelona, for a visiting professorship in 2007 that proved especially stimulating for the project.

My thinking has also been shaped from participation in various publications. Earlier versions of parts of this book have been published as: 'El «desarollo atrofiado» de la cultura móvil: el extraño caso de los contenidos móviles', in Juan Miguel Aguado and Inmaculada J. Martínez (eds) *Sociedad Móvil: Tecnología, Identidad y Cultura*, Madrid: Biblioteca Nueva, 2008, 215–30; 'Mobiles becoming media', in Kristof Nyíri (ed.) *Towards a Philosophy of Telecommunications Convergence*, Vienna: Passagen Verlag, 2008, 205–12; 'Mobile digital television: *Dancing with the Stars*, or dancing in the dark?', in Andrew T. Kenyon (ed) *TV Futures: Digital Television Policy in Australia*, Melbourne: Melbourne University Press, 2007, 27–53; 'Adapting the mobile phone: the iPhone and its consumption'. *Continuum: Journal of Media and Cultural Studies* 23 (2009): 231–44; 'Assembling media culture: the case of mobiles', *Journal of Cultural Economy* 2 (2009): 151–67; 'Geomobile web: locative technologies and mobile media' (with Alice Crawford), *Australian Journal of Communication*, 36 (2009): 97–109; 'The models and politics of mobile media', *Fibreculture Journal*, 12 (2008), http://journal.fibreculture.org/issue12/issue12_goggin.html (accessed on 5 May 2010); 'Regulating mobile content: convergences and citizenship', *International Journal of Communications Law and Policy*, 12 (2008): 141–60; 'An Australian wireless commons?', *Media International Australia* 125 (2007): 118–30. I am indebted to the editors and contributors of these projects for extending my ideas regarding mobile media.

Finally, and foremost, my deepest thanks as always go to my wonderful lover and partner, Jacqueline Clark, whose patience, humour, generosity and intelligence have sustained me, as have the unconditional love and marvellous lives of our children, Liam and Bianca.

Gerard Goggin
Journalism and Media Research Centre
University of New South Wales, Sydney
April 2010

Abbreviations

CDMA	code division multiple access (digital transmission system)
EV-DO	Evolution, data optimized (or 'only'), a wireless high-speed broadband standard
FCC	Federal Communications Commission
1G	first generation (analogue mobile system)
4G	fourth generation (digital cellular mobile system)
GSM	global system for mobiles (originally Groupe Spécial Mobile)
IMT-2000	International mobile telecommunications, a group of standards for 3G mobiles
ITU	International Telecommunications Union
MMS	multimedia message service
PDA	portable digital assistant
PSTN	public switched telecommunications network
SIM	subscriber information module (card)
SMS	short message service
2.5G	second and a half generation (digital cellular mobile system)
3G	third generation (digital cellular mobile system)
TDMA	time division multiple access (digital transmission system)
Wi-Fi	wireless location area technology, based on IEEE 802.11 standards, used widely in households and public places for internet access
Wi-Max	Worldwide Interoperability for Wireless Access, successor technology to Wi-Fi

Permissions

All tables and figures have been reproduced with kind permission. Whilst every effort has been made to trace copyright holders and obtain permission, this has not been possible in all cases. Any omissions brought to our attention will be remedied in future editions.

Tables 2.1 and 2.6

The data in these tables is sourced from OECD (Organisation of Economic Co-operation and Development) material, and has been reproduced with kind permission from OECD.

Tables 2.2, 2.3, 2.4 and 2.5

The data in these tables is sourced from ITU (International Telecommunication Union) material, and has been reproduced with kind permission from ITU.

Figure 7.2

This photo has been taken from the flickr page for Dennis Crowley, the founder of dodgeball.com, and is reproduced here under a Creative Commons license.

Chapter 1

Introduction

Cell phones as global media

In late 2008, the International Telecommunications Union (ITU) declared that the number of cell phone connections in the world had passed the four billion mark (GSM World 2009). In 2010, the figure will soon exceed five billion subscribers. Driving this growth are countries like Brazil, Russia, India and China, with their momentous economic and social changes. Also responsible for the rise and rise of the cell phone are those living in smaller, poor, developing countries, and indeed across continents such as Africa, where the technology is finding not only new users, but new uses too. In Europe, the US, Canada and the Asia-Pacific, subscribers have embraced the cell phone even more intensely. Already taken-for-granted the cell phone comes with a welter of new applications, and has achieved an even more prominent place in commerce, work, intimacy, family, social networking, culture and politics. In the second decade of the twenty-first century, the remarkably plastic technology of the cell phone continues its seemingly unstoppable career – emerging largely unscathed even from the prolonged and profound world financial crisis that hit in 2008.

In Japan, people read cell phone novels on the way to work. In Tanzania, a farmer finds out market information, and sells produce with his phone. In Bangladesh, the famous 'phone ladies' of the GrameenPhone provide a communications service for all and sundry. In Seoul, avid social networkers upload photos and updates on their mini-hompy. In the US, Iran and many other countries, friends, colleagues and celebrities micro-blog with Twitter. In Belarus an underground theatre company performs its plays in people's houses, and other clandestine venues, and audience members are contacted by cell phone to let them know details of where the night's performance will be. In the city of Barcelona three North African immigrants listen to music on their cell phones, swapping tracks via Bluetooth. In Australia, avid fans follow the cricket on mobile television. In trains, planes and automobiles, people watch short video, and downloaded programs on their handsets. Pretty much everywhere people take photos with their cell phones, and show them to their friends, families and colleagues – or message the images on, and upload them to their blogs or photosharing site. Devotees brandish their iPhone like a Nintendo Wii, playing a bowling game, or revelling in the download of yet another application.

Walking or driving, people in motion navigate with their various mobile location technologies, whether SatNav, Google Maps or mobile location finders. Standing out front of a store, a would-be customer receives an ad on their phone. People wake up to text messages from their lovers, and fall asleep bathed in the consoling blue light of the console, beeping to signal the arrival of another communiqué.

Mobiles as global media

These are a few vignettes to evoke the rich and prosaic, complicated and everyday facets of mobile media. In my 2006 book *Cell Phone Culture*, I sought to provide a biography of the cell phone to that point in time. Many of the features of this new culture of cell phones still hold. However, the scale, complexity and depth of the imbrication of cell phones in contemporary society requires a different perspective. The approach that I have chosen is to look at cell phones as a species of global media. There are four main reasons why I think it is important to undertake an inquiry into mobile media.

First, the cellular mobile phone has moved beyond being a communications technology, in a way that is still recognizably an evolution from the telephone. From at least 2001 onwards, the mobile has been imagined, discussed and shaped as a form of media. By the middle of the decade in 2005, media industries were regarding mobiles as an integral part of cross-platform media businesses (Groebel et al. 2006). Old and new media, entertainment and communications companies were increasingly taking a stake in mobile companies, mobile content and media ventures, and were creating or modifying programmes and materials for delivery on more and more advanced mobile handsets. This was a period when camera phone culture became well and truly entrenched, mobile television emerged worldwide, and cell phones became used in tandem with YouTube and other video-sharing internet architectures to create new forms of audio and televisual experience. In the process cell phones became a serious part of mainstream media business, policy, social life and public debate.

Second, thinking about cellular phones as media is a useful move for trying to comprehend the changes they bring to established ideas of how different communication and media technologies relate to each other, and how they connect with the social. My focus on mobile media is not just about large-scale corporate attempts to fashion recognizable forms of television for small screen viewing. It is about the durability and inventiveness of very basic forms of mobile culture as they become media: text messaging as low-cost mobile media in India; local mobile news for communities in Kenya; user–producers using media capabilities of phones to create their own content, and distribute via the internet. There are new uses of cell phones that question and extend our typical understandings of media: the role of cell phones in community development; as crucial to small, micro and medium enterprise; the importance of mobiles for healthcare (for instance, notification of newly discovered HIV–AIDs status to a person's partners); and, not least, the way that cell phones redraw the boundaries between private, intimate communications and media, and larger public under-standings and expectations. Many of these transformations are neither solely due to, nor the exclusive province of, cell phones – but the technology plays an indispensable role in them.

Third, as handsets are shipped with media and internet features, computing, handheld and portable media devices are taking on capabilities formerly restricted to the world of telecommunications. Microsoft's Zune, Apple's iPhone, Google's Android, Research in Motion's Blackberry, not to mention voice and video over Internet Protocol on laptops are all examples of technologies from the world of computing and internet that have been adapted to incorporate elements of cell phones. What are these things? And what has happened to the object we call the cell phone as it has had a metamorphosis into media? What are the relationships between cellular mobile networks and the panopoly of affiliated reconfigured networks? For instance, the circuit-switched fixed-line telecommunications networks moving to Internet Protocol-based networks; the wireless networks, whether corporate or home Wi-Fi, or new Wi-Max networks; television networks, being reworked through digital broadcasting; radio networks, and digital audio broadcasting initiatives; satellite networks (still important, if not widely used by consumers); private networks, of corporations, governments, or educational institutions; the ad-hoc networks created through transient, local Bluetooth connections.

Fourth, what is the relationship between the cell phone as media, and other forms of media, whether older forms such as television, radio, newspapers and publishing, or newer forms such as internet and games? If mobile media is starting to be taken seriously by consumers and producers, and is emerging as an important part of culture and society, what are the implications for the traditional ways we understand the role of media? What is the role of cell phones in media diversity, long regarded as the *sine qua non* of citizenship and democracy? Are new audiences and publics being created with mobile media? Where do cell phones fit into new approaches to media, such as ideas about innovation and creativity? What are the implications of the salience of cell phones in media for how we formulate and tackle questions of access and participation? What, finally, of the pressing questions that cell phones raise for policy and public debate, calling for urgent debate and fresh models associated with intellectual property, privacy, content regulation and cultural and media policy?

Updating global media

Cell phones are an exemplary global technology, as their worldwide diffusion suggests (Castells et al. 2007; Edgerton 2007; Law, Fortunati and Yang 2006). The field of mobile studies is flourishing, with many helpful accounts now available.

A strong focus among many recent accounts, seeking to advance social and scientific knowledge, is particularly on understanding mobile communication (Haddon and Green 2010; Katz 2008; Koskinen 2007; Ling and Donner 2009; Qiu 2009). How does mobile communication differ from other forms of communication? What are its typical contexts and characteristics? How does study of the emerging, even novel, aspects of mobile communication deepen our understanding of human communication theories? While mindful of these new theories of mobile communication, and hoping to contribute to such debates, my focus in this book is upon mediated communication. That is, I approach mobile communication with a particular interest in how it is transforming media.

Thus what I hope to add to the understanding of cell phones is twofold: firstly, I hope to provide a comprehensive account of the cell phone as media; secondly, I wish to highlight the importance of a global approach to mobile media. My rule of relevance is how various incarnations of mobile media relate to the cellular mobile phone. Thus my starting point, and main focus, is the cellular mobile phone, its networks, dedicated applications, affordances (Gibson 1977 and 1979) and cultures of use. I am interested to show how the cell phone developed to encompass various forms of media, whether mobile internet, mobile games or mobile television, or uses of mobile technology for reinventing place or community. While I fully recognize that the cell phone is entangled in – and constitutive of – a larger, messier media and communication ecology, I am interested in looking at media convergence from the point of view of cell phones. Thus I look at how cell phones are being disassembled and then reassembled into these new digital, networked systems, that have been the subject of so much attention. My attention will be directed to how other media systems are interacting with cellular mobiles; the interzones, borders, exchange and trading places, and new domains of innovation among mobiles and internet, mobile networks and Wi-Fi; the adaptation and transformation of the cell phone into the new objects of smartphones, iPhones and open source phones; the new policy debates that straddle and cross-fertilize the traditional agenda associated with telecommunications and cell phones, on the one hand, and those of press, publishing and broadcasting, on the other.

As I hope to show, cell phones need to be understood as an important part of the contemporary global media system. Yet, as is also the case, local settings, including the national, are very much key to how media do their public and private work (Goff 2007). There is a substantial literature, which places local, national and regional media in a global framework (Balnaves, Donald and Donald 2001; Cunningham and Sinclair 1994; Demers 2002; Flew 2007; Gerbner et al. 1993; Hackett and Zhao 2005; Herman and McChesney 1997; Machin and van Leeuwen 2007; McPhail 2010; Miller et al. 2005; Murphy and Kraidy 2003; Raboy 2002; White 2005). The strength of this literature is that it does seek to comprehend media in a global context, and to identify the particular global forms, structures and organization of media. While different approaches are adopted to the investigation of global media, the political economy approach has dominated (Babe 1995 and 2009). It has sometimes been criticized for taking a monolithic approach to media – focusing too much on the imperialism or dominance of particular countries (especially the US) in media – at the expense of adequately characterizing the complex relations between culture and economy, something that has been a great topos of the debate between political economists and exponents of creative industries (for instance, see Cunningham 2008; Flew 2009; Flew and Cunningham 2010; Garnham 2005; Miller 2002 and 2009). Global media approaches have also been faulted for lack of subtlety in capturing the relationships among national or international actors, the interplay of the global and local captured in theories of 'glocalization', 'hybridity', or even the intercultural and cross-cultural. While acknowledging these debates, and hoping to do justice to the combination of different factors, I believe that it is productive to undertake a treatment of global mobile media. We still know little of what is distinctive about cell phones as media; how they fit into global media generally; and how, when we consider this seriously, the inclusion of cellular phones changes our understanding of global media, its structures and implications.

My starting point is the political economy of cell phones. There exists quite a literature on the economics and policy aspects of cell phones, but still little that focuses on the political economy of mobile media (for a fine exception on mobiles and advertising, see Wilken and Sinclair 2009a and b). There is an evergreen body of work on political economy of media, and even newer media such as the internet (Mosco 2004; Schiller 1999 and 2007), but as yet this approach has not been extended systematically to mobile media. I draw upon the tradition of political economy of telecommunications in the 1990s, with its fine studies undertaken by Robin Mansell (1993), Jill Hills (1986, 2002 and 2007), Vincent Mosco (1982, 2004 and 2009), Dwayne Winseck (1998) and others, and set out to investigate forms of power as they are unfolding in mobile media.

To investigate how mobile media are placed at the transactions between culture and economy, I also offer a preliminary exploration of the cultural economy of mobile media. There seem to me to be two closely interrelated and mutually constitutive parts to understanding the media–political nature of cell phones: an economy that needs to be grasped as both political and cultural. The benefit of thinking about the cultural economy of mobile media is that it immediately brings into relief the large and pressing questions of cultural politics today and into the future: participation and culture; cultural policy; innovation; the figure, powers and limits of the user; cultural citizenship; the commodification and controls of ideas and intellectual property; and how to design cultural technologies for democracies. My approach to cultural economy is an eclectic one, drawing across various traditions in the area (Anheier et al. 2008).

Elsewhere the book's design and itineraries are very much influenced by the desire to take a *media* approach to cell phones, so drawing upon the work of various media studies traditions and writers – especially those concerned with new media (such as Bruns 2008; Burgess and Green 2009; Hjorth 2009;

Lovink 2008). Also, however, I am especially interested in theorizing media as *technology*, so I am informed by theories of social studies of science and technology (Brown 2009; Flichy 2007; Latour 1996 and 2005b). A further thread through the book relates to policy studies; at various times I draw upon work in tele-communications and media policy and regulation in particular, but also new work and concepts generated around the movements associated with the commons and open source software (Deek and McHugh 2008; Feller et al. 2005).

A roadmap of mobile media

Ahead of the itinerary of the book, first a note on terminology. My main focus is upon media based upon cellular mobile telecommunications technologies, with their associated handsets and other devices, manifold applications, technologies, organization forms, and institutions. By 'mobile media' I principally mean the types of media that are based on cellular mobile phones, devices and networks. However, I am also aware of a range of other potential 'mobile' – or indeed 'portable' media – from radios, newspapers, and books to game consoles and handhelds, portable digital assistants, e-books and e-readers and laptops. So as the book proceeds, I discuss other kinds of non-cellular mobile media, especially as they vie with, connect to and form hybrids with their cellular counterparts. While 'wireless' is a term that can refer to cellular mobiles – especially in North America – I use it to mean a range of standards and technologies associated with other networks (notably Wi-Fi networks that many people use to connect to the internet in home, offices, airports, hotels, cafés, or public spaces). Again, these kinds of wireless networks are very much involved in a process of convergence with their cellular counterparts – so they very much feature as dramatis personae of this story. With all the array of technologies encountered in the book, I hope the reader will bear with me as I try not to dwell overly on the technical details – simply giving the essential characterization as clearly and economically as I am able.

The book falls into three parts. Part I, 'Cell phones and the new media economies', sets the scene, outlining the key features of the production and consumption of mobile media, and how these are intertwined. In Chapter 2, 'Power and mobile media', I aim to sketch the key facets of power in mobile media, as it is shaped especially by patterns of corporate ownership, control and cultures. The chapter opens with a discussion of telecommunications and cell phone carriers. With a focus on regional multinationalism, it provides short case studies of new kinds of carriers significant in the development of mobile media, such as the Hong Kong based '3' (Hutchison Whampoa), China Mobile and the Mexican giant América Móvil. Then I discuss some new kinds of companies providing application and content for cell phones. Here there are a bewildering array of businesses, from very small start-ups or niche companies, to large media and entertainment companies. Next I discuss cellular handset and equipment manufacturers, considering the long-standing dominant firms, emergent competitors, those promoting new technologies (from smartphones to e-readers) and the rise of informal 'copycat' production of cell phones in countries like China. The third section looks at the dynamic area of mobile content, services and applications, where new firms and cultural intermediaries have emerged, very much pioneering the first established, profitable forms of mobile media. After a brief consideration of computer and internet interests moving into mobile media, I explore the emerging network infrastructures, such as the rapid rise of mobile broadband, the cross-overs between cell phones and wireless, WiMax, fourth generation cell phone handset (4G), and internet protocol based next generation networks, which promise to fundamentally reshape the nature of boundaries of cellular mobile networks.

In Chapter 3, 'Cultural economy of cell phones', I shift focus to considering consumption of mobile media, and how this is closely linked to – and indeed altering – what we understand by production. First, I look at what we know about who consumes and use what kinds of mobile media, where and how. Second, I discuss the valorization of consumption, and the creative role of the consumer in shaping, indeed co-producing, technologies. New forms of participative culture have emerged, notably in gaming, but mobile media also has its own distinctive forms of creative consumption that need to scrutinized. Third, I look at the area of 'user-generated content', which has rapidly emerged as a strategically important area in internet cultures. In one sense the forms of user-generated content allied with mobile media have been more easily captured for revenue because of telecommunications billing systems, or through the wholesale and retail merchandising and sales chains of handsets and accessories (upon which are based user customization of cell phones); on the other hand, the kinds of new cultural activity of mobile media, in which users are key, have not yet been registered.

Having introduced some key features of the political and cultural economy of global mobile media, in Part II I offer four case studies. Chapter 4 is devoted to the growth and nature of mobile music, and the kinds of forms, business and imaginaries that have underpinned this. The chapter opens with a brief history of sound and music in the development of telephones and telecommunications, then looks at the first and still very lucrative form of mobile music: ringtones. From ringtones, we move to the development of cellular handsets as portable music players, vying with the Sony Walkman, MP3 players and iPods, and then discuss the transformation of cell phones into music stores. Once 'cell phones' were established as popular devices for purchasing, collecting and storing music, their status and potential as a distinctive technology for sharing this important cultural activity and artifact came into stark relief. After tracing the technologies of sharing developed by mobile media entrepreneurs and companies, in the final section of Chapter 4 I take up the topic of making music – something that offers revealing insights on the constraints and possibilities of mobile media networks.

The changing shape of broadcasting and the politics of audiovisual material is the subject of Chapter 5, 'The mobile invention of television'. The chapter begins by reviewing the development of mobile television in its first five years, and considering what characterizes it as a media form, and how it has been received by its audiences. The difficulty of firmly establishing mobile television has in no small part resided in competing standards, which vary across countries and regions, and the trajectory of the previous media form (television, radio or computing). The welter of standards has not made the job of policymakers and regulators any easier, but here again they have lacked enthusiasm, motivation and clarity to carve out a place for mobile television. From standards and policy, I proceed to discuss mobile television cultures, where we encounter the most striking feature of the strange career of this media form: namely, that it is morphing from an 'official' mobile television, constructed by an alliance of carriers and broadcasters into a kaleidoscope of 'unofficial' do-it-yourself televisions, courtesy of video sharing sites and technologies, and the velocity and pull of social media.

In Chapter 6, 'Mobile gaming', I discuss the relatively new media form – if ancient social and cultural practice – of games. First, I sketch a history of mobile gaming, from its humble beginning with rudimentary games such as the Nokia snake game. Second, I look at the various initiatives cellular companies, entertainment providers and game developers have undertaken to offer a distinctive cell phone gaming experience, and discuss the mainly lukewarm user response to date. This contrasts, third, with the many ludic uses of mobile and wireless technologies created by artists, educators and others, especially around locative media, and in hybrid and alternative reality games, that have generated a great deal of excitement and possibility.

In Chapter 7, 'Mobile internet', we encounter perhaps the most significant contemporary area of mobile media. No longer associated with the slow speeds and tiny screens of early mobile internet experience, the connections between cell phones and the internet produce distinctive new forms of global mobile media that take many and various guises. I commence with mobile social software, a relatively early development that has taken some years to be widely used – and which now, of course, is undergoing a tidal wave of user enthusiasm and industry development, because of the general turn to social media. Mobile media platforms are very much engaged in, and defining, these logics, as the case of Twitter shows, and also the 'Facebook moment'. From social software on cell phones, I turn in the second half of Chapter 7 to consider the way that mobile internet is being shaped by a vast new groups of users – those who live in the 'global South' (often referred to, no less problematically, as the developing countries). Here I discuss the initiatives to fashion the mobile web for development, as well as the innovative uses and imaginaries of the mobile internet emerging in societies where the cell phone *is* the first means by which many users experience the internet.

Following these four case studies of mobile music, television, gaming and internet respectively, Part III delves into the overarching issues that go to the heart of the politics of mobile media networks. I do this through a discussion of the technology that in the minds of many has fundamentally changed the world of cell phones: Apple's fabled iPhone. In Chapter 8, 'The computer, the internet and the cell phone', I show that the grand claims accompanying the iPhone have been both true and false. I review the development of the iPhone, and its rapturous reception upon launch. I discuss how the much vaunted design and emphasis on the iPhone's new kind of touch fall well short of revolution when it comes to users with disability. From the disabling face of the iPhone, I move to the phenomenon of iPhone apps, which have galvanized the languishing smartphone market – but which have, more importantly, highlighted the cultural potential of mobile media networks. Finally, I consider the significance of the widespread modification of the iPhone, something that opens up into a general discussion of software, licensed, free and open source, among the iPhone, Google's Android, BlackBerry and other kindred devices.

In Chapter 9, 'The mobile commons?', I take up the concept of the commons to see what light it casts on the politics of cell phone networks – especially the ideals of open network cultures in which mobile media now play a strategically critical role. However, as I shall argue, drawing on the work of a range of thinkers, the idea of the commons when it comes to mobile media is suggestive but also has significant problems. Thus having sketched an idea of mobile commons, I note its limits and move instead to a consideration of mobile publics. In doing so, my argument is that we need to move well beyond commons, to draw upon ideas in the heritage of telecommunications as well as unfolding cultures of mobile media – in order to develop an unconstrained idea of open, mobile, networked cultures.

It is the vision of open mobile networks that I elaborate upon in the conclusion to the book in Chapter 10, 'Culture garden'. I suggest that we now need to seize upon a pivotal moment to imagine, devise, design and safeguard this vital area of contemporary digital culture and technology. There is an interplay of commercial and non-commercial forces and spaces that we need to map, work with and regulate to make our mobile media networks the rich, fertile places they stand to be. This culminating argument of the book is that the development of such visions, and debates, about the possibilities of mobile media deserves much more centrality, on a par with those concerning the internet, than the subject currently enjoys. This is important not just for those of us concerned with mobile or online media – but indeed for all of us who care about the future of media and culture generally.

Part 1

Cell phones and the new media economies

Chapter 2

Power and mobile media
Structures, networks and control

Evolved from the late nineteenth century, the architectures, structures and processes of telecommunications are relatively familiar. Telecommunications has experienced great transformations for the past three decades from the early 1980s (Curwen 1997; Curwen and Whalley 2004). Broadly speaking, privatization of formerly government owned telecommunications carriers is now almost complete – though many issues and struggles remain. Ironically, just as privatization is taken for granted, the role of the state in telecommunications has re-entered policy debates and become a live issue. This is especially the case when it comes to perceived market failure in providing universal – or even widespread – access to advanced broadband services.

Broadly speaking, as markets have failed to provided sufficient, pervasive communications infrastructure of sufficient quality, an acceptable price, desired capacity, data rates and speeds, all sectors have turned to governments to underwrite, instigate or indeed supply such necessary networks. After the classic era of universal service (golden age myth as it was), the form and character of state agency, ownership and control, however, is different. While in some countries there are proposals for government to take ownership over facilities, what is emerging is an emphasis on public–private partnerships in telecommunications (a hybrid form common in other infrastructures, such as roads, railways and airports). The formerly government owned telecommunications carriers remain dominant in many markets – often with new owners and shareholding arrangements. Many of these carriers also offer mobile services; they need to be in this business because fixed-line services revenue is fast declining, while income from cell phones is still rising. The historically dominant carriers still enjoy a strong advantage in providing mobile services as part of an integrated – or at least more comprehensive – set of services and networks. This is ironic, given that cell phones have featured heavily in an important area of competition and deregulation, especially as a way to introduce more competition into telecommunications markets formerly believed to be natural monopolies. The commercial introduction of cell phones nicely coincided with the rise of neoliberal policies, and so in a number of markets licences for mobile services were some of the first awarded – ushering new entrants into telecommunications markets. There are now well established national, regional, and global firms that specialize in cellular mobile services (Buellingen and Woerter 2004). The past 30 years of the twin projects of telecommunications liberalization and beginning of mobile services have certainly seen many new firms created and older corporations adapt and successfully assume new kinds of dominance.

If this broad account of the recent evolution – co-evolution – of tele-communications and cell phones over the past three decades (roughly late 1970s to late 2000s) holds, there are clear patterns of ownership, control and struc-tures that relates to this. The challenge to our understanding of such patterns presents itself forcefully in the present phase of development. For some time telecommunications firms have been in great transformation, auguring their futures amid media convergence. Many telecommunications and mobile com-panies have interests in other areas of media and entertainment. Conversely many media companies own stakes in the telecommunications enterprises. The interests that bind the different stakeholders are most clearly evident in the 'triple' or 'quadruple-play', centring on the main services and infrastructures into households: telephony, internet, subscription television, cell phone. Accordingly, boards of telecommunications companies feature directors with interests and expertise in media, entertainment, internet and other now allied interests.

The great investment challenge of telecommunications companies is bound up with the difficult questions about network infrastructures and their futures. For some years, there has been discussion of next generation networks, and a recognition that the internet protocol and technologies will need to be incorpo-rated in the very architecture of what comes next. If we are to leap-frog, or just catch up, from copper-based, circuit-switched telecommunications networks, to ultra-fast broadband networks to the home, or person, then such networks will be packet-switched, internet protocol-based. This immediately pits the tele-communications industry against powerful competitors from other sectors which also possess experience in building and operating networks – internet providers and technology firms, and television and media interests, to name just two groups.

For mobile carriers, there are a set of questions about what comes next with their network infrastructures. As we shall see, the question of what follows 3G networks (which really evolved bit by bit from their 2G predecessors) is bound up with a pot-pourri of different mobile and wireless networks (for instance, see Bohlin, Burgelman and Casal 2007). There is the little discussed question of what is the relationship between fast growing mobile networks and the next generation networks (of which an important component will still be wireline, cable networks – or else desired speeds will not be reliably delivered, at this stage at least). The large, not well understood questions of networks, however, are now only one part of global mobile media. Famously, the capabilities, computing power and intelligence are no longer centred in traditional nodes of networks. Such intelligence has been redistributed elsewhere: to the 'edges', as many the-orists suggest; to the devices themselves; to the users; to new intermediaries in the value chains.

This is the broad scene of contemporary networks in which mobile media is set. It is the argument of this book that to understand the emerging forms of communication and media designated by mobile media, then we need to take a global perspective. Further, that at the heart of such a global perspective is the question of power. I draw on a range of theories and concepts, but especially aim to illuminate how power is being shaped in the economies, processes, institutions, contexts, media forms, communicative architectures, cultural practices, use and apropriations that make mobile media.

In this chapter, especially, I am broadly informed by the concepts and tools of political economy, which remain very useful for grappling with these overlapping changes – a 'cornerstone' of this endeavour. The 'centrality of *power* in the analysis of communication' is something nominated by Vincent Mosco as an abiding preoccupation of the political economy approach (Mosco 2009: 220). Mosco offers two definitions of political economy, a less and more constrained meaning, respectively that are worth quoting to orient my discussion here:

> In the narrow sense, *political economy is the study of the social relations, particularly the power relations, that mutually constitute the production, distribution, and consumption of resources, including communication resources.*
>
> (Mosco 2009: 2)

> A more general and ambitious definition of political economy is *the study of control and survival in social life.*
>
> (Mosco 2009: 3)

In Mosco's renovation of his theory of political economy of communication, he focuses upon three overarching logics: commodification (content, audiences, labour), spatialization (space, time, communication) and structuration (class, gender, race, social movements, hegemony). Power and communication, or rather communication power, is something that the pre-eminent theorist of global networks, Manuel Castells, has also offered an account of – with 'a new approach to understanding power in the network society' (Castells 2009: 5). Castells is interested in the 'social structure that characterizes society in the early twenty-first century: a social structure constructed around ... digital networks of communications' (4). He argues that:

> the process of formation and exercise of power relationships is decisively transformed in the new organizational and technological context derived from the rise of global digital networks of communication as the fundamental symbol-processing system of our time.
>
> (Castells 2009: 4)

While very much interested in communications, my own exploration of power is focused upon media – and the new dynamics of power in mobile media in particular. It is evident that the transformations in contemporary media are occurring at a number of levels simultaneously. When we are thinking of television, radio, press, publishing or advertising, or even music, there is a rich trove of information and scholarship that helps us gauge the changes that are underway (Albarran and Chan-Olmsted 1998). The same is true of tele-communications, to some extent, and there we also have at least one important study on mobile media (Feldmann 2005). In economics and policy literatures, we have a great deal of information about ownership and control of corporations, their technologies, infrastructures and services (Gruber 2005). We know much less about the contemporary political economy of telecommunications, or inno-vation (Cowhey and Aronson 2009), let alone that of mobile media. Accordingly, as a preliminary sketch of one facet of such an endeavour, this chapter focuses on (mostly) commercial corporations. The aim is to trace the structures of power in the mobile media industries, especially as such power is shaped by patterns of corporate ownership, control and cultures. This will provide a starting point for exploring the interactions among economy, culture and policy, and, ultimately, calling for a new debate about mobile media, their uses and publics.

Structure of the cell phone industry: the carriers

My first task in this chapter is to identify and characterize key companies in mobile media internationally. The starting point is obviously baseline informa-tion on telecommunications and mobile carriers, virtual mobile carriers, handset, network and other equipment manufacturers. Then it is important to consider available data on new kinds of companies providing application and content for mobiles. Here there are a bewildering array of businesses, from very small start-ups or niche companies, to large media and entertainment companies. Finally, I am especially interested in identifying involvement of traditional, or recogniz-able, media companies in the new business of mobile media.

Before undertaking this task, a brief note on the threshold difficulty: namely, the lack of reliable, longitudinal data on relatively established mobile and telecommunications companies, let alone new entrants and ventures. Important data sets are made publicly available by the International Telecommunications Union (ITU) and Organisation for Economic Co-operation and Development (OECD) respectively. However, the kinds of organizations about which data is collected have changed, especially with the changes in telecommunications, media, entertainment and information and communication industries over the past 20 years. There is a wealth of other data available from industry asso-ciations, national governments and regulators, market research firms and some academic studies; however, it tends to be selective in its coverage and purpose, or, in the case of much market research, unclear about its methods and reliability.

For this and other reasons, I am indebted to Peter Curwen and Jason Whally's excellent *The Internationalisation of Mobile Communications* (2008a).

Interestingly Curwen and Whally find the existing data so inadequate, they create their own databases on mobile operators – a task, unfortunately, well outside the constraints and resources of my own project. Curwen and Whally's book offers the most systematic and accurate data on particular aspects of structures of ownership and control, and market strategies of mobile operations around the world. In their book, and a series of papers published elsewhere, Curwen and Whally offer a series of analyses of mobile telecommunications companies that greatly enrich our understanding. Their focus is upon the cell phone operators themselves, and their patterns of collaboration, partnership, investment and ownership across countries – hence the emphasis upon internationalization. Nonetheless, their findings are very important correctives to the assumptions – on the part of both analysts of power and managers and promoters of companies – about the uniformity and reach of cell phones as media companies. What Curwen and Whalley show is that the internationalization of cell phone operators is more limited that one might suspect. Companies like Vodafone, or the American baby Bells, or even France Télécom, the company they find present in the most countries around the world, are not as uniformly omnipresent globally as their marketing and advertising discourses, or even management cultures, suggest. Rather they have quite specific investments or undertakings in particular countries or parts of the world. Indeed, in the case of the baby Bells, such companies might even at times 'de-internationalize', or retreat to their home market (case in point: Bell South selling its interests in Latin America to Spain's Telefónica). Quite a number of companies thought to be seeking global or regional domination of mobile markets, in fact at closer inspection turn out to discern their best interests as sticking close to their domestic markets – as in the case of China Mobile's moves towards, and then retreat from, investments in African mobile markets (Curwen and Whalley 2008a: 98). Curwen and Whalley's work cues us to be careful about how we postulate what is global about mobile media. Accordingly, what I wish to do in this chapter is to draw attention to, and critically discuss, some important features of the corporate and commercial organization and control of cell phones – a feature of this stage of its thoroughgoing commodification. I will draw upon various data but will also discuss particular cases – aiming to sketch the grounds and vectors of power, its areas of future transformation, and also discontinuities, gaps and dissonances.

Let us start, then, with a list of the top ten telecommunications service companies in 2006 (the most reliable publicly available figures, current late 2008).

It is difficult to make a historical comparison, using equivalent figures for an earlier period, because different things were measured in the publicly available data spanning this period. In 1998, for instance, the figures gathered by the ITU related to the top ten fixed-line carriers – clearly the predecessors of their counterparts a decade on.

What has changed in the intervening decade, however, is that while fixed-line telephone services remain important and profitable, the margins for this class of

Table 2.1 Top ten telecommunications service companies, 2006 (OECD 2009)

1	NTT (Japan)
2	Verizon Communications (US)
3	Deutsche Telekom (Germany)
4	Telefónica (Spain)
5	France Télécom (France)
6	AT&T (US)
7	Vodafone (UK)
8	Sprint Nextel (US)
9	Telecom Italia (Italy)
10	China Mobile (Hong Kong, China)

Table 2.2 Top ten fixed-line telecommunications operators, 1998 (ITU 1998)

1	China Telecom (China)
2	NTT (Japan)
3	Deutsche Telekom (Germany)
4	Bell Atlantic (United States)
5	SBC (United States)
6	France Télécom (France)
7	BT (United Kingdom)
8	Telecom Italia (Italy)
9	BellSouth (United States)
10	GTE (United States)

service have been steadily, if not dramatically, eroded by competition. Depending on competition policies, market size, structure and characteristics, and a range of local factors, wholesale and retail competition has intensified in fixed-line services. While facilities-based competition in telecommunications has been difficult to realize in many jurisdictions, the internet provides an excellent, cheap alternative with voice and video over internet protocol services, widely used by 2010. For our purposes, here, however, the most dramatic development is the substitution of mobile services for fixed-line telephony and associated telecommunications services (voicemail, intelligent network services such as caller ID and a range of new services). Thus the surviving, in some cases thriving, but definitely still powerful former monopolies have diversified across telecommunications services – with cell phones as an important part of what they offer.

The league table of top ten cell phone companies gives a different picture compared to telecommunications service countries. In 1998, China and Japan rank at the top, and the Korean Republic at ninth place, but the remainder are four US companies, two Italian companies and one German enterprise. Already in 2004, we can see the emergence of new European players (notably Telefónica), a dedicated global mobile company (Vodafone), an additional Chinese company and the emergence of a Latin American mobile giant (América Móvil). In 2009, there are some very interesting changes: América Móvil up in the ranking; China Unicom down; Orascom, the Middle Eastern mobile carrier, enters the

Table 2.3 Top ten mobile cellular network operators 2008 – 2004 – 1998 (Source: ITU, 2004 and 1998, and company reports; based on numbers of cellular subscribers)

	2008	2004	1998
1	China Mobile	China Mobile	NTT DoCoMo (Japan)
2	Vodafone	Vodafone (Britain)	China Telecom
3	Telefónica	China Unicom (China)	TIM (Italy)
4	América Móvil	Deutsche Telecom (Germany)	AirTouch (U.S.)
5	Orange/France Télécom	América Móvil (Mexico)	AT&T (U.S.)
6	Telenor	France Telecom	SBC (U.S.)
7	T-mobile	Telefónica (Spain)	Bell Atlantic (U.S.)
8	TeliaSonera	NTT DoCoMo	Omnitel (Italy)
9	China Unicom	Verizon (U.S.)	SK Telecom (Korea (Rep.))
10	Orascom	TeliaSonera (Sweden)	Mannesmann (Germany)

top ten. Not listed in this table, but even more interesting perhaps is the next ten carriers with most subscribers: Bharti Airtel (top Indian carrier) in 11th place, South Africa's MTN group 12th, Russia's MTS 13th-ranked, then Verizon Wireless and AT&T Mobility in 15th and 17th spots respectively.

Unfortunately, robust, longitudinal data sets are not publicly available, as I have noted, nonetheless what the available data shows is that telecommunications service overall is dominated still by companies based in Europe, the US, Japan and China. Mobiles are now the largest segment of telecommunications revenue. However, when it comes to dedicated mobile carriers, by subscribers at least, there are significant new regional forces, as well as reconfigured traditional, or even colonial interests, dominating mobiles worldwide – it is worthwhile gaining a sense of the contours of this new mediascape. Before I do so, I will briefly look at a casestudy of a new kind of global company that has specialized in many of the early forms of mobile media: Hutchison Whampoa's '3'.

The global 3 generation mobile company: Hutchison

One of the first companies to specialize in third-generation cell phones, and a company that styles itself as eminently global, is Hutchison Whampoa, which trades as '3'. In developing a global presence, especially in Europe and selected countries in the Asia-Pacific, Hutchison places special emphasis on pioneering third-generation cellular handsets. In Europe it was a heavy purchaser of 3G licences from 2000 onwards, allowing it to become a new entrant in telecommunications markets. Moreover, Hutchison held onto these licences while others struggled with the debts incurred in obtaining licences, and the slow take-up of the services:

> Hutchison Whampoa is something of an oddity within the European mobile communications industry … it is axiomatic that, since Hutchison Whampoa

has no installed 2G customer base to fund its expansion into 3G, it must rely on other sources for funds. The foray into 3G has been financed by a very deep-pocketed parent company that seems willing to suffer huge short-term losses and to persevere against the odds that have led incumbents like Sonera and Telefónica to abandon most or all of their 3G new entrant investments.

(Whalley and Curwen 2006)

As Whalley and Curwen note, without the base, and comfort, of an existing 2G network, Hutchison needed to launch as quickly as it could – and so was first to offer 3G services in six European countries. Its difficulty, however, was that its overall subscriber base remained relatively low in the first few years – compared to the existing mobile companies. Hence it was heavily reliant on its parent company, something that led Whalley and Curwen to be pessimistic about Hutchison's prospects – as well as critical of such restrictive licensing auctions as a way to introduce and sustain new entrants into telecommunications markets (Curwen and Whalley 2009; Whalley and Curwen 2006: 632).

Despite these shaky foundations, Hutchison has been an important pioneer in offering mobile media globally centred on 3G:

3G fuses together two of the most powerful consumer technologies in history – the interactivity and depth of the Internet with the convenience and freedom of mobile telephony ... Hutchison Whampoa believes that 3G will change the way people communicate and the way they access information and entertainment. This will be as significant as the birth of television after a generation of radio. We are not in the business of selling phones. Our mission is to enhance people's lives – we are creating a service that, upon demand, shows you where you are, what you want and how you want it – and puts it in the palm of your hand.

(Hutchison Whampoa Ltd 2003)

Hutchison was one of the first companies to market mobile videotelephony – as yet an unsuccessful undertaking itself. However it was important in the imaginaries of mobile media. Hutchison has also been an innovator in the area of mobile content, especially entertainment and sport. In a number of markets, Hutchison has strongly pushed mobile television, built particularly on dedicated sport programming. Hutchison also created its own handset subsidiary INQ, perhaps best known for its 'Facebook' phone. With the popularity of voice over internet protocol, Hutchison launched a '3 Skyphone' handset in October 2007, offering free calls from cell phone to other skype users. Hutchison sought to capitalize on the consumer penchant for social media.

Like Vodafone, Hutchison operates in a number of jurisdictions around the world – though its coverage of markets is nowhere near as comprehensive. However, there are some significant differences between the two. As it is much remarked, Hutchison Whampoa is controlled by Li Ka-shing, often called 'Asia's richest man'. There is a body of commentary about the nature of substantial private, familial control in such a large, powerful corporation (Chan 2008). Mobile telecommunications is a relatively new area for Hutchison, which acquired one of Hong Kong's first mobile licences in 1992. In the early 1990s, Hutchison was also a backer of public access cordless telephony (CT-2 technology) – then tipped to be a pervasive and popular wireless technology rivalling mobile cellular, but this was not to be (Goggin 2008b). It also has very substantial holdings in real estate and property development, energy, infrastructure and retail, and has been the world's leading port investor, developer and operator. While based in and still strategically controlled from Hong Kong by Li Ka-shing and family, Hutchison's modus operandi is to develop suitable partnerships and joint-venture arrangements in the particular countries in which it operates. These relationships are shifting, contingent and highly strategic – much more so perhaps than many, as a shrewd way to continue rivalry (Chan-Olmsted and Jamison 2001). While Hutchison shows a propensity to use its deep pockets to subsidize 3G services in some markets – notably Europe – it is also continually selling stakes and reforming partnerships. In 2009, '3' in Australia joined forces with Vodafone to form Vodafone Hutchison Australia, enabling the two to boost their market share against the other two main mobile carriers Telstra and Optus. '3' was happy to adopt Vodafone as the lead brand, with a slow phase-out.

Regional mobile multinationalism

Hutchison's '3' is an example of a new global firm in mobile media, its forays into new markets and technologies underwritten by the vast wealth from other sectors such as property. However, there remain, as we have seen, a select number of extremely powerful global interests in mobile media, that derive their influence from historical dominance in telecommunications. Then there are new very big interests that have built their capital, reputation and power globally in the cell phone area. Vodafone is one example of such a company, which has built further on its world dominance in cellular phones (Curwen 2002; Anwar 2003; Goggin 2006), with concrete strategies in mobile data areas carefully extended into key sites in emerging mobile media. Another such company is China Mobile, building upon the largest national market of all. Listed on the Hong Kong stock exchange, China Mobile was the cell phones division of China Telecom, where it originated. With the break-up of China Telecom in 1999, China Mobile was created. China Mobile is a so-called 'red chip' company, based in mainland China, but listed and incorporated in Hong Kong. It is a state-owned enterprise, that effectively maintains control in China Mobile through 70 per cent equity stake – held through China Mobile (HK) Group Ltd (which is 100 per cent owned by the Chinese government controlled holding company China Mobile Communications Corporation).

Companies such as Vodafone, China Mobile and others have investments, presence and substantial control, and a major shaping role in the political economy of global mobile media. There is a complex interplay among the global and local in emerging global mobile media, in which the meso-level inter-mediation of the region plays a critical role. First, we can observe regional patterns of ownership and control that build directly on historical patterns. The most stark are the spheres of influence of empires and their colonies. Take, for instance, the case of patterns of regional investment in mobiles in Africa (depicted in Table 2.4 below).

The influence of the former colonial powers of Britain (in Vodafone and Vodacom, for instance), France (France Télécom) and Portugal (Portugal Tele-com) are still very much apparent, if on the wane (Curwen and Whalley 2008c). There has been a complex process of de-colonialization, the emergence of new imperial powers and the re-arrangements of relationships among old and new centres of power (Obadare 2006). This can be observed in the case of the US, the most powerful actor in telecommunications policy since the mid-twentieth-century. As documented in Jill Hills' study of international tele-communications policy, *Telecommunications and Empire* (2007), the US has worked assiduously to shape the post-World War II telecommunications dispensation, contested variously by the British, Europeans and the newly decolonized, devel-oping countries.

The patterns of old and new global actors can also be seen in the case of another region, Latin America and the Caribbean (outlined in Table 2.5 below).

Notable here is the Spanish telecommunications giant Telefónica (Guillén 2005), second biggest strategic investor in mobiles in this region. The new kinds of work and labour being created through these cheap phone developments, as well as the more organized co-design ventures between companies in different countries need much greater attention (Qiu 2009). The extent and depth of Telefónica's control of Latin American telecommunications has been dubbed a 'conquest' in a full-length study devoted to the topic, further emphasizing the enduring colonial roots to this political and economic set of relations

Table 2.4 Strategic mobile investors in Africa, 2008 (ITU 2009c: 19)

Strategic investor	Subscriptions (000s)	No. of countries	Revenue (US $m)
MTN (South Africa)	64,306	15	12,088
Zain (Cellnet) Kuwait	41,018	15	4,169
Vodacom (South Africa)	44,995	5	6,841
Vodafone (UK)	21,090	2	1,609
France Telecom	16,962	14	2,300
Millicom (Luxembourg)	9,039	7	711
Portugal Telecom	6,032	4	1,661
Moov (UAE)	1,500	7	n/a
Vivendi/Maroc Telecom	1,011	2	202

Table 2.5 Strategic mobile investors in Latin America and the Caribbean, 2008 (ITU 2009d: 9)

Strategic investor	Subscriptions (000s)	No. of countries	Revenue (US $m)
América Móvil	182,724	17	26,692
Telefónica	123,385	13	32,441
Millicom	18,642	6	2,396
Digicel	6,540	26	1,500
Cable & Wireless	3,797	15	635

(Martínez 2008; Chapter 5 of this book is devoted to Telefónica's systematic investment in media between 1996 and 2003). Set against Telefónica's powerful influence on the political economy of Latin American cell phones, it is fascinating to note which company is the top investor, with interest in no fewer than 17 countries in the region: Mexico's América Móvil.

América Móvil was established and is still controlled by Carlos Slim Helú. In March 2010, Slim became the world's richest person – the first time a Mexican had claimed this dubious honour. In 1990, during the presidency of Carlos Salinas, Slim benefitted handsomely from the privatization policies of the government, heading a consortium that purchased Telmex (Teléfonos de México) and Telnor (Mariscal and Rivera 2005 and 2006; Rhodes 2006). Slim subsequently acquired and controls Telcel, the Mexican mobile carrier. Slim is a very interesting figure, not least for his range of business, civil and political ventures. In 1997, he acquired the early online service company, Prodigy, and in an alliance with Microsoft launched a Spanish-language portal. A key innovation in cell phones that underpinned Slim's early success in the area was a new pre-paid system 'Amigo de Telcel', launched in 1996. The largest corporation in Latin America, América Móvil is a holding company. América Móvil controls subsidiaries that trade under various names including TracFone (in the US), Claro (in Brazil, Chile, Peru, Columbia, and Central America), and Concel (Ecuador) (América Móvil 2008). Slim's three sons play key roles in América Móvil, its subsidiaries and various entities in the family's empire – notably with Patrick Slim Domit serving as chairman of the board of América Móvil, and Carlos Slim Domit leading that of Telmex (América Móvil 2008; Telmex 2009). For a time Carlos Slim was also the US mobile carrier MCI's biggest shareholder, selling his stake to Verizon in 2005.

Handset manufacturers and vendors

In all instances, global, regional, national and sub-national, the mobile telecommunications operators retain a critical important force. They remain very important, if not decisive, in questions of the investment, control, roll-out, commissioning (and closure) of network infrastructures. Crucially, the carrier still remains the largest bloc of interests in connecting subscribers, with strategic control of billing systems. However, in the realm of cell phones especially – rather than simply telecommunications in general (a distinction rapidly losing its relevance) – there is a second significant power bloc: the handset and associated equipment manufacturers. First, let's begin with the classic, dedicated cellular mobile handset companies – such as those that regularly feature as the top vendors, and that have exercised an early, strong influence on the shaping of mobile media. In late 2009, these were, in rank order: Nokia, Samsung, LG Electronics, Sony Ericcson and Motorola (IDC 2009a). A number of the top mobile device firms – such as Nokia, Motorola and Ericcson – are also significant competitors in the wider communications equipment and systems. For instance, the Swedish firm Ericcson is a firm with a long history in provision of switching and telecommunications equipment. Its rivals are older North American and European companies such as Alcatel-Lucent (merger of long-standing French telecommunications switching company and the spin-off of the famous Bell Labs) and Nortel Networks (Canada), and new firms from emerging markets such as Huawei Technologies.

Looming large in this landscape of telecommunications equipment, especially when it comes to cellular mobile handsets, are what are called smartphones (that is, multimedia or converged mobile devices). From 2008 onwards, we have witnessed the genuine emergence of new players in the handset market – with the reprise of the Smart Phone, and new technologies from quite different areas of media culture. Apple, with its iPhone, is the most obvious of these. In this area, established handset companies such as Nokia and Samsung contend with Apple and other rising forces such as Research in Motion (Blackberry) and HTC ('Touch'). The top five converged mobile device vendors in late 2009, in rank order, were: Nokia, Research in Motion, Apple, HTC and Samsung (IDC 2009b). There is a bewildering array of new handsets, many of which are driven or commissioned by the carriers, rather than originating from the

Table 2.6 Top ten communications equipment and systems firms (USD millions in current prices; OECD 2008: 59)

	Country	Revenue 2007	Net income 2006
Nokia	Finland	69,895	2,992
Motorola	United States	36,622	3,661
Cisco Systems	United States	34,922	5,580
Ericsson	Sweden	27,788	3,537
Alcatel-Lucent	France	24,356	−741
L-3 Communications	United States	13,961	526
Nortel Networks	Canada	10,948	28
Huawei Technologies	China	11,000	512
Qualcomm	United States	8,871	2,470
Avaya	United States	5,279	201
Total		243,641	18,766

traditional vendors. An example is the 'Facebook phone' – manufactured by Hutchison Whampoa subsidiary INQ. Another case is Taiwanese HTC's Touch Diamond (sold under label by the likes of T-Mobile and Orange). A third is Prime, an initiative of Japan's NTT Docomo.

In this new wave of handsets, there are very interesting developments driven by 'co-design', or co-operation in design of cell phones and user interfaces by manufacturers and operators, especially in East Asian countries, such as China, Taiwan, Korea and Japan. As one expert in this area notes:

> ... the easiest route to massive UI [user interface] customization is for an operator to work with OEM or ODM manufacturers who will dedicate resources to operators' needs. The majority of such manufacturers reside in Far-East Asian markets. Developments in codesign have therefore brought a number of previously unknown manufacturers into the hands of Western users, providing greater choice and promoting earlier adoption of advanced features that are prevalent in Asian markets.
>
> (Williams 2006)

The role of working class consumers is important in how this process of co-design unfolds, as Jack Qiu points out in his study of wireless communications in China. In order to attract consumers, firms have been forced to design and market cheaper phones (Qiu 2009). A fascinating area that gives co-design a new meaning is the black art of grey-market phones: that is, the quick, ubiquitous and unauthorized copying of cell phones and media devices for unofficial sale, especially in emerging markets and developing countries. The trade in copied phones, and indeed the 'copycat' culture around appropriation, adaptation (201), and reworking of brands (especially Western ones) is a significant part of consumer culture and economy in China (Keane 2007; Wang 2008), where it is called 'Shanzhai'. Manufactured by companies as small as three employees in places like Shenzhen, the 'capital' of Shanzhai cell phones, the business model turns on readily available components, especially the chip:

> Most of these 'Shanzhai mobile phone' companies are using chips from a Taiwanese company MTK. These chips integrate various functions such as camera, MP3, MP4, touch lens, JAVA and Bluetooth and can be regarded as 'turn-key' solution with not only chips but also SDK (software development toolkit) and application software.
>
> (Wu and Zhang 2009: 7)

Such informal assembling and copying of cell phones is rare in Western countries, though with the iPhone, as we shall see, in Chapter 8, modification and hacking – mostly by individuals – has finally achieved a wide popularity in mobile media, to rival that of its important place in internet and digital culture and technology generally. The Shanzhai adaptations of the iPhone, however, were much more varied, faster and widely sold. They also have their parallels in many other countries, not least in Asia and Africa, related no doubt to the well-established and relatively informal cultures of repair, maintenance and customization of mobile phones (see, for instance, Hahn and Kibora 2008). There is also an interesting comparison to be drawn between the function and place of copycat culture in China and how it mediates technology and design transfer relationships with other countries, and the many years of discussion on Japanese supposed proclivity for copying and adapting design in the 1980s. Nonetheless, currently, because cellular mobile handset design copying is a somewhat informal, 'grey', area of commerce, there is little reliable information on its firms, revenue, organization and contribution to Gross Domestic Product or trade. However, consumer electronics research firm GFK estimated in mid-2009 that up to 30 per cent of the Chinese mobile phone market could be Shanzai phones (Xing 2009). The economic share of Shanzai is so significant that commentators worried that the stimulus package crafted by the Chinese government in response to the global financial crisis could see subsidies to rural dwellers simply boosting the profits of the Shanzai producers (Ernst 2009). The new kinds of work and labour being created through these cheap phone developments, as well as the more organized co-design ventures between companies in different countries need much great attention (Qiu 2009).

In addition to these new kinds of cell phones and the panoply of smartphones, there are earlier predecessors from the field of computing, notably Qualcomm (famous for the email package, Eudora, now in terminal decline), with devices that especially compete in the field of mobile media. Some portable digital assistance manufacturers still maintain their interest in mobiles, notably Palm. Then there are the new entrants focused on mobile email, the best known being Canadian firm Research in Motion's Blackberry. The cornucopia of cell phone, multimedia phones and other devices from old and new handset vendors is not all. There are other new products produced by firms originating in other areas of convergent, networked portable devices. Most obvious perhaps, with an enormous customer base already, are games equipment companies. Many of these companies have launched game consoles and handhelds with mobile and wireless connectivity – including Nintendo DS and Sony Playstation Portable (PSP).

A new example comes from the field of publishing. Cell phones are already well established as devices for reading and publishing, as the celebrated case of flourishing cell novel culture in Japan illustrates (Hjorth 2009b). However, the investment and consumer interest in different portable technologies such as e-readers has increased – especially with the appearance of the Kindle, a much discussed e-reader device from Amazon.com. Until late 2009 the Kindle was confined to the US only. While figures on these sections of the mobile media industry are difficult to find, one estimate has it that three million e-readers were sold in the US in 2009 – with Kindle taking 60 per cent of market share, compared to Sony e-reader's 35 per cent (Epps 2009a). Kindle also uses the cellular mobile network, offering purchase of books using the built-in connection – using 3G to offer connectivity internationally as well as in the US. Before the Kindle launched in 2007, the dedicated e-reader market had been slow to develop. Like other areas of mobile media, it has been spurred on by the iPhone, with its many e-book and e-reading applications – and Apple is now reportedly developing a tablet-style e-reader of its own. The Dutch Ixread device, launched in October 2009, also has a mobile connection. From China, there is the Hanwong, launched in 2008, and by the end of 2009 claimed to be the world's second largest producer – with 800,000 sold of its PC plug-in device and plans to expand into Europe (Hongyan 2009). Hanwong joined with China Mobile to develop an e-reader that uses the China domestic 3G standard (TD-SCDMA), and another technology that uses Wi-Fi, to allow download via mobile and wireless (Fletcher 2009a). China Mobile is seeking to establish itself as the e-book retailer of choice with other companies – such as equipment supplier Datang also developing an e-reader using the 3G standard (Fletcher 2009b). As commentators note, cell phones are already widely used to read books and other reading material, often pirated, in China – so dedicated e-readers will face challenges establishing themselves (Fletcher 2009b). The mobile and internet companies are not the only sector cross-competing in publishing. Games companies are hedging their bets in this new area of mobile media by creating their digital reader applications: Nintendo DS offering a reader application aimed at eight-to-eleven-year olds, and Sony Playstation announcing a digital reader app featuring Marvel comics (Epps 2009b).

The rise of mobile data and services: content, programs, applications and software

From carriers and handset manufacturers, I now want to move to the various mobile content, programme and application companies. The distinguishing feature of mobile media, if anything, must surely reside in the advent of mobile data and services. The development of mobile networks and devices has required, encouraged and allowed the development of software and applications – many of which I will discuss in detailed case studies later in this book. There has also been a new area created of mobile services. While carriers and vendors have certainly been in the vanguard of mobile data and services development, this is very much an area where, from the late 1990s onwards, there have been significant new entrants, including the creation of new firms – something that innovation and business theorists called for and welcomed:

> Innovation on the mobile platform has focused on the development of infrastructure and devices with mobile carriers and device manufacturers leading the effort. With the commoditization of voice traffic, there has been a shift toward content innovation. In order for innovation to continue to

flourish on the mobile platform, a new paradigm must be adopted. Rather than the current linear approach in which carriers dictate the terms to content providers and users, this new paradigm is more networked and ecological in structure.

(Ziv 2005)

This new area was variously called mobile data, mobile commerce, mobile entertainment or mobile services. Regardless, it made for much more complex intermediate layers of technology – such as 'middleware', applications layer and so on – and, once profitability was established, far more complicated value chains – indeed networks (Benn and Kachieng'a 2005; Chan-Olmsted 2006; Li and Whalley 2002; Maitland et al. 2002 and 2005; Olla and Patel 2002) and business models, the subject of much debate by researchers and industry. Many of the new mobile data and service companies have now accrued sufficient power and revenue to counter, or even trump, the power of carriers and vendors. Here reliable data is even more difficult to find, so what I will do is sketch some different types of enterprises, what they do and what their typical characteristics are.

While there are many small firms offering mobile content – ringtones, music, videos, screensavers, games – there are now relatively well-established, large-scale international businesses. Privately owned British-based firm Mobile Interactive Group (MIG) is one such firm, claiming to be the 'largest supplier of next generation mobile interactive solutions servicing the mobile and digital markets in the UK, Ireland, Europe and the USA' (MIG 2009). One of the best-known international mobile service companies is Jamster International, operating in 35 countries, including western and eastern Europe, South Africa and Canada. Jamster was established in 2000, under the name Jamba (by which it is still known in some countries). Jamster bills itself as 'one of the world's leading mobile entertainment brands, delivering the best content directly via mobile phone to consumers around the world' (Jamster 2009). Headquartered in Berlin and Beverly Hills, California, Jamster has now been acquired by News Corporation. It is now a wholly owned subsidiary of News, and in August 2008 was renamed Fox Mobile group. Thus Jamster has become an official brand of Fox Mobile, which claims to be:

> The global leader in mobile content distribution, production and services, offering more of the benefits of mobile entertainment to consumers and business partners than anyone else. A division of Fox Entertainment Group, FMG distributes and produces more mobile entertainment to more people and business partners in more ways and in more places than anyone else in the world.

(Jamster 2009)

As these corporate metamorphoses suggest, the epitome of global media – if actually an atypical rather than exemplary company – very much wished to cover the mobile market, hence its acquisition of Jamster. In doing so, Jamster has made an extraordinary transition from a small start-up company established by two German porn entrepreneurs to a respectable subsidiary of the Fox and News stable. In their middle period, however, lies a tale. For some years, Jamster was a very aggressive marketing of premium mobile content, certainly pioneering such services – especially ringtones (famous for its 'Crazy Frog' ringtone and song, discussed in Chapter 4) – but doing so with scant regard for consumer rights.

Premium services in telecommunications was a market that existed from the early 1980s, but the advent of the cell phone saw consumers prepared to pay small, but cumulatively significant, sums for cultural, informational and experiental goods. More so than wallpapers, screensavers and even games, ringtones were the mobile content 'killer app'. Premium rate service providers were skilled at entering the emerging markets for content around the world, advertising and promoting their products in traditional media – for example, popular magazines read by various demographic and target groups interested in ringtones – as well as online media, and cell phones also (for instance, text messages). Many of these providers were very entrepreneurial, and not so familiar with, or respectful of, the norms and regulations that had developed around telecommunications, many of which were being slowly extended to mobiles. Operating across national jurisdictions, a significant number of the premium rate providers – most notoriously Jamster – did not bother with well established consumer information and protection norms. Rather such providers saw an opportunity to enter markets fast, saturate advertising and stimulate quick take-up, then exit, or modify, sharp practice once regulators caught up with them. There are many examples of the shonky ringtone purveyors, but perhaps the earliest to be widely exposed was the case of Jamster's Crazy Frog ringtone. The preference for self or co-regulation made matters worse – as governments' response for some years was to allow the market in ringtones to rip, asking industry to put rules in place. What unfolded, however, and still obtains, almost a decade on, is a blatant disregard for consumers' right, if not scams, rip-offs and deceptive practice. Regulators have finally acted, often prompted by governments – evidenced in various reports and reforms. For its part, Jamster has sought to rehabilitate its reputation, by remaking itself not just as a mobile company but part of a broader media ecology. Also by presenting itself as a responsible corporate citizen – especially via the association with acceptable branded content, courtesy of Fox. The old miscellany of Jamster content lives on – safely corralled within the confines of this brand.

There are now many other large and small mobile data and services companies, not least the myriad of software and applications developers, which the establishment of the Apple apps stores, and various other apps stores and platforms have made possible. This is perhaps the most dynamic area of cell phone innovation, and also the one least controlled and dominated by large, integrated firms – at this stage at least. Those engaged in this area of the industry congregrate at the various 'Mobile Monday' meets regularly held around the world, and also consider themselves part of internet, computing and interactive media industries.

Computing and internet interests

From its shaky beginnings in Wireless Access Protocol (Goggin, 2006), there are now a multitude of ventures by internet companies that specifically link to mobile platforms.

As one of the world's largest internet companies, Google dominates the strategically crucial area of search. In approaching the cell phones market, its first move has been to adapt its famous search engine for mobile platforms. So in early January 2007, to take one instance, Google joined with China Mobile to create the leading mobile search service in China. Later in 2007, it launched a Google search application for the iPhone. It followed up in November 2008 with a new version of the iPhone search application that allows voice search. The second area, and again a natural extension of its dominance of search, is moving into mobile advertising with its AdSense product. Google had already moved into advertising in online games, so mobile offers fertile possibilities. The third area is that of cell phone design and production, already noted with Google's Android phone, and commitment to a new open source operating system for mobile handsets. While search and advertising are two well established strengths for Google, and cell phones are an obvious direct rivalrous move with respect to the cell phone manufacturers and carriers, the new area, where it has a particular edge, is in location based services and the movement of geoweb services to the cell phone (discussed further in Chapter 7). Google Earth and Google Maps have been two phenomenally successful applications, and obviously lend themselves to portable, mobile media devices – where they can be melded with the new location – sensing, mapping, authoring, tagging – and data technologies for mobiles.

Another large internet firm strategically positioning itself in mobiles is Japan's largest internet company, Softbank. Japan pioneered mobile internet, so it perhaps came as no surprise that in 2008 Softbank's Chief Executive Officer Masayoshi Son set a goal for the company to become the world's large mobile internet company (actually in a speech given to a Chinese business audience) (Schwankert 2008). At the time Softbank was already the largest internet company in Asia by size of market capitalization.

Google and Softbank are but two of many internet companies with interest in mobile media, and we shall encounter others, such as Facebook, in Chapter 7. Before we leave this topic, however, I will just briefly note the companies active in the area of operating systems for cell phones. Operating systems are a strategically critical area of computing – witness the power of Microsoft, enthroned by the dominance of its ownership of MS-DOS, and then development of the Windows operating system. In the cellular mobile phone area, Windows Mobile is a significant if minor player, but Symbian has dominated. Symbian was acquired by Nokia in December 2008, in order for it to evolve into the not-for-profit Symbian Foundation. Apple, of course, is now a forceful new entrant with its iPhone operating system, and a number of others are promising open source operating systems of uncertain hues – from the more established Linux, through Google's Android already mentioned, and fledging systems such as Open Moko. Of these Android is shaping up as the most promising competitor to Symbian, while Apple's system does not, of course, work across other mobile devices or platforms. What this highlights is not that the operating system itself is especially lucrative in mobile media, as it obviously is in the realm of computing; rather, the operating system offers the keys to the kingdom, the promise of controlling access to lucrative technology development and customers – exactly what Android is starting to do for Google.

Internet, cell phones and wireless: enmeshed access technologies

As well as mobile internet, wireless and mobile networks themselves have become important access technologies for the internet. There are two broad developments that have a significant bearing not only on the relationship between the mobile and the internet, but also in the question of how we understand and map global mobile media.

First, the widespread coverage of cell phone networks, and sheer number of subscribers worldwide, means that there is a potential network available to offer access to the internet, for other devices than a cellular phone. One of these devices is something called mobile broadband. The predominant form of mobile broadband is a card that a user buys or leases to plug into their laptop computer. Once configured, and with an activated customer account, the card allows the user to connect their computer to the internet via the cellular mobile network. Many providers also offer a stand-alone modem designed to be placed next to a desktop computer, or laptop – larger than the card, and designed for use in the home or small business. Due to the availability of 3G networks, especially, the data speeds offered can compare favourably with fixed-line options. What is especially significant about mobile broadband is that, especially with the card or 'dongle' version, it offers a mobility solution for people wishing to access the internet from different locations, or while travelling. It is the sheer coverage of cellular mobile networks that makes this such an attractive option – the fact that a user can pretty much access the internet with a mobile broadband card where she can find mobile coverage (especially in countries with 3G or other advanced networks).

The second main access technology for accessing the internet without cables is Wi-Fi (or wireless internet). Wi-Fi works by transmitting within a radius of a transmitter (or 'hot-spot'). Devised by an Australian scientist, working for the government Commonwealth Scientific and Industrial Research Organization (CSIRO), Wi-Fi is associated with the Institute of Electrical and Electronic Engineers (IEEE) 802.11 x standards, especially the well known 802.11b standard. Equipped with Wi-Fi, computers or handheld devices are able to connect to a wireless local area network within a relatively short range (usually up to 300 feet) (http://wi-fi.org/ accessed on 6 May 2010).Wi-Fi relies upon a dedicated chip to allow a computer (typically a laptop) to be connected to the internet. Wi-Fi has been quite a phenomena in its own right, spawning quite distinctive internet cultures and practices, something theorized under the concept of 'wirelessness'. It is offered commercially by a range of internet service providers, telecommunications and mobile companies, as well as municipal and city authorities (Ballon et al. 2009), community networking organizations and non-for-profit organizations. Its diffusion is attested by the fact that a traveller can have every expectation to find a café with Wi-Fi in many cities and towns, in hotels and airports, in universities and many other settings (now including planes). As well as its commercial and institutional varities, Wi-Fi has also featured heavily in alternative community and citizen's media – part of a grass-roots movement around computing and iInternet. In addition, Wi-Fi has been used in fascinating ways in developing countries, not just to offer access but in the dynamics of information and communication technologies for development, known by the acronym ICT4D (for example, see Tacchi and Grubb 2007). However, because of its relatively short range, and the cost of installing sufficient base stations, Wi-Fi suffers from patchy coverage. Ironically, where Wi-Fi is most ubiquitous and popular is in the home. A high proportion of users accessing cable broadband internet rely on a Wi-Fi router or modem within their house, property or its environs. Typically the cable broadband service plugs into the router, which then makes it available to a number of Wi-Fi-enabled devices – such as laptops or smartphones – to connect to the internet. Some users, whether by accident or design, also allow other users in the vinicity to share their internet connection. Wi-Fi devices can also be combined together in a 'self-configuring network'. In at least some countries Wi-Fi via household routers has been very popular, whereas commercial implementations and offerings have languished in comparison.

If to date such domestic appropriation of Wi-Fi has been its prevalent mode, this provides a rare opportunity to reverse the usual binary between commercial/public versus domestic/private use of communications technology. While Wi-Fi can be seen as pioneered by researchers and 'early adopters' in commercial or corporate settings, there is a case to be made that diffusion to wider populations has come through its non-commercial use in households. The everyday use and shaping of WiFi in the domestic setting overlaps with the adoption of wireless technologies in voluntary, community networks (though it might serve as a foil to this also). Wireless community networking involves citizens banding together to use open source technologies and wireless transmitters to construct wide-area metropolitan networks, as an alternative to commercial broadband networks. It has been celebrated by a range of activists and advocates for alternative and community media around the world, and received attention from scholars also (Mackenzie 2005 and 2006; Sandvig 2004). It has also been an important feature of the 'invention' of WiFi by users and collectivities. The legality of community networks falls into a grey area, with citizens essentially taking advantage of unmetered, or at least reasonably cheap, broadband access, and then repurposing it to share with others. This is something I will discuss further in Chapter 9 in relation to the notion of the 'wireless commons'.

The other burgeoning area of Wi-Fi, already mentioned, is actually in the cellular mobile telephony area. Here, many phones are now shipped as dual-mode devices, that inconspicuously – other than via the appearance of the wireless symbol – connect a smartphone to the internet, but still allow it to exercise other cell phone functionality, such as SMS or making and receiving calls. The use of Wi-Fi to connect cell phones to the internet is important to many users because this is a proven way of minimizing or avoiding the still relatively high rates charged by providers for mobile data.

The significance of both these access technologies is that they show the evolving structures, politics and complexities of mobile media when it comes to the lucrative and vitally important domain of broadband internet. There is a widespread expectation in rich countries that broadband access should be a right of every citizen – almost a new species of universal service obligation. Naturally, this obscures the reality that for the majority of the world's population some form of public access to broadband, let alone individual fixed or mobile access, is very far from being a reality.

Mobile media evolutions: the politics of 4G

Mobile broadband has proved a profitable, influential way for mobile companies to deal themselves back into the broadband environment, ahead of 4G mobiles. Mobile broadband, in the form it has eventuated, was largely unanticipated, and remains relatively expensive for the bulk of users. Yet it is an important part of the broadband ecology, of the hybrid platforms that constitute contemporary high-capacity internet – when technology infrastructure companies, internet companies, investors, voters and governments in wealthy countries struggle to find and strike suitable arrangements to make broadband widely accessible or even universal.

Wi-Fi, as we have seen, has played an important role, especially before, and even after, the advent of mobile broadband. It taught users to expect to be able to connect laptops and phones to the internet, and enjoy reasonable, media-rich experiences, at a time when cell phones struggled to provide – and in some sense still do – user experiences comparable to the computer-based use of the internet. If Wi-Fi has been a little eclipsed in the recent rise of mobile broadband, its supporters have been insisting that this will change with the availability of the successor technology, WiMAX. WiMAX is a new adaptation of wireless broadband technology, providing an alternative to existing broadband access technologies (such as ADSL and cable) for the 'last mile' of access to networks. WiMAX is an evolution of WiFi, however it also is a technology that bridges wireless internet and advanced cellular mobile networks. The WiMAX Forum, for instance, supports the development of technologies based on the harmonization of the IEEE 802.16 and the European Telecommunications Standards Institute (ETSI)'s HiperMAN standard. The organization describes itself as a 'catalyst for open Internet, anywhere, at true broadband speeds' (http://www.wimaxforum.org/about/ accessed on 6 May 2010). In this way, WiMAX offers a long-range, robust form of wireless broadband access, that could foreseeably overcome problems in widespread, commercial deployment of broadband. WiMAX Forum's board features directors representing players in computing and internet equipment – Intel Corporation, Cisco – together with leading telecommunications equipment and mobile manfacturers (Alcatel-Lucent, Fujitsu, Nokia, Motorola, Samsung, ZTE) as well as providers and carriers (Comcast, Huawei, Sprint-Nextel, KDDI, Korea Telecom, Tata).

In 2009 in the US, Clearwire offered 4G WiMAX, with the adage 'Clearwire will give you faster internet at home, at work and on the go, so that people everywhere will have the magic of the internet with them all the time' (http://www.clearwire.com/ accessed on 6 May 2010). The leading promoter of WiMAX has been Intel, which has its own Intel® WiMAX products. Intel had successfully identified itself with WiFi, registering and branding its chip, and then partnering with manufacturers to make themselves the default for the vast majority of computers shipped. Intel built upon the successful development and marketing of its processors – and the 'Intel inside' campaign and sticker – to do the same with WiFi. WiMAX networks can be accessed through indoor or outdoor units, PC cards, modules embeded in notebooks and laptops, and integrated interfaces in handhelds and PDAs (Intel 2007). For its part, Korean companies developed their own version of wireless broadband, called WiBro (Nam et al. 2008). It is a version of WiMax that particular includes specific requirements for providers, focusing on quality of service, among other things. KT launched a commercial service in 2006, expanding it to all areas of Seoul in 2007.

WiMax represents the most thoroughgoing effort by forces in the computer equipment and internet service provision industries to intervene into the future of mobile broadband networks. It is a large-scale organized attempt to create high-speed mobile data networks to force the telecommunications industry to modify its long-standing developments centring on mobile cellular networks. This confrontation of interests, and its vast implications, are on display in the posturing around the decisions regarding 4G. Take, for instance, this reported comment of the WiMAX Forum's Vice-President Mohammed Shakouri (a a representative of Alvarion, one of the world's largest WiMAX specialists, headquartered in Israel):

'WiMAX is not a cell phone,' Shakouri said. 'You're not going to go to the telephone store to buy broadband services; you're going to go to consumer electronics, to the retail store.'

(Barthold 2009)

WiMax is the most prominent attempt to provide an alternative network infra-structure to the rough consensus that emerged with 3G networks. The history of 3G has been well discussed elsewhere, but suffice to recall that the revolutionary claims of advanced mobile networks articulated by its proponents, especially the European developers and promoters, but also East Asian counterparts, were modulated by the turn of the twentieth century. Various factors were at play, but especially the vast losses crystallized in the telco 'tech wreck'. Early auctions of 3G licences had seen successful bidders pay enormous sums, much to the delight of governments. However, auctions held later were not so successful. The overall result was that companies holding licences struggled to see how the required investment to implement 3G networks could quickly recoup their costs. Telcos and mobile carriers around the world looked at how they could eke revenue from enhancements to existing 2G networks, through so-called '2.5G' and '2.75G' technologies. Investments in 3G networks occurred steadily along-side this, with some companies, such as Hutchison, specializing in 3G – and developing products and marketing based upon its virtues. By and by 3G net-works have become the basis for mobile networks in developed countries espe-cially – though 2G networks (basic and enhanced varities) still predominate elsewhere. The difficult questions now centre on what the building blocks for future mobile networks should be.

A clear technical consensus emerged through many futures and planning exercises, that things called 'next-generation networks' would be packet-switched networks based on the internet protocol (IP) (rather than classic circuit-switched telephone then telecommunications networks). The starting point for most dis-cussions of future networks, then, is this centrality of the internet, and how to properly design and dimension networks to offer the bandwidth, reliability, capability and quality of service that users now require (Alleman and Rappoport 2009). The discussion about mobile media fits into this broader setting. It is a discussion about the relative weight, and investment, to be given to fixed rather than mobile components of the networks. It is also a conversation, or really a battle, about which kind of networks actors should support. For those in the telecommunications and mobile industry that have already invested heavily in 3G networks, it makes financial sense – at least in the short- or medium-term – to look at an evolutionary path building on this expertise and technology. Here what has emerged is something called long-term evolution (LTE). Its roots are in moves by 3G supporters to fashion a way forward in the late 1990s, notably with the formation of the third generation partnership project (3GPP) in 1998. (3GPP now bears the motto 'setting the standard for mobile broadband'). The Long Term Evolution project was commenced in 2004 'focused on enhancing the Universal Terrestrial Radio Access (UTRA) and optimizing 3GPP's radio access architecture' (3GPP 2009). Participants now envisage the LTE Advanced version, to properly take the technology into the 4G era. The trajectory is imagined as an evolution, more or less smooth, to 4G networks. The idea of 4G has been under discussion and development for sometime. No overriding idea regarding 4G has yet triumphed over others. International Mobile Telecommunications-Advanced (IMT-Advanced) is the most coherent standards initiative in the 4G area, but there are quite a few others. As well as various implementations of WiMAX, LTE and LTE Advanced, there are also HC-SDMA ('iBurst'), and Flash-OFDM. The babel of standards and implementations constitutes a collective attempt to grapple with the key ingredients of 4G. The recurring elements include: packet-switching; very high data rates by today's standards, up to 1Gb (while stationary, less if in motion); support of network for many internet-connected devices (so use of the next internet standard, IPv6, is necessary, to provide a greater number of addresses); much longer range of communications; high reliability; seamless handoff of devices among various networks; roaming; efficient use of spectrum.

Clearly 4G functions as a horizon for imagining, and perhaps realizing, various dreams associated with mobile communications for at least 20 years now. What is clear is that whatever 4G eventuates as, it will be a collection of standards, devises and a hybrid of networks. The new entrants from the world of internet and computers shaping mobile media are likely to achieve their objectives, and gain a substantial part of the 4G markets. This view is supported by the fact that the telco and cell phone players themselves are having a bet either way (so to speak), and taking a stake in developments such as Wi-Max. Further, we see telecommunications equipment companies, such as Alcatel-Lucent (inheritor of the famous Bell Labs), making substantial investments in the internet infrastructure options – notably IP TV – and seeking to lead industry, policy and regulatory debates also. If 4G looks complicated enough already even at this early stage, there are various other networks and technologies now well established and significant enough to warrant serious contemplation for how they fit into mobile media. These include wireless sensor, mesh and radio frequency identification (RFID) networks, that I can only mention here. Evidence for the importance of these networks can be seen in the fact that a number of regulators around the world have commissioned research upon these, or are seriously taking them into consideration for future planning.

The prospects of these various networks, and how they will knit together, or diverge, depends critically upon availability of the radio waves to carry their signals – and so upon spectrum, its licensing and use. Always important, if underrated, the allocation of spectrum for future mobile services has become a topic of intense debate and scrutiny. Mobile media has been placed at the crossroads of old and new media through what has been dubbed the 'digital dividend'. That is, the spectrum that was formerly used by analogue television will become progressively available for other services, as the switchover to digital television occurs around the world. Digital television uses spectrum more efficiently than its analogue counterpart, and regulators and governments have managed to curb the enthusiasm for existing television interests to simply soak up the extra spectrum freed up (for instance, through additional spectrum needed for high-definition television). As analogue television networks are shut down, attention has been focused upon the new spectrum bands, which could support the various new mobile networks. The prospect of new spectrum bringing out new entrants and services has preoccupied policy makers, who have sought to promote availability, coverage and access to broadband internet, mobile and media services, balancing the rights and prospects of existing players with the need to create genuinely viable and new alternative infrastructures to the continuing monopolies, or at least dominant infrastructures, built upon copper telephone networks and then cable pay television.

New mobile media businesses

In this chapter, I have sought key features of the ownership and control of cell phones and media businesses interested in cell phones. In some sense, this is the more or less known, or at least knowable, terrain of mobile media. This terrain is shaped out of the albeit dramatically changing structures of mobile telecommunications, as these grow in complexity at national and regional levels, yet still constitute a global system (Rugman 2005; Rugman and Verbeke 2004). It is also shaped by the interplay of various forces that I have not been able to foreground and analyze here, but which are very much central to the politics of globalization, media and cell phones: gender (Cohen and Brodie 2007; Ng Choon Sim and Mitter 2005); the relations of work and labour (Mosco and McKerher 2007; Mosco 2008); affect and emotion; bodies and difference – for example, the production and reproduction of disability (Goggin and Newell 2003), and the reshaping of working and middle classes through the process of technology construction (Qui 2009).

The shape of this terrain is shifting again with the convoluted evolution of 2G and 3G mobile networks, the real potential for opening up of markets with 4G networks, and the move to IP networks, now constituting the battle over wirelines services. The substrata of mobile media also includes the significant market power and technology design and supply forces constituted by the handset and equipment manufacturers – especially evident in the battles over intelligent devices, themselves important nodes in the mobile media ecology. Involved in networks, handsets and services are the media and entertainment companies – rising forces expanding the horizon of telecommunications, most companies now an admixture of media interests. Finally, there are even more enterprises and projects that are also important, if nascent, parts of global mobile media. These are new kinds of media, expanding our ideas beyond the joining of previously well recognized media to mobiles. These are the fertile new areas of global mobile media that I will explore in the second part of the book, discussing in turn mobile music, mobile television, mobile games and mobile internet. Before we turn to this, it is important first to consider the demand, or user, side of mobile media – and to do so to make a broad shift from political to cultural economy.

Chapter 3

The cultural economy of cell phones
New relations of consumption and production

As a way of understanding media, political economy is relatively well established. It offers clear ways to approach questions of power and media, especially helpful with its emphases on ownership, control, structures and arrangements of power. In approaching mobile media from the standpoint of political economy in Chapter 2 – however loosely – I sketched the kinds of firms that largely organize mobile media production. As well as power, and media, the other cardinal concept of this book is culture. There are many ways to draw the relationships between power and culture, long debated, for instance, across those committed to political economy approaches in the study of media and communication (Chakravartty and Zhao 2007), and those who are interested in a range of other approaches, developed in cultural theory and studies especially. At some peril, I will skirt those debates here, and consider the recently developed approach of cultural economy.

Cultural economy offers a range of approaches to thinking about culture, value and policy (for instance, Aitken 2007; Ash and Thrift 2004; Best and Paterson 2009; du Gay and Pryke 2002). There are economists who have long studied the arts, who also consider the broader concept of culture. The question of cultural policy, rather than say arts policy, emerged during the 1990s. It represents an attempt to grapple with the wide range of kinds of culture, and the value that accrues and is placed upon these across a society. It remain controversial because it involves a de-centring of so-called 'elite' arts or cultural forms, in favour of research and policy that seeks to do justice to, say, computer games, handicrafts and festivals, as much as opera, literature and theatre. Cultural economy is worth pursuing precisely because of the heightened role that culture plays in contemporary economies. This is thematized in the policy and intellectual movements around creativity, notably in 'creative industries' discourse. Theorists of creative industries argue for the need to move beyond old understandings – pejorative and neutral alike – of cultural industries, to a recognition of the role that creativity plays in everyday life, and in the creation of economic value. The importance of cultural economy has grown rapidly in the past decade, especially with developments in globalization, and digital cultures and forms play a significant role in this. Though there has been little work to date on cell phones and the cultural economy, cell phones are likely to feature significantly in this (Cunningham and Potts 2009).

We might start by measuring how much digital technologies, and in our case here, mobile media, might contribute to cultural goods and service, and so to our economy. Cultural economy, however, signifies other things too. In political economy we are accustomed to looking for the new ways in which power is arranged, brought together and functions in a system (hence the connotations of the word 'economy'). There is a similar resemblance evoked by the economy of culture. What are the new kinds of systems – economies – that construct our relationships with, around, and through culture forms? What new cultural practices and characteristics arise in this? What are the systems of value arising from these? Here cultural economy offers a way to bring together central questions about digital technologies and cultures – especially to do with the role of use and the new role consumption and creativity is believed to have in new media. Again, less has been written to date regarding cell phones in this – attention has focused upon internet based technologies and cultures, with an assumption that cell phones add to, or extend, such developments.

Against this background this chapter seeks to consider implications of cultural economy of mobile media. First, I investigate the economy of consumption and use of mobile media. Who consumes mobile media? How is mobile media being used in different regions of the world? How are cell phones figuring as media in developing countries? How do forms of mobile media relate to other forms of cultural undertaking, value and distribution, such as traditional television, film, music and newspapers? Having discussed some indicators of mobile media use in the second section, I discuss the valorization of consumption, and the creative role of the consumer in shaping, indeed sometimes co-producing, technologies. New forms of participative culture have emerged, notably in gaming, but mobile media also has its own distinctive forms of creative consumption that need to be scrutinized. Third, I look at the area of 'user-generated content', which has rapidly emerged as a strategically important area in internet cultures, especially with the meteoric rise of music (Napster), photo (Flickr) and video (YouTube) networks and sites. In one sense the forms of user-generated content allied with mobile media have been more easily captured for revenue because of telecommunications billing systems, or through the wholesale and retail merchandising and sales chains of handsets and accessories (upon which are based user customization of mobiles – Fortunati 2006, and Hjorth 2009b); on the other hand, the kinds of new cultural activity of mobile media, in which users are key, have not yet been adequately registered.

Consumption of mobile media

The world figures on the total consumption of cellular phones reveal an astonishing quantity of devices and subscriptions. The most reliable statistics are those gathered by the International Telecommunications Union, from national bodies, and chart indicators of telecommunications from 1960 onwards for over 200 economies (Sutherland 2008). If we look at the most recently available data for the past decade, 1998–2008, the phenomenal growth of cell phones is evident. In 2008, there were some 4.045 billion mobile cellular subscribers in the world, with an average of 59.75 cell phone subscribers per 100 inhabitants (ITU 2009b). Overall, access and use of cell phones by the world's population has grown significantly. From the early 2000s onwards, with the saturation of markets in early adopter countries, notably in the global North, evident or anticipated, the focus of mobile companies turned in earnest to markets with potential for growth. Therefore across all regions we can see a shift in 2005 especially with the uptake of subscriptions.

Nonetheless, great variation across countries remains. The most cell phone saturated country is United Arab Emirates with 208.65 subscriptions per 100 inhabitants, or about two cell phone subscriptions per person – presumably helped by its relative wealth, small size, relatively even topography and modest population (almost three million people). The honour for the lowest rate of cell phone subscriptions is taken by Myanmar (Burma), with 0.74, or less than one per 100 inhabitants – despite the important role that cell phones have played in human rights activism in that country. The second lowest rung is occupied by Eritrea with 2.2 cell phone subscriptions per 100 inhabitants.

There are broad disparities in cell phone distribution between regions – OECD countries, for instance, eclipsing others, or Europe, North America, Japan and Korea well ahead of the rest. Such differences continue, but over time have become less stark. Where the great contrasts really lie now are among various countries in the same region. Europe, for instance, has countries with very high cell phone ownership and use (Finland, Sweden, Denmark, Estonia, Italy, Germany) but others with relatively moderate, if accelerating, recourse to cell phones (France, Serbia). There are telling comparisons to be drawn between European access to and use of cell phones – and that of internet, especially broadband internet. Africa is the locus of much activity by the cell phone industry (as we have already seen in Chapter 2), yet this continent is a real mix of those with intensive use of cell phones and those with much less intense use, or indeed little access:

> In 1998, there were some 8.2 million fixed telephone lines in Africa, which corresponded to a penetration of 1.4 per cent, the lowest of any region. Between 1998 and 2008, the region added only 2.4 million telephone lines … In 2000, the number of mobile cellular subscriptions surpassed that of fixed telephone lines in Africa … reaching a total of nearly 246 million subscriptions by 2008. The high ratio of mobile cellular subscriptions to fixed telephone lines (the highest of any region in the world), and the high mobile cellular growth rate suggest that Africa has taken the lead in the shift from fixed to mobile telephony, a trend that can be observed worldwide.
>
> (ITU 2009c: 3)

Thus, the scale of access to mobiles in Africa has altered dramatically over the span of less than a decade:

> Between 2000 and 2008, mobile cellular penetration has risen from less than two in 100 inhabitants to 33 out of 100 ... [though] penetration rates are still considerably lower in Africa than in other regions. Over time, mobile cellular subscriptions have become more evenly distributed across the region. This is illustrated by the situation in South Africa which, in 2000, accounted for 74 per cent of Africa's mobile cellular subscriptions. Yet by 2008, only 19 per cent of Africa's mobile subscriptions were located there. The growth in Nigeria is most notable, but [also in] other countries including Kenya, Ghana, Tanzania and Côte d'Ivoire ...
> (ITU 2009c: 4; cf. Gray 2006, James and Versteeg 2007, and Minges 1999)

Diffusion of cell phones varies greatly still, with subscription rates varying from 'more than 90 in the Seychelles, Gabon, and South Africa to less than five in Eritrea, Ethiopia and the Central African Republic' (ITU 2009c: 15). Nonetheless, with many of the 400,000 villages and rural areas lacking fixed telephones (less than three per cent penetration) and public internet (less than one per cent), by contrast mobile signals now cover some 40 per cent of such populations (that is, rural dwellers at least have potential access to the infrastructure, if they can overcome income and other issues) (ITU 2009c: 13–14; cf. Chabossou et al. 2008). Latin America and the Caribbean also offer a stark example of countries with a range of levels of GDP, great disparities in wealth across and within the country's population, with rising but differentiated levels of mobile use.[1] Argentina claims 117 subscribers per 100 people, relatively poor Guatemala has 109, Chile has 88, Bolivia approximately 50 and Cuba only three per cent.

Despite this unevenness of diffusion what is remarkable is the way that cell phones now figure so heavily in the telecommunications ecologies of developing countries. To understand these developments, we need to consider the changing role of cell phone networks and operators, and how these form part of a much larger, mixed telecommunications and convergent media environment. Recalling the development of cell phones reminds us that universal service in telecommunications – the idea of availability of telecommunications for all citizens in a country – was first imagined on the model of fixed-line voice telephony (Mueller 1997; Goggin 1998). From the late 1980s and through the 1990s there ensued heated debates on universal service, the upshot of which was to achieve a more detailed and comprehensive understanding of the concept – and new ways to secure its funding in competitive environments (OECD 1991; Sawhney 1994). What was also unfolding in the processes of telecommunication reforms was the new form of provision represented by cell phones (Goggin 2008c). In many places, cell phones were an early form of private sector, competitive provision of telecommunications. Moreover cell phones represented an intense area of competition and innovation, because they introduced new intermediaries, especially retailers, micro-enterprises, resellers and handset vendors into telecommunications (as discussed in relation to copycat handsets in Chapter 2). For consumers, what this meant in practical terms was the availability of a whole range of telecommunications services that were relatively easy to access and affordable to purchase. These new mobile products and services revolutionized telecommunications for many less well-off consumers, especially in poor countries. For instance, pre-paid phone cards coupled with cheap phones – a consequence of mass diffusion, competition in manufacturing and provision, as well as technical and design advances – have seen the widespread use of cell phones by people on low incomes (Mahan 2003). With the advent of new pricing products and possibility through cell phones, their billing systems and software utilised, barriers to use have been significantly reduced – with relatively low handset phone prices, reduction of upfront access and ongoing rental, and budgeting that can be managed through a range of options (especially pre-paid). Indeed a great deal more can be done by companies and regulators to use the capacities of cell phones to address affordability issues for poor users (Milne 2006).

Particular groups of consumers – for example, young people in wealthy countries, low-income groups and micro-entrepreneurs in developing countries – developed new systems of social and user innovation centring on the affordances of cell phones (Haddon et al. 2005). While associated with the individual in many developed countries, the cell phone was reworked and activated as a collective, shared device in developing countries – a substitute for payphones, or shared household phones, in the famous case of the village 'phone ladies' (Sullivan 2007). Users developed new techniques for controlling or sharing costs of cell phones through missed call messages, beeping (Donner 2007), or SMS. In turn, operators have used these opportunities to develop new services, blending fixed and mobile, as evidenced in the success of the South African 'please call me' free SMS service (funded by advertising attached to the text message). Also the cell phone has become entwined in the new social and economic patterns, especially regarding small and micro-enterprises and entrepreneurship (Donner 2008). Finally, cell phones have been highly significant in the social maintenance and micro-economic, credit and banking patterns of users in developing countries (Hughes and Lonie 2007), notably the migrant and diasporic workers wishing to keep in touch or send remittances to their relatives in their home country (GSM Association 2007).

Cell phones are also offering different kinds of services now widely used by consumers every day in conjunction with, complementing, or substituting fixed-line telecommunications. Substitution is worth remarking upon here, because it has been quite a phenomenon in advanced economies, where groups of users, notably young people in shared households, have decided to retain a cell phone as their only phone – rather than also, or solely, maintaining a fixed-line subscription (cf. Wirzenius 2008 on the advanced abandonment of fixed lines in Finland).

While there is good evidence of the widespread use of cell phones, and the trends in which they are embedded and to which they contribute, there is only patchy information available on the diverse aspects of mobile media. Firstly, the ITU data, as can be seen, focuses on cellular phones as a general category. Depending on our definition, however, mobile media requires various capabilities: messaging; camera function; internet; music player; video watching; location technology (mobile or GPS); sufficient computing power to run advanced graphics, video and audio; operating systems, interfaces and applications. As well as the functionality of the handset, network capabilities and features are important. Advanced 2G networks offer good data capabilities, sufficient to underpin many mobile media. However, 3G networks make advances in distribution of content and connectivity possible that are especially important for mobile multimedia and networked mobile cultures. What do we know about the diffusion of advanced cell phones and the development of 3G networks? Finally, if handset and network capability exists, what data do we have about the kinds of mobile that media users actually consume, or engage with?

Figures on ownership of different brands and types of handset are gathered by vendors and also by market research companies. They are uncertain, however, given the built-in obsolence, turn-over and existence in households of extra phones, which consumers are actually using. Some research is also available on the brands of consumers' use (for example, AIMIA 2009). There is also research in which consumers report whether they have 2, 2.5 or 3G capable phones (such as Ofcom 2009b), however, not surprisingly, many are unsure regarding this.

Data on availability of networks is probably most reliable (although again it is not always clear that the existence of infrastructure translates into consumer use). Regarding the kind of networks that underpin the further development of mobile media, 3G networks have only developed relatively slowly. In the OECD countries, the percentage of 3G subscribers reached 18.2 per cent of all mobile subscriptions in 2007 (OECD 2009). Korea had the most 3G subscribers (nearly 100 per cent), followed by Japan (82 per cent) and Italy, and then the remaining OECD countries each had less than 25 per cent (OECD 2009: 103).

The uneven diffusion of 3G networks is much more evident when we consider other country groupings and regions. In the Americas there were around 25 million 3G subscribers in 2008 (with W-CDMA being the preferred technology). However, some 80 per cent of these were in North America, with Latin American and the Caribbean only accounting for some 4.7 million subscribers (43 per cent of these being in Brazil) (ITU 2009d: 22). Interestingly, if we look at the extension and upgrade of existing 2G networks (specifically, CDMA 2000 based EV-DO technology), we find another 5.9 million subscribers in Latin America and the Caribbean and almost 63.2 million in North America (ITU 2009d: 22). While not fully-fledged 3G mobile, these advanced 2G networks still offer broadband data, especially, with the appropriate spectrum, to rural consumers (García-Murilloa and Rendón 2009). In Africa, present

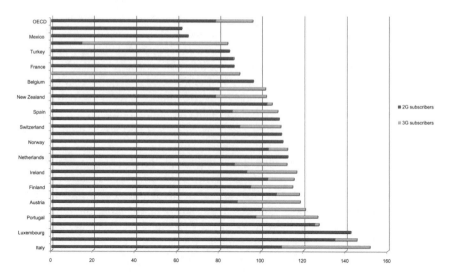

Figure 3.1 2G and 3G mobile subscribers per 100 inhabitants (OECD 2009: 103).

Note: Portugal's 2G data includes both 2G and 3G subscriptions

diffusion of 3G networks is low, but this is the area where investment is now occurring:

> As an increasing number of countries in Africa are deploying IMT-2000/ 3G networks, and fixed telephone line networks remain underdeveloped, mobile broadband has the potential of becoming Africa's main broadband Internet access method in the future.
>
> (ITU 2009d)

Why have 3G networks been slow to develop? A multinational study of diffusion of 3G mobile found that contributing factors were 'multiple standardization policy, lower level of 1G and 2G penetration, and a higher level of income' (Lee et al. 2008: 1; cf. Henten and Nicolajsen 2009, and Koski and Tobias 2007). To which, one would certainly wish to add factors such as market and institutional structure (a strong emphasis of ITU competition and development discourse – see ITU 2009c and d; also Curwen 2002), and socio-technical factors (Goggin 2006; Vincent 2004; Gao and Rafiq 2009a and b).

After this brief look at patterns in the global diffusion of mobile devices and networks, what then does the available data tell us about the consumption of mobile media? Who actually views mobile television, listens to music on their cell phone, browses the internet or uses search on a cell phone, downloads apps, or deploys their device for navigation and wayfinding? Well, unfortunately, not a lot of reliable, comprehensive research exists. Useful data is available from some national regulatory bodies and industry associations, otherwise it is scattered through the academic literature. Doubtless cell phone carriers, vendors and other industry players hold invaluable data, but rarely make it available publicly. As yet there is no cell phone equivalent of the World Internet Survey, a co-ordinated longitudinal exercise to chart the use of and attitudes towards the internet, that is undertaken by university researchers in various countries. What data does exist – to hazard a gross generalization – indicates that certain kinds of mobile media are well established (namely, cell phone data such as ringtones, music and graphics downloads), but that many kinds of mobile media are only just beginning to find their adherents. I will briefly sample some indicative research, drawn mainly from the English-language literatures, especially nationally, from the UK, and Europe, the US and Australian research.

Mobile internet is becoming an important part of mobile media consumption. A 2009 British study revealed that 22 per cent of respondents use their cell phone for web or data access, and 19 per cent for listening to audio content (Ofcom 2009a). A Pew Centre study of the US found that accessing of the internet via cell phones has sharply increased: 'In December 2007, 24 per cent of Americans said they had at some point used the internet on their mobile device. By April 2009, 32 per cent of Americans said they had at some point used the internet on their mobile device' (Horrigan 2009: 3). The study also found that African Americans were leading users: '48 per cent of African Americans have at one time used their mobile device to access the internet for information, emailing, or instant-messaging, half again the national average of 32 per cent' (Horrigan 2009: 4). Interestingly also, Pew found that, compared to cell phones, 'other access devices – iPods, game consoles, or e-books – for now play a small role in people's wireless online habits' (Horrigan 2009: 5). Also, 17 per cent report having used one of these four devices to access the internet, but the 'pool of users on these devices adds just 5 percentage points to the pool of wireless users' (Horrigan 2009: 5). Another Pew study on Twitter use found that:

> as of September 2009, 54 per cent of internet users have a wireless connection to the internet via a laptop, cell phone, game console, or other mobile device. Of those, 25 per cent use Twitter or another service, up from 14 per cent of wireless users in December 2008.
>
> (Fox et al. 2009: 6)

A 2009 Australian industry study showed that 60 per cent of respondents had accessed a website via their mobile (AIMIA 2009: 52). Email was used by 36 per cent, chatrooms by nine per cent, instant messaging by 18 per cent and social networking by 32 per cent (the latter a substantial growth area). These forms of internet communication were all eclipsed by MMS, used by 57 per cent. When it came to frequency of use, however, respondents said they used social networking (46 per cent) and email (42 per cent) daily, whereas MMS was only used daily by nine per cent and video calling by a dedicated seven per cent (AMIA 2009: 59). While mobile internet use grows, well established types of entertainment content still hold sway in mobile media. For instance, in Australia the top-ranked services and content in 2009 were, in order: games, ringtones, music, wallpapers. Screensavers dropped to sixth position, with videos being more popular (AIMIA 2009: 5).

As discussed in Chapter 2, mobile broadband has been a fast growing area, but still concentrated in the wealthy countries to date: 'While many developing countries (e.g. Indonesia, the Maldives, the Philippines and Sri Lanka) have launched 3G mobile broadband networks, the vast majority of broadband sub-scribers remain concentrated in the developed world' (ITU 2009a: 71). British research shows that: 'Use of mobile broadband appears to be being driven by the more affluent demographic groups ... Mobile broadband connection also increases with household income' (Ofcom 2009a: 34). Slightly more men than women had mobile broadband (with the extra one per cent being men who also had fixed-line broadband) (Ofcom 2009a: 33). Where available, a constraint on mobile internet takeup has been pricing of data. Whether the internet is accessed over a mobile device (such as a standard phone, a smartphone or an iPhone), or mobile broadband card, data rates have dropped to stimulate demand, but generally remain quite high compared to fixed-line broadband:

> Unlike fixed broadband which is sold based on speed, mobile broadband is typically marketed by data allowance ... most mobile operators segment subscriber groups by the amount of data included in the subscription each month. Typically mobile operators include a limited amount of traffic per month with the subscription and then charge users for each additional megabyte of traffic transmitted. Data caps are commonly much lower on mobile broadband than on fixed networks due to the inherent scarcity of spectral capacity.
>
> (OECD 2009: 284)

Or, as the ITU reassuringly puts it: 'The speed, quality and throughput of mobile broadband can all be varied to optimize investment budgets' (ITU 2009a: 44).

Mobile television take-up has also been sluggish. While the OECD does not give figures, it comments:

> Despite growth in the Korean and Japanese markets, the growth in video over cell phones has been slow across the OECD. The services offered by carriers are still in their infancy and subscribers must transition to new handsets and pay for new subscriptions in order to benefit from the enhanced service offerings. Television on mobile handsets is available in other countries but take-up has not been as significant as in Korea and Japan. In Italy, operators have been successful selling mobile-TV enabled handsets but television usage remains low.
>
> (OECD 2009: 194)

Australian data shows that 16 per cent of respondents used mobile television in the past 12 months, with nine per cent of these using it every day (AIMIA 2009: 64). British research across the nation and regions found only one per cent of respondents saying they used their mobile phone for TV streaming, compared to six per cent who downloaded games, three per cent to find out sports scores, receive news, listen to podcasts or download a video clip, and two per cent who used their mobile for video streaming or calling (Ofcom 2009b, see table 36).

As we can see from this mosaic of information, there is a lack of good data on mobile media in markets where these are already established to some extent as 'rich' mobile media. The state of knowledge is even more scant in emerging markets and developing countries, where those with an interest in providing such data have many fewer resources to do so. There is little study or data on learning, social software or gaming in mobile media in developing countries, for instance (an exception is Adesope et al. 2007). There is some research available, either from market research or stand alone industry studies, but from this it is difficult to compose a meaningful aggregrate picture – and it is beyond my scope here. Clearly, though, in the markets for 'rich' media, some of which have been noted, as well as markets where 'low-end', or 'poor' mobile media predominate, there are already good reasons to ask probing questions about what the future of global mobile media will look like from the perspective of consumers and users. Such discussions are already underway by those rethinking the concept of information and communications technology for development (ICT4D):

> Current growth rates will likely carry usage to well over 90 per cent of the world's population, leaving the questions as those of reaching the last half-billion, and of the spread of Internet-enabled phones, given that most phones in poor communities are currently calls-and-SMS-only. For both these questions, the need for hardware innovation may re-emerge. There are also likely to be innovations as iPhone-and-apps-type developments on mobiles converge with netbook-type attempts to produce lower-cost PC-like terminal devices; ending with something like a 'Blackberry-for-development'.
>
> (Heeks 2009a)

The difficulty faced in understanding these developments and reflecting these in appropriate design is the paucity of data, information, user and critical perspectives to shape, inform and support the conversations and action needed (Blum et al. 2005; Bouwman et al. 2008; Brewer and Dourish 2008; Green et al. 2001; Van de Kar and den Hengst 2009).

Creative consumption and the cell phone

Much attention has been paid to consumption in recent years. In digital cultures, creativity has been especially valorized – not only seen as central to dynamics of the kinds of participation believed to be characteristic of digital technologies, but also of great significance to the wider economy. Various theorists have sought to capture, and often to celebrate, what occurs in these processes. Governing concepts include 'participatory culture' (Jenkins 2006), 'crowdsourcing' (Howe 2008), 'produser' (Bruns 2008), 'user customization' (Hjorth 2009b). Then various accounts of the new kinds of economic relationships have also been generated, ranging from the 'new', 'creative' or 'hybrid' economy (Lessig 2009), to Anderson's now famous argument for the importance of the 'long tail' (Anderson 2006 and 2009). One of the difficulties of sorting through these theories is their conflation, especially in almost naturalized discourses such as Web 2.0. As we have already seen, cell phones are certainly assuming a growing importance in the area of cultural economy – registered in the many new forms, if not all successful or well-subscribed, of media. Yet there are some very interesting threshold questions about how creativity and consumption work in mobile media.

A useful starting point is Axel Bruns' account of the principles of online 'produsage' communities (Bruns 2008), that reach their apex in projects like Wikipedia. Interestingly the principles Bruns discerns that are crucial to the viability and sustainable flourishing of creativity in various online settings have a vexed relationship to industrial forms of organization, typically represented in most large corporations. There is great contention about the implications of such communities, and their potential for distributed, collaborative, generative work, and what they mean for important social functions – such as that of journalism (Allan 2006). Various theorists, including Bruns, strongly argue for at least some significant substitutability between conventional journalism – upon which repose important functions for democracy of information, truth-telling, scrutiny, critique and investigation of the social – and open source, distributed news, blogging, social media and other affiliated projects. The future of journalism, on such accounts, is not so dire – in fact, the openness inherent in such collaborations can transform such media for the better. In response, many critics suggest that journalism still needs particular kinds of expertise to be sustained by skilled professionals, resources, networks, and the relationships and contexts that existing media organizations, such as newspapers, bring together.

Where do mobile media fit into these emerging patterns about active, creative consumption and the discussions about how to gauge and measure them, and what do they mean? Mobiles are often annexed to such accounts. A good example of this can be observed in the typical accounts of citizen journalism (Allan and Thorsen 2009; Rosen 1999). Many of the theorists and promoters of citizen journalism offer the cell phone camera user as the epitome of this new paradigm (Gillmor 2006; Gordon 2007), as too do enthusiasts for the paradigm shift that mobile journalism ('mojo') can offer (Quinn 2009). The difficulty we face is discerning what is the genuinely new and different kind of relationship to cultural production, consumption and economy to be found here.

Cell phone users and content generation

A leading instance of the heightened importance of consumption for production itself can be found in user-generated content. In the contemporary internet, there are at least two obvious general senses in which use and users are generating content. First, because of the technical nature of the internet, a great deal of data is generated by users doing quite everyday things. Signing up for websites, or social networking sites. Posting photos on Flickr, or videos on YouTube. Blogging on WordPress, and tweeting incessantly or discreetly on Twitter. While users can be more or less informed about protecting their privacy, and such technology can be less or more configurable to afford this, a great deal of data is being generated – that, in turn, has its unforeseen uses, and enormous commercial as well as public value. Second, much of the popular technologies of the internet since at least 2001, if not having their antecedents before this, revolve around users making non-trivial investments of time, money, and dare one say it, creativity, and making this available to others online. Indeed many of these technologies could not exist in the forms they do without sharing, modification, swapping, downloading, uploading and reworking of material among users.

User-generated content raises pressing questions for those interested in understanding the nature of mobile media, but also for policymakers. First, there is the question of the nature, depth and extent of the phenomena. The European Union, for instance, commissioned a 2008 study that mapped the growth of user-generated content in Europe, suggesting that it was outstripping that observed in the US – the focus of much international attention at that time (Le Borgne-Bachschmidt et al. 2008). What is not so clear, however, is how cell phones fit into these patterns of user-generated content. It is especially unclear whether the burgeoning future of mobile media – outside the early adopter, global North countries – fits into both discussions of user-generated content, and the gathering of data regarding it (see Watkins and Tacchi 2008 for a UNESCO-commissioned pioneering study of user-generated content for development). The focus of researchers, and public discussion too, has been on the internet as a prime site for user-generated content. As well as particular technology and user characteristics of the internet, it has also allowed – serendipitously – the generation of much data, as we have observed, but also the harvesting of such data. It is possible to get a range of numbers that measure internet-based user-generated content, even if the interpretation and significance of such data lags behind.

In comparison, the measurement of volumes and incidence of cell phone user-generated content poses some tricky challenges. The problem is that much of the data about cell phone media traffic, application and uses lies in the hands of the various industry players – especially those who control the networks, such as carriers and service providers, who always have detailed traffic data, billing data and now data from an increasing range of online and mobile services they offer or in which they have a hand. A useful example is provided by mobile television. Who has the usage statistics on mobile television? The carriers and the commercial partners, such as programme and content suppliers, who play a part in offering the service. Who has information on, say, iPhone usage and apps? Again, the carriers and service providers on mobile usage, and a new group of intermediaries with respect to iPhone apps: namely the apps store controllers (Apple) and individual apps developers and providers. These groups control the release of this information. As we have seen, other data, of course, is gathered by usage and ratings agencies (such as Nielsen NetRatings), industry associations with an interest in keeping tabs on, and promoting, mobile media, regulators (who wish to understand emerging technology use and the potential policy issues it raises), and various university, institute or thinktank-based researchers. If a mobile media application or service has an internet aspect to it, then it is likely that data relating to it can also be gathered through the new internet technologies for doing this.

This threshold issue of gauging the extent of mobile user-generated content points us to some pertinent, substantive questions in this area that arise from cultural economy. There is a longstanding debate on how we approach questions of participation in a society where information and communications technologies play an important role. With creative consumption, rhetorics of Web 2.0 and user-generated content, the problematic, as we have seen, becomes one in which participation is greatly expanded and takes on a new sense. Rather than being termed 'the information society', a concept with an almost four decade, evocative and ambiguous lineage, we speak of 'participatory cultures', the 'participative web', or 'supporting a participative information society' (Le Borgne-Bachschmidt et al. 2008). The structure of the technologies themselves, and their assumed cultures of use, now suppose themselves inherently participatory – and this changes, it appears, our account of the information society, or indeed of society itself.

Such claims are contentious, to say the least, and not without their critiques. If we take them at face value, however, we are surely required to understand what kinds of participation are actually occurring, possible or suggested by media (Carpentier and De Cleen 2008) – in this case, mobile media. Then we need to explore what kinds of participation we think are desirable – from a variety of economic, social, political, cultural or even ethical and moral standpoints. Many of the available discussions actually do carry governing assumptions about the kinds of participation their proponents envisage. Innovation, for instance, is prized at present, and access to and use of mobile media, as much as online media, is often urged to foster user-generated content, spreading this kind of participation in 'creative economy' activity for the economic welfare benefits it might bring. Far less well discussed, in relation to mobile media, are their concrete implications for social, political and cultural participation. This is surprising, when one considers the wide range of discussions of such kinds of participation in relation to the internet. As well as many accounts of how participation actually does occur, and what are the affordances of internet tech-nologies in relation to traditional and new structures of participation, there are quite a number of accounts that explicitly offer a normative view on participa-tion. Not so for mobile media, where discussions of participation, its encoding and 'hard-wiring' in cell phones and mobile media technologies, and the norms that might govern it, are few and far between. These are the important issues concerning mobile media that I will now proceed to investigate in Part II of the book, with case studies of mobile music, television, gaming and the internet.

Note

1 The use and understanding of this data has been greatly improved by the use of visualization technologies, freely available via the internet, such as Google Motion Charts. The use of such data to contest myths around development was popularized by Swedish development researcher Hans Rosling, through his Gapminder foundation (see his cult presentation to the 2006 TED forum – Rosling 2006). Useful visualiza-tions of the ITU 1998–2008 data have been created by various cell phone scholars (Heeks 2009b; Ling 2009; Qui 2009).

Part II

Mobile media cultures

Chapter 4

Mobile music
Ringtones, music players and the sound of everything

If a song can survive being transposed from live instruments to a cell-phone micro-chip, it must have musically hardy DNA ... Ringtones, it turns out, are inherently pop: musical expression distilled to one urgent, representative hook. As ringtones become part of our environment, they could push pop music toward new levels of concision, repetition, and catchiness.

(Frere-Jones 2005)

Imagine a future where you have a little cloud above your head and in that is everything you think is groovy, and you can carry that along with you and pull it down to either watch or share, and it's all controlled by this little device in your pocket.

(David Stewart of the Eurythmics, quoted in Bruno 2008d)

What are the forces and constraints that limit present-day usage on the mobile to simply parallel what we do in the living room or on a stationary computer? Instead of replicating traditional media in a portable package, can we not look at the mobile phone and high-bandwidth mobile networks as an artistic canvas on which to create entirely new forms of art?

(Tanaka and Gemeinboeck 2009: 174)

Call-bells and ringers

Music was perhaps the first widely accepted form of mobile media – and the mobile has steadily been consolidating its place in the music industry, embedding itself in the consumption of music not to mention in people's musical practices. Of course, music has an intriguing place in the history of the telephone, indeed the reproduction and transmission of sound over distance generally. Alexander Graham Bell is the figure most widely associated with the invention of the telephone – our understandings of science and technology still revolving around myths of heroic, solitary inventors. However, there were other important figures in the origins of the telephone, one of these being Elisha Gray. Gray had established himself as an important figure in the development of the telegraph in the US, and began to experiment with the transmission of sound – what he called 'vibratory currents' (Hounshell 1975: 133). Gray experimented with transmitting sound, creating single and double tones, using variously his bathtub, a violin and diaphram electronic magnetic receivers. He concluded that music telegraphy was as much possible as voice telegraphy, or something called multiple telegraphy. Gray's music telegraphy system consisted in a 'one-octave music telegraph transmitter' that he connected to a 'washbasin receiver', which he demonstrated in 1874 in public exhibitions. Although Gray was quite close to inventing what we now know as the telephone, he was perhaps too absorbed in the telegraph as a technological system – and it was Bell who ended up making, and being credited with, key breakthroughs (Hounshell 1975).

The first kind of popular music associated with the cellular phone has to do with a slightly different history: the telephone's ring. The ring signifies that a call has been received, and it is ready to be answered. In picking up the receiver, the circuit is completed and the two parties may speak. (Of course, with party-lines, people could stay on the line for as long as they wished, overhearing other conversations – lurking, as one might do with online chat and social media environments now). A telephone call was signified by the striking, and ringing, of a call-bell. From early on, this bell was recognized as an important part of the telephone system, as in this late nineteenth-century legal discussion:

> A telephone exchange consists of a larger or smaller number of persons ... each of whom is furnished with a telephone and *call-bell*, with a wire running therefrom into a central office ... [so] that any two persons so equipped can be put into speaking communication with one another. These are the essential elements of an exchange; everything else is an accessory.
>
> (Tyler 1884: 165; my emphasis)

From very early on, the cacaphony and stridency of the bell raised public concerns, as witnessed in an 1899 Hartford scheme for 'stopping bell ringing':

> The more the subscriber rings the telephone bell when he gets nervous the more noise he makes for his own care. He does not 'bustle' the telephone girl with any noise at all ... If, every time a subscriber, or any number of subscribers, rang up, the bell sounded in the ears of the girl at the central office, she would be in the midst of a pandemonium of jingle jangles that Edgar Allan Poe never dreamed of when he wrote his poem on 'The Bells.'
>
> (*Hartford Courant* 1899)

The ring of the telephone, however, could also be used for other purposes – such as the morning wake-up call. Or even the alarm, as in the service we can find in Sydney in 1933: 'Next Monday it will be possible to arrange with the telephone exchange to ring a bell at whatever hour the subscriber wishes to be awakened in the morning' (*Canberra Times* 1933). With the advent of the electronic telephone system in the middle of the twentieth century, it was possible to replace the customary, indeed iconic, bell ring, with a range of other sound signals:

> A bird-like whistle may soon replace the telephone bell ... The familiar ring will disappear when Britain's new electronic telephone system is installed through the country. To save the power necessary to provide the present ringing of telephones, new call sounds, including a bird-like whisper, are being tried out, the post office said.
>
> (*Age* 1960)

In the US, new telephone sounds were translated into design and marketing possibilities to help users navigate the gendered architecture and demands of their suburban households:

> As the family looks over blueprints for their new home, each member will have ideas about telephone planning. Illinois Bell Telephone Company has experts to help and advise the planners, many of whom are providing for home communications centers ... Another telephone service is the bell chime. A flick of the switch changes the telephone ring to pleasant, musical chime. It also provides a low ring, ideal during baby's naptime, and a loud ring, best when you're out in the garden. Mom will want a wall phone in the kitchen.
>
> (*Chicago Daily Tribune* 1962)

An auditory signal did not always suffice. The Hartford proposal of 1899 featured the glowing and flickering of electric lights, and the advent of automatic exchanges (where subscribers dialled the desired number themselves) brought with them lamp signalling (Mueller 1989). Once messages were able to be recorded, visual ring indicators were devised. These were monitors with a light-emitting diode (LED) showing a call had been received, and message was available (as in an IBM device circa 1972). Flashing indicators were also needed for telephone users with hearing impairments, or people in noisy environments where it is difficult to hear the phone ring. With cell phones came a panopoly of ways to manipulate telephone culture: for instance, a facility to mute a ringing call, as in a Motorola invention for cordless CT2 telephones in the early 1990s (Spring, Brown and Marko 1993), something we now take for granted.

As telephone instruments and telecommunications network technology developed, it became possible for different combinations of sound to be available. For instance, companies offered 'distinctive' ringtones to distinguish between a number of telephones in a room. Rather like flashing lights, ringtone technology was developed to alert subscribers with hearing impairments to an incoming call.

As the telephone equipment and carriage markets opened up, new kinds of ringers were developed. This was especially in the wake of the 1968 Federal Communication Commission Carterfone ruling that allowed third-party equipment – that is, equipment that was not sold or rented by the phone company – to be connected to the telephone network, as long as such a device did not damage the system (FCC 1968). Not only did equipment manufacturers design and sell a wide range of telephones, including many novelty options, they made accessory ringers that could be connected to the telephone – especially electronic ringers that played tones or melodies. The electronic tones took over from bells, and ringers, as the standard in most equipment.

Ringing the tones

Because of the interest in improving sound, acoustics and voice reproduction and transmission with the telephone and telecommunications, there emerged significant and close links between the development of electronic and recorded music and telephone technology in the twentieth century, such as the role of Bell Laboratories in high-fidelity classic music recording (McGinn 1983). The links, however, did not become so direct until the emergence of the cell phone. In its first phase at least, the technology was not so much hi-fi as low-fi in the form of the ringtone. While the telephone had different kinds of ringtones, as we have noted, and music had been created using telephones as instruments, or making music with telephone sounds, the ringtone had not featured recorded music – nor, despite the accessories mentioned earlier, the facility to compose or create ringtones easily. Such capabilities in ringtones were pioneered by Japanese developers. NTT offered handsets with preset ringtones in 1996, followed by competitor IDC (now KDDI) which offered simple personalization of ring-tone (a phone that allows the user to programme their own ringtone through keypad input):

> The personalized ringtone soon became popular as a way to personalize the *keitai*; in 1998, the *Keitai Chaku-mero Doremi Book*, which showed how to program melodies, sold 3.5 million copies. In the same year, karaoke companies started to develop polyphonic MIDI ringtones. Astel Tokyo opened the first commercial *chaku-mero* download service in 1997, followed by J-Phone in 1998, and sound quality saw steady improvement, as Yamaha Corporation developed sound chips that could play an increasing number of chords.
>
> (Manabe 2009: 319)

Credit for the most important pioneering effort in early mobile music lies with the Japanese NTT DoCoMo i-Mode adding Xing and other polyphonic ring-tone suppliers to their menu in 1999 (Manabe 2009: 319). The genius of i-Mode lay in its ability to provide a successful ecology, including a successful platform for development, a system of micro-payments and digital services, application and environment that the users valued sufficiently to pay (Anwar 2002; Natsuno 2003a and b).

The breakthrough in ringtones came when sound was harnessed to an important development in cell phone culture: messaging. A Finnish inventor, Vesa-Matti Paananen, devised a service called Harmonium (Frere-Jones 2005). One part of Harmonium was already implicit in the Japanese developments in ringtones, based on the MIDI tones of electronic music, and allowing users to customize them, creating their own simple music. Thus Harmonium allowed users to devise monophonic ringtones. The other, critical part lay in the distribution path. Harmonium used the mechanism of SMS to be able to deliver the ringtone over the network to a mobile device. This, then, was the service that Radiolinja, the Finnish mobile operator (now called Elisa), commenced in 1998 – although it took Paananen some months to convince the carrier of the potential of the service (Steinbock 2005). Parallel developments were underway in Japan. In the next few years, we witness the development of formats associated with ringtones. Gopinath outlines 'a model for ringtone development, whereby functional tones become: (1) monophonic ringtones or simple melodies; (2) polyphonic tones (MIDI synthesizer music); and (3) digital sound files (True Tones or other company-specific formats, and ultimately MP3 files)' (Gopinath 2005). Reminding us of the importance of attending to the international career of the ringtone, Gopinath notes that:

> These developments in the ringtone have not progressed uniformly around the world. Instead, particular convergences of national legal systems, consumer preferences, and the interests of local wireless firms and handset manufacturers have led to differing rates of acceptance for each type of ringtone, as well as ringtones generally.
>
> (Gopinath 2005)

While the development of ringtones has taken specific paths and shapes in different parts of the world, and among different groups of users, by 2000, ringtones were highly audible in many countries, and already representing a significant market. In the next six to seven years, ringtones were perhaps the most popular and commercially lucrative part of a burgeoning mobile content market. Ringtones offered a new way to promote music, as a teaser, for instance, for music not yet released in other channels:

> If you want your finger (and phone) firmly on the pulsing nub of youth, try www.ministryofsound.com/music/ring-tones/. The South London super-club lets you download the latest tunes. These repetitive, beat-based ditties are not even in the charts yet and you can snap up five dancefloor monsters for a tenner if you're quick.
>
> (Trueman 2001)

In the area of music publishing (selling rights for music to be used in performance, recorded music, broadcasting, and so on), ringtones provided a new stream of revenue:

> While the recorded music business sees new technologies as a threat – unauthorised music file sharing and CD burning, for example – in music publishing, technology is creating real opportunities. The proliferation of mobile telephone ringtones is the best example.
>
> (Hardy 2002)

While record labels considered changing their business models to gain a share of ringtone revenues, cell phones also played an important role in reconceiving marketing and personalizing customer relations:

> Conversations with fans are no longer purely based around pushing a new single or album, as in the days when the insert postcard was the dominant form of communication ... EastWest worked with mobile marketing company Aerodeon to recruit fans through posters, CD inserts and the web by offering them incentives of free ringtones, logos and news.
>
> (Adegoke 2002)

Commentators and scholars alike debated the cultural significance of ringtones. Early on, some commentators rued their appearance:

> Once, ringtones were limited to a few ready-programmed melodies (give or take a few Barry-from-EastEnders-style geeks who wore the phone clipped to their waistband and reckoned The Entertainer made them an instant hit with the ladies) and life was pretty aurally bearable. But though we may have vowed, when we put away our pashminas, never to fall prey to another ridiculous fad, we have succumbed once more. Hence there is nothing cooler than to have Britney, Sisco or Puffy blasting from your handset. And the naffer the better.
>
> (Bolle 2000)

The reflex reaction – part of a broader response to mobile culture and indeed the changes wrought by the internet – was to dismiss ringtones as another otiose, irritating fad in popular culture (Drescher 2008). However, ringtones cannot be so easily wished away – and are indeed a significant cultural development.

We might consider three ways that ringtones have been important for cultural practices and understandings. First, ringtones can be grasped as part of the complex social and cultural changes in which cell phones are involved: the redrawing of the boundaries between the public and private realms. This raises the question of what kinds of communicative and cultural practices are appropriate in public spaces, and what are the rules regarding this? Second, there is the matter of the relationships to the body and self that cell phones suppose – for instance, the customization and personalization of the cell phones through ringtones that is related to specific performance and constitution of gender (Hjorth 2009b). Third, what do ringtones signify for how we create, listen to, perform and remix music? Here we have the debates on how ringtones fit into the genres and taste formations of contemporary music. Do ringtones simply distill the essence of pop music? From the three minute 'single', or track, we have moved to the ten-to-thirty second excerpt of music contained in the ringtone. What kinds of composition and music-making are characteristic of ringtones? These are all important questions for understanding where mobile music fits into broader cultural transformations and music. However, while still the unique and most popular kind of mobile music to date, ringtones are only part of a larger set of developments that now bring cell phones closer to the central dynamics of what is occurring with music internationally. The rest of this chapter will explore the entwining of mobile and online music, but before this it is important to discuss the fall, as well as rise, of ringtones – or how, at least, ringtone providers brought themselves into disrepute.

As we have seen, ringtones quickly grew in sophistication as a format, service and musical genre. Theoretically users could create their own ringtone – whether from scratch using methods of electronic composition, or remixing existing tracks – and this was very much in the contemplation and design of the first ringtone applications. What emerged, however, in the heyday of the ringtone, was that for most users ringtones were a commodity. Users would purchase them from a commercial provider, then download the ringtones onto their phone to be played when a call was received. One reason for commercial provision of ringtones becoming the dominant mode was the business model that underpinned music. As well as novelty, retro, cool or satirical possibilities, ringtones were very much about exhibiting and broadcasting one's musical preference and taste – like humming a tune, turning the volume up on the music at home, driving around in a car with your stereo blaring, or walking around with a portable stereo. Music copyright owners had already negotiated regimes for recouping rents for various forms of recorded or performed music, and ringtones were no different. For this set of reasons, users became accustomised to purchasing ringtones, strange as this may seem:

> Ringtones have become a badge of passage, particularly having one of the latest ones – though how long the cult will last is a moot point. At the moment, the producers can't believe their cash machines. At a time when everyone else is unsuccessfully trying to work out ways of making punters pay for the web, young consumers are paying twice over – royalties for the content as well as the (premium-rated) telephone calls. If such a business model could be transplanted to the mainstream internet, it would transform the commercial prospects of the web.
>
> (Keegan 2002)

Because of the nature of cell phones as a relatively closed technology, copying and remixing of music to create ringtones was not as simple as it might have been thought (or indeed later became), although some disputed this:

> My 15-year-old son has found a way to add new ringtones without exhorbitant charges. He downloads midi files on a PC and opens a music program (EVA Audio) to show the musical score. He then copies the musical notes onto his Sagem mobile. He put *Mission: Impossible* on to his phone last week.
>
> (Stafford 2002)

Others felt that the cost was justified:

> It is no mystery why people pay handsomely for mobile ringtones, when they want content on the web to be free. The mobile is an entirely different kind of device to the PC or digital TV. It is more than personal – it is an intimate object that is part of your identity, in both physical, emotional and psychic terms. This is why mobile telephony is one of the most important communication channels both now and in the future.
>
> (Kimball 2002)

It was at the point of the user assuming a productive and influential new position in the cultural economy, however, that new intermediaries entered the political economy of global mobile media. One of the first forms such new intermediaries took was that of premium rate content and service providers (introduced in Chapter 2).

As the examples from the early history of ringtones indicate, cell phone carriers were prime movers in developing or commissioning ringtone technologies to make these available to their customers. With the booming popularity of ringtones, the carriers expanded their efforts, especially through 'portals', that provided a way for their customers to browse, select and pay for such cell phone content. The carriers enjoyed a historical advantage of well established customer bases, relationships and billing systems – allowing ringtone downloads to be simply added to the subscriber bill. For their part, the handset manufacturers also sought to expand into the provision of ringtones. 'Club Nokia', the Finnish giant's mobile content portal, was a leading example of this (Brown-Humes 2001). However, neither the carriers nor the handset manufacturers were necessarily so well placed to advertise and market this new kind of consumer entertainment service:

> In Europe ... wireless operators have sought to attract mobile internet users to their portals with the 'carrot' of free content. Their business models are based on boosting traffic and thus call revenues to the portal rather than putting a value on the content ... Nevertheless, a new mood of realism seems to be settling on the wireless industry ... there is now a realisation

that the 3G industry will need to offer a wide range of content and package it in different ways.

(Nairn 2001)

In doing so, the carriers especially faced stiff competition from new entrants, in the form of premium service providers.

Companies specializing in ringtones and other content very quickly established themselves as profitable, or at least commanding attention on stock exchanges. These included companies such as Vizzavi, created in 2000 and operating across Europe (*Guardian* 2002). There are many examples of the shonky ringtone purveyors, but perhaps the earliest to be widely exposed was the case of Jamster's Crazy Frog ringtone. Released in Britain in 2005 the Crazy Frog ringtone featured an extremely annoying yet catchy tune promoted by a computer animated character. The ringtone became the Crazy Frong song, which in turn spawned various videos and remixes, topping charts. Because it was such a bestseller, and indeed the first ringtone to achieve such prominence and notice, the problems with the terms and conditions upon which Crazy Frog were offered to customers were also brought to public scrutiny – and, eventually, attracted widespread condemnation and a fine (ICSTIS 2005). (Crazy Frog was also the subject of British advertising standards complaints, on the grounds that the creature was sporting a visible penis – but which were ultimately not upheld; ASA 2009). Crazy Frog was the most high-profile case among many that followed around the world. As mentioned in Chapter 2, the overdue imposition of consumer protection regulation helped to bring to a close the heyday of ringtones – though it certainly remains a very profitable section of the mobile media industry. Now I shall turn to discuss how mobile media expanded beyond ringtones, to become an important device for storing, playing and sharing recorded music in all its forms.

Portable music player

The portability of music has a long history, with the portability of recorded music taking a leap forward with the celebrated Sony Walkman (du Gay et al. 1997), digital music players and the iconic iPod (Bull 2007). As cell phones developed in sophistication, especially adopting computer processors, operating systems, applications and storage capacity, handset companies quickly saw the potential for handsets to be positioned in the portable music player market. Once it became possible for cell phones to store music – rather than being restricted simply to sounds associated with operating functions, commands and keypads, or the burgeoning ringtone music culture – companies developed and marketed cell phones as music players. However, this took some time to develop.

In 2001, Nokia developed a digital Music Player. The Player combined an FM stereo radio and facility to download audio files in two formats (MP3 and the Advanced Audio Coding format, the latter with built-in digital rights management)

(Nokia 2001c). The Music Player could be used with a number of Nokia hand-sets, and also served as a hands-free kit. With the appearance of such devices, cell phones started to become used as a music player, but still only by very few:

> On the one hand, you have a mobile phone. It's portable. It's built for sound. It can receive digitised data over the airwaves. The network opera-tors are desperate for cash. On the other, you have the music companies. They have vast databases full of music in digital form. Faced with falling CD sales, they are desperate for more cash. Surely a match made in heaven? … Shouldn't we all be abandoning our Walkmen in favour of a single mobile multimedia device: a phone? And yet only a tiny number of the most technically adept are actually listening to music over mobile phones, and most of them are downloading MP3 files to specialised handsets that incorporate a small MP3 player.
>
> (Harvey 2002)

At this point, various consumer electronics companies joined their cell phone counterparts to devise phones that would be attractive as music players also. This revealed a central tension in the forces of convergence that have shaped mobile media – namely, the relationships between technologies and intellectual property. In large, integrated corporations such as Sony Ericsson, the tensions between intellectual property and technology are internal, as much as external. To deal with these contradictions, Sony, like many other companies, have put a strong emphasis on embedding digital rights management systems:

> Sony Europe's president has said the group's consumer electronics and entertainment divisions are increasingly working closer together to combat music piracy: 'Unless we are careful, the hardware group will sell products with features that can copy music,' he said. 'Naturally we have a little pro-blem that will kill not only Sony music but the rest of the (music) industry …' Mr Tsurumi said Sony was also trying to incorporate copyright protect-ion software known as digital rights management (DRM) technology in cell phones produced by its Sony Ericsson joint venture as well as in the group's PCs.
>
> (Malkani 2002)

Here we see the inscription of intellectual property regimes in the technology itself, something that is the great battleground of contemporary digital cultures, in which mobile music is steadily becoming more important.

The battle for the music store and the collection

Among media, music has undergone as profound a change as other areas, if not more so. The music industry has an enduring hierarchy, represented in its dominance by the 'majors' – the handful of global giants, which, as labels, controlled the recording industry through horizontal and vertical integration, the development of music groups and performers (as well as their material and its recording), performance and distribution. The development of new online systems of distribution, in both commercial and non-commercial realms (Duckworth 2005; Fox 2004 and 2005; Fox and Wrenn 2001; Peitz and Waelbroeck 2006), posed serious challenges to this dispensation. The distribution of digital music via the internet represented what has been termed 'disintermediation', or the ability of those creating content, such as music, to make it available directly to consumers (Flew 2008). Or for consumers to bypass the traditional intermediaries – retail stores, record labels, venues – to find and obtain the music they would like directly. In reality, what had been unfolding was a new set of channels and intermediaries, creating new relationships among the different interests and actors in music. In this, cell phone carriers and handset providers have seen a real opportunity to gain revenue and profit from music consumed via cell phones.

As a media platform, cell phones have some distinct advantages, compared to what has been available for the first 15 years of the commercial internet (roughly 1990–2005). As I outlined in Chapter 2, cell phones build on the systems established by telecommunications to minutely identify consumer use of communications services, to log transactions and to bill customers. Furthermore, mobile handsets and networks offer quite good systems for maintaining regimes of intellectual property, so copyright owners and licence holders can extract suitable rents. In the face of the difficulties copyright owners of music experience on the internet – causing them to resort to the incredible doomsday scenarios conjured up in advertising and lobbying campaigns by recording industry association (music downloading and swapping = piracy = theft = revenues for terrorist organizations). Because of their security, billing systems and relatively closed nature, mobile platforms – to date at least – have looked very attractive. Handset manufacturers see not only an opportunity to sell more, and higher-value (viz. more profitable) devices. They also see an opportunity to gain a share of music, as a music and entertainment industry. This desire to muscle in on music is one shared by the cell phone carriers and content service providers, whether taking a cut of providing music to customers, or moving into the business of being a music provider. A threshold problem for those with a stake in mobile music has been how to grow the market beyond ringtones (Andersson and Rosenqvist 2006; Bouwman et al. 2008; Vlachos et al. 2003 and 2006). Ringtones remain well established and profitable, but downloading of full-length tracks or albums is something that lacked genuine innovation and has met with consumer disinterest:

> The problem is that most mobile music services – as implemented –
> did not take advantage of the unique capabilities mobile phones had outside

of instant access. The existing models are nothing more than wireless stores ...

(Bruno 2008b)

There are also real differences between the genre of the ringtone and that of the song or album:

Ringtone purchases are impulse-driven, chart-/hit-driven, and are not necessarily representative of the music buyers love the most, he says, whereas full-track sales are more deliberate. Additionally, full-track customers tend to buy more than one song at a time and browse longer for songs than for ringtones ...

(Bruno 2008c)

In Japan, a real pioneer of mobile music, as we have seen, ringtones remained more lucrative than full-song downloads for some time:

The market for paid cellular phone content in Japan was 315 billion yen ($2.6 billion) in 2005, half of which came from music. Specifically, 105 billion yen came from polyphonic ringtones (*chaku-mero*), 46 billion yen from mastertones (ringtones sampled from the original recording, or *chaku-uta*), and 10 billion yen from full-track downloads (recording of the entire song, or *chaku-uta full*). As of 2006, 55 percent of KDDI's content revenues came from music ... for NTT Docomo, which was late in offering *chaku-uta full*, 20 percent of web access was for music ...

(Manabe 2009: 318)

Indeed due to peculiarities of the music industry (Takeishi and Lee 2005), and reluctance to allow PC downloads, the *chaku-uta* took on a life of its own and played an important role in promoting Japanese popular music (J-pop), with record companies, for instance, releasing the ringtone in the weeks preceding the release of the full album:

Originally meant as a ringtone, *chaku-uta* was detected early on as a product for listening pleasure, thus inspiring the rollout of *chaku-uta full* and a whole industry of search and download functions. These products grew despite their price premium relative to CD rentals, illustrating the power of the instant gratification offered by the anytime, anywhere mobile phone. *Chaku-uta* eventually became a major promotional tool for record companies.

(Manabe 2009: 329)

In other places, such as Europe, the ringtone market was lucrative, but the mobile internet uptake had been slow, and also the rollout of 3G, where again Japan was a leader in both of these areas (Breuer 2009). Hence, aside from the ringtone, the mobile media industry was in many respects reacting to the developments of online music via the internet – especially with file sharing and then the popularity of iTunes (Kärrberg and Liebenau 2007). Interestingly iTunes was also popular on PCs in Japan, but its catalogue concentrated on Western and Japanese independent tracks, rather than J-pop, which was the focus of mobile music (Manabe 2009: 323). In Europe in 2006, then, we find Jamster, the purveyors of Crazy Frog we encountered previously, offered customers three options for buying their music: SMS premium service, WAP page or dual delivery via PC as well as mobile (Bruno 2008c). Jamster was trying to differentiate itself from other mobile music interests (as well as its own chequered premium mobile services past):

> 'There's a very fundamental difference between a technology company, a telco company and Jamster,' [Markus] Berger-de León [CEO of Jamster/ Germany] says. 'We don't use premium content to sell hardware or phone contracts. We generate more new content and give incentives for generating new content every day. The more content there is, and the better I can sell it, the more the whole industry – and particularly the artists – will profit. They shouldn't be afraid of us. They should make more use of us.' Indeed, Jamster wants an industry with a lot of music. 'I live from the Long Tail … '
>
> (Butler 2006)

Precisely due to the characteristics of the mobile platform, not least the potential for control of intellectual property, the interest from the music industry has been keen. A study of the German full-track mobile music market has shown that there are certainly markets where over the air downloads – that is, cell phone music downloads – did generate some level of profit over and above that potentially lost by cannibalisation – that is, substituting for sales what would have occurred in a music shop, or from a free or 'illegal' channel, whether peer-to-peer filesharing, free MP3 downloads, copying of CDs, or recording from the radio (Konig et al. 2006). Nonetheless the music store in the online and mobile world has become a complicated thing indeed.

Big, integrated cell phones and telecommunications carriers have sought to market music directly to consumers, just as they have done so with television or games, as we shall discover shortly. For example, Australia's Telstra, the dominant carrier, conducted an advertising campaign in 2005–6 to market its music downloading services over mobiles. This coincided with the growing availability of third-generation mobiles, and Telstra's own proprietary 'NextG' mobile system.

Typically most carriers have developed a mobile music offering, prominently marketed, often through a joint partnership between the handset manufacturer and the carrier. In this climate, wedged between the iPod and MP3 players, on the one side, and the cell phone, on the other, the Sony Walkman certainly

Figure 4.1 'One touch, two downloads', Telstra, c. 2006 (source: author photo).

looked vulnerable – hence the attempts by the newly merged Sony Ericsson to promote its 'Walkman Phone'.

Thus, an ongoing, overarching battle in the political economy of global mobile media is being waged between the carriers on one side and equipment manufacturers on the other. Sometimes for particular purposes strategy may dictate a joining of forces, as in the example of Vodafone and Sony Ericsson just discussed. At other times, other strategies may be tried. A well publicized example may be found in Nokia, the corporation that has perhaps most tried to

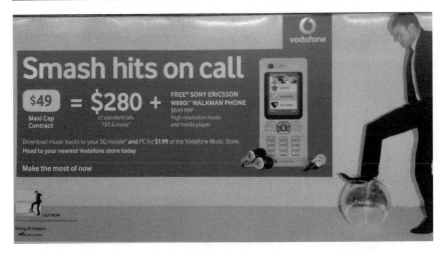

Figure 4.2 'Smash hits on call', Vodafone, Australia, 2006 (source: author photo).

systematically cover all aspects of mobile media. At the time of writing Nokia's website welcomed visitors with the tagline: 'Welcome to a world of mobile music, games, maps, photos, email, conversation and more' (www.nokia.com accessed September 2009). Not content with designing and selling cell phones on which music can be played, stored, recorded, created, swapped and shared, Nokia has sought directly to set up its own music store tied to its handsets. Nokia's 'Comes with Music' was launched first in the UK in September 2008. Although Nokia was marketing this new service, it was provided as a pre-pay channel run by Carphone Warehouse (a big mobile phone retailer, operating across nine markets) for customers who purchased the Nokia 5310 XpressMusic (Nokia 2008b). To enhance its service Nokia signed up Sony BMG, Universal and Warner. Previously it had signed an agreement with EMI to provide and market their content via Nokia handsets and stores. (Nokia 2007b). As well as the dedicated channel, content was also available through Nokia Music Stores:

> With millions of tracks from major artists and independent labels, the Nokia Music Store lets people enjoy music directly on their Nokia device or personal computer. The Nokia store, with its compelling combination of download and streaming services, empowers fans to connect to music they want, in the way they want.
>
> (Nokia 2008d)

Warner praised the convergence between major interests in music and mobiles:

> 'Nokia's Comes With Music service will be a significant step forward in the evolution of digital music. It's the first global initiative to fundamentally

align the interests of music companies with telecommunications companies', said Edgar Bronfman, Jr., Warner Music Group's Chairman and CEO. 'Through this innovative service and business model, all parties are equally driven to create the best and most comprehensive music offering designed to meet the ever-expanding consumer appetite for music and music-enabled devices.'

(Nokia 2008d)

Once a consumer had purchased one year's subscription to 'Comes With Music', they could choose, listen to or download the music they desired. After the year was up, they were allowed to keep the music permanently. Purchased songs could also be transferred to compatible Nokia devices via the customer's PC (Nokia 2008a).

As it launched around the world, Nokia marketed content to local music tastes. In Singapore, it partnered with independent Asian labels – Ocean Butterflies, Rock Records Singapore and Thai music label RS digital – to offer a mix of local, regional and global content. In such ventures, Nokia underlined that: 'Consumers now have instant access to millions of songs from a very wide gamut of genres ranging from pop to dance to Asian like Mandarin, Malay and Indian music' (Nokia 2008c). Further that with 'the rising demand for digital music in Singapore, Nokia Music Store increases the options for consumers by leaps and bounds, as well as brings the artists closer to their audience through their mobile device, an intimate platform that is always with them' (Nokia 2008c). In Brazil, the first launch in the Americas, Nokia was keen to show its respect for national cultural sensitivities, hosting labels such as Tratore, Som Livre, Deckdisc, ST2, Building Records and Atração:

> The local music content represents a very important component inside the catalog, to both, the domestic audience and enthusiasts of the Brazilian music throughout the world where Comes With Music is available. 'We know that the Brazilian consumer is among the world's top consumers of national music, consequently we made sure to contact major labels and local independent labels as well,' says Almir Narcizo, president of Nokia Brazil. 'With Nokia 5800 Comes With Music we are making available the opportunity to have access to this content to them and to everyone that enjoys our music, with a product that will revolutionize the ways of digital consumption.'
>
> (Nokia 2009)

In August 2007, Nokia announced its Music Store, forming part of 'Ovi' – the company's internet services brand name (Nokia 2007a). On New Year's Eve 2006, Nokia organized a five-city music event, with artists following on from each other in Hong Kong, Mumbai, Berlin, Rio and New York. In a lead-up piece of research, the corporation emphasizied the memorable nature of music and its link with picking up the phone: 'if a piece of music reminds you of a place and time and makes you want to connect with someone, you're not alone' (Nokia 2006). For the event, Nokia:

> offered music lovers several innovative ways to use their mobile phones, including the opportunity to send in messages (and a few marriage proposals!) that were displayed on screens around each stage throughout the night. Party-goers could also send messages to the other Nokia New Year's Eve cities as well as use the bluetooth 'beam-zones' on site to receive a host of free content including wallpapers, links, gig guides, ringtones and artist content.
>
> (Nokia 2007c)

Earlier, Nokia had sought to design and market its handsets as the 'mobile jukebox'. Its N-series range were specifically designed to cater for the range of emerging uses and preferences for mobile media. The N91, for instance, was 'optimised for mobile music consumption', with special music keys on its handset, a stereo headset, ease of file transfer from PC, and dedicated accessories from leading audio technology brands such as Bose, Harman Kardon and Sennheiser. According to Jonas Geust, Nokia's Vice-President of Music:

> What sets the Nokia N91 apart is the fact that it is always connected – you can download new music while on the move, add it to your favorite playlist and then share your playlist with friends. It's truly the world's best mobile connected jukebox.
>
> (Nokia 2005b)

The development of smartphones and the intensifying imbrication of cell phones with the internet saw cell phones playing a larger role in the transformations of digital, networked music. Like in other areas, the appearance of the iPhone in 2007 galvanized mobile music interests. Top-selling 'music-enabled' phones (that is, those able to play music in at least some of the major formats) include: LG's V8300, Samsung SGH A707 and Motorola RAZR V3M and KRZR (Bruno 2007). Nokia's 95 most comprehensively covered the musical bases. It supported MP3, WMA, RealAudio and other digital music formats; allowed streaming to other speakers through Bluetooth; access to the internet via Wi-Fi, as well as WAP; Ovi music and entertainment store on its European models; 8GB internal storage capacity; and an FM radio tuner (Bruno 2007). Key to competing with iPhone was, of course, gaining consumer acceptance of the digital music interface and business model. This has proved quite difficult, because up to 2006 at least, most companies had struggled to offer a digital music service able to effectively compete with Apple's iTunes.

The transformations in music distribution have seen other significant new online ventures that rely upon mobile services in different ways. Cell phone carriers, service providers and vendors have not been the only ones leading mobile music. Music labels have viewed mobile media as an important new arena for maintaining their relevance and profits. In April 2008, the label Island Def Jam launched two new mobile initiatives, featuring Mariah Carey's new album $E = MC2$:

> Mariah Carey embraced her inner tech-geek for laughs in the 'Touch My Body' video with *30 Rock* actor Jack McBrayer. But her label, Island Def Jam, is dead serious about using today's mobile technology for promotion and profit … 'For us this is an attempt to capture a bigger part of the off-deck world with exclusive content you can't get anywhere else for the true fan' IDJ senior VP of new media and commerce Christian Jorg says. 'There are things we wouldn't necessarily sell on-deck and sell millions of, but that we know will be interesting to a fan.'
>
> (Bruno 2008a)

Island Def Jam offered a subscription service giving access to a wide range of Universal Music tracks, as well as exclusive ringtones, ringback tones and other content from the label's acts (Bruno 2008a). It also launched a mobile website with more ringtones, artistic information, tour dates and social networking features:

> Carrier content strategies tend to target the widest audience possible and focus on refreshing content on a regular basis. A label-run mobile Web site, while certainly focused on promoting the newest release, can maintain niche communities of fans around a specific artist indefinitely.
>
> (Bruno 2008a)

Here mobile platforms offer the opportunity for music companies to side-step the carriers or handset vendors and directly market services to customers, meaning they retain a greater share of revenue (only needing to split profits with their technology partners). Nonetheless while developing their own portals and services, the music labels also spread their risk with targetted arrangements with cell phone carriers – exchanging Mariah Carey ringtones for prominent marketing placement, or tie-ins with *American Idol* and AT&T Mobility (Bruno 2008a).

Other companies also saw potential to move beyond the simple downloading model for finding, storing and playing music. In 2007, a company called mSpot introduced an application called Remix, which allowed cell phone users to access their whole digital music collection remotely, then allow the creation of a select playlist for the mobile device, for which songs are downloaded automatically to the handset (Fitchard 2007b). Music identification services, now termed 'music discovery', are another distinctive aspect of mobile music – 'right here and now' (Kärrberg and Liebenau 2007) – that again were pioneered in Japan:

> Should a user hear a song in a café or on television, he or she could identify it by punching in the name of the artist onto a music portal on the mobile phone … If the consumer did not know the name of the performer, he or she could point the cell phone in the direction of the music, whereupon the phone would 'hear' it and identify it through its sound-wave patterns. Once the song was identified, the consumer could immediately download it to his or her cell phone or buy the CD on a mobile Internet shopping site.
>
> (Manabe 2009: 326; cf. Funk 2004)

Now the technology has spread to the rest of the world. Shazam, a company started in 2002 and headquartered in London, bills itself as the world's leading 'mobile music discovery provider'. By the end of 2009 it claimed over 50 million customers in over 150 countries. Shazam's technology is either integrated and embedded into mobile devices, or is available as apps: 'Loving that tune? With Shazam you can identify music tracks, store them, send them to your social networks, share them with your friends and buy them' (Shazam 2009). Music streaming is another way that distribution has been conceptualized and implemented. In late 2009, Spotify, a rising star in music streaming, sought investment from cell phone companies and music labels. The carrier 3 (encountered in Chapter 2) invested sufficiently to receive a seat on the board, taken by its INQ CEO Frank Meehan (Andrews 2009). 3 was also interested in the potential of Spotify to sell music to the mainland China market.

Sharing music

As we have seen, since at least the mid-1990s, the mobiles, music and entertainment industries have been evolving distinctive forms of mobile music – some forms enjoying more success than others. Critical to gauging the significance of and prospects for mobile music is the question of how those interested in producing mobile music have comprehended and grappled with the modes of its consumption (du Gay et al. 1997).

What people do with music is often regarded as a quintessentially personal experience. For many, this is something personal music players highlight, and so these are decried by their detractors for being excessively personal, isolating and evacuating the listener from their surrounds and social connections. For all its personal investments and dispositions, however, music is constituted by social relations, experiences and spaces. Furthermore, with music, as with mobile media generally, there is an intriguing interplay between the individual and various kinds of collectivities – in the consumption, as well as production, of music (Bloustien et al. 2008). Playing and listening to music is not in fact the 'privatized', individualized experience detractors and buffs alike may assume.

Consumption of music can be quite a collaborative activity (O'Hara and Brown 2006). This is highlighted in everyday consumer practices (Laughey 2006). With mobile music, this intensely social and collaborative dimension is highlighted by the desire of listeners to share their preferences and music, and also swap with each other's recommendations and favourites. What unfolded with the intersection of cell phones and music was a range of ways that cell phone and music companies sought to cater to, and capitalize on, this new mobile music sharing – creating new affordances to support and commoditize it.

Here mobile music has closely interacted with the new listener habits and music distribution options associated with the internet. The most controversial new development was online music sharing and downloading through peer-to-peer (p2p) technologies, notably the simultaneously celebrated and reviled technology of Napster, followed by a range of other p2p technologies, such as Kazaa, Gnutella and then bittorrent which opened the floodgates of downloading and filesharing to even bigger global audiences (bandwidth permitting). There is much to be discussed about online music that is not able to be touched upon here, but suffice to say that p2p established new user cultures in which the sharing of music cheaply and easily became an expectation.

What cell phones initially added to this online music sharing was the sharing of files via Bluetooth. When users connected their phones with close range via Bluetooth, they were then able to swap music files without incurring any charges – something that was enormously significant. These users were also able to share files without the notice, regulation or intervention of cell phone or music companies, or the intermediaries involved in mobile content. Bluetooth quickly became the preferred mode of music sharing of many young people (Haddon 2007). As we have seen, cell phone vendors, especially, have marketed the Bluetooth protocol as part of their suite of features of music-enabled phones. However, carriers and service providers have certainly not been so keen on it. In many ways, music consumption via Bluetooth is something of a 'grey' area in the business models of mobile music. It is, however, really important to know how consumption actually occurs – very much a case of domestication, if not co-creation, of media technology by their users. Though there is little dedicated research on Bluetooth and mobile music generally, it is an important area because the phenomenon points to the unexplored area of how users take cell phones into their own hands. Music sharing via Bluetooth is part of 'unofficial' cultures that are actually constructing mobile media – but in ways little recognized, let alone credited, by mobile or media companies themselves. Bluetooth uses unlicensed, uncontrolled radio spectrum, albeit for quite short-range purposes. Such uses are contingent on users being in close promixity. These transactions are neither tracked by software or systems in the handsets or network, nor being tariffed or billed to customers. This sphere of mobile music sharing, then, escapes the logic of music commodification we see structuring the political economy of mobile music – and indeed the internet also.

Because it is relatively small-scale, local, select circle file exchanges, if with some limited potential to send to multiple users (a rough kind of broadcasting), Bluetoothing music has not attracted the public outcry of music downloading via the internet.

The question of sharing mobile music has attracted quite some interest from researchers and companies alike. For instance, there have been fascinating developments around the playlist. Once new genres of music had been established on cell phones, such as ringtones, and the device had been recognized by producers and users as a viable, even attractive music player, the question of the organization, selection, arrangement and consumption of music came into sharp relief. In music, such questions – which ultimately are to do with matters and politics of taste – can be usefully approached via the concept of the playlist. Once listeners assemble a collection, how do they select songs, or whole albums, to play? How do they easily construct lists of their favourite tracks? Given the work that goes into a playlist – now familiar to millions of music lovers through Apple iTunes, digital players and other software and handware devices – what about the idea of accessing and sharing other people's playlists? Apple itself developed such a technology with its Rendezvous software. One of the most popular social playlist websites is Last.fm, which aggregrates recommendations and playlists from songs actually listened to by its subscribers. When a Last.fm subscriber listens to a song on their computer, iPod or other digital device, the name of the song is sent to Last.fm, added to the user's individual profile, but then aggregated with the data from other users to recommend music or make available a 'personalised radio station' (www.last.fm, last accessed on 10 May 2010). Sharing playlists is also the underlying concept of an experimental software called 'TunA', a protoype which allowed users in a vicinity to access playlists of others and listen to their music at the same time they do (Bassoli et al. 2006). Another experimental application, Push!Music, allows users to send a track to someone else, without them realizing it:

> Delores enters a café to grab a coffee to go. On the screen of her Push!Music player she notices that another user is nearby. At a table sits a cool-looking guy with headphones. Before leaving the café, she decides to send this person her current favorite song! As Johan continues to listen to his playlist he discovers a new song he has not heard before …
>
> (Jacobsson et al. 2005: 1)

New software also makes it easy to share music using messaging from PCs to cell phones, for instance that offered by Messaging International (Allen 2009). In late 2009, the popular music creation application Beaterator was released on the iPhone, to high hopes: 'With Beaterator, though users will be able to share their tracks with others via the Rockstar Social Club, there must surely be a way of getting the best user-generated music onto the iTunes Store … ' (Stuart 2009). Interestingly, Beaterator started life on the Nintendo DS.

Making music

The rise of sharing as an important aspect of contemporary culture, especially when it comes to music, has an increasingly close relationship to the subject of making music. As is evident from our discussion of music sharing, much of the investment and design in mobile music to capture and catalyse these cultural currents has to with acknowledging and materializing the role listeners and consumers play not only in making lists or collections, but explicitly in sampling, mash-ups or edits of music itself. The creation of music is, therefore, a vitally important issue when it comes to mobile media. Mobile media companies have recognized the importance of music creation to consumption, but also the potential of cell phones for creating music, with phone design and application.

As well as the efforts of mobile media companies to devise music products and services, cell phones have been used for some years by musicians and composers to make music, with many works, ensembles and performances around the world. A relatively new venture, spurred on by the programming possibilities of the iPhone, the Stanford Mobile Phone Orchestra extends electronic music into the smartphone realm:

> Far beyond ring-tones, MoPhO's interactive musical works take advantage of the unique technological capabilities of today's hardware and software, transforming multi-touch screens, built-in accelerometers, built-in microphones, GPS, data networks, and computation into powerful and yet mobile chamber meta-instruments.
>
> (Stanford Mobile Phone Orchestra, http://mopho.stanford.edu/, accessed 25 May 2010)

The Mobile Phone Orchestra instigators remark on the distinctive acoustic characteristics of mobile devices:

> Like traditional acoustic instruments, the mobile phones are intimate sound producing devices. By comparison to most instruments, they are rather soft and have somewhat limited acoustic bandwidth. However, mobile phones have the advantages of ubiquity, strength in numbers, and ultramobility, making it feasible to hold jam sessions, rehearsals, and even performance almost anywhere, anytime.
>
> (Wang, Essl and Penttinen 2008)

Other experiments in mobile music seek to enlist the new possibilities of a range of mobile media devices to connect with people, things, processes and environments. For example, the idea that mobile devices could harness the sonic potential of cities (Gaye, Mazé and Holmquist 2003). Many of those involved in these mobile music endeavours to date have required strong artistic, musical and technical expertise (as part of a broader movement around mobile technologies) as the technologies are not so open and easy to use:

> the effort to provide a broad platform for designing and facilitating inter-active musical expression on these devices is still very much in its infancy. The ongoing effort described in this paper is part of a larger field of mobile and locative music performance that involved not only mobile phones but also other mobile technologies such as PDAs, GPS and custom made sensing devices.
>
> (Essl, Wang and Rohs 2008: 11)

Cell phones still have quite different operating systems, interfaces, characteristics, applications and software that make any-to-any connectivity for basic voice and data telecommunications difficult. Hence the project of devising a common software to consolidate all mobile devices – cell phones, PDS, GPS, sensing technologies – into an integrated, available platform for music making (Essl, Wang and Rohs 2008: 13).

Expanding the ways of creating mobile music has been the motif of a rich movement of researchers, designers, music producers and listeners. Undertaken by Atau Tanaka, among others, through a series of international workshops on mobile music technology, it suggests a much broader definition and account of mobile music than we see promulgated by the various efforts of cell phone, music and entertainment companies:

> Mobile music as a term covers any musical activity using portable devices that are not tethered to a specific stationary locale; in particular those where the activity dynamically follows users and takes advantage of the mobile setting, thereby leveraging novel forms of musical experience. Mobile music devices might possess properties such as context awareness, ad hoc or dis-tributed network connectivity, or location sensing, sometimes combined with technology embedded in the physical environment. Therefore, they can be used anywhere and on the move, and take advantage of people's displace-ments, location, and of the changes of social and geographical context that mobility implies. Examples of mobile music activities include pushing music to people nearby, sonifying local Wi-Fi coverage while riding a bike, or remixing music tracks with remote friends across peer-to-peer networks. Mobile music goes beyond the iconic Walkman^{TM}, and does not need to imply individual use, headphones or passive music listening. It spreads over a large spectrum of musical interactions, ranging from consumption to creation, and with mobility increasingly blurring this distinction. Mobile music resonates with practices of both … musicians and everyday users of consumer audio products.
>
> (Gayle et al. 2006: 22)

What emerges from various experiments with mobile music, especially those that radically seek to enlarge the concept, is the availability and affordances of cell phones as platforms for consuming and making music.

The technical standards and systems level of mobile music are intimately interwoven with the commercial and control imperatives. The trajectory of commercial mobile media discussed in this chapter shows the difficulty the converging industry has experienced in imagining and capitalizing on music beyond the ringtone. The welter of only partly if at all successful mobile media initiatives around moving music distribution online and engaging with new modes of media consumption, not to mention changing social concepts of media, is testament to the restrictive political economy of mobile media in this area. At play are the different visions of the social functions of mobile music, as Tanaka and Gemeinboeck note:

> There are increasingly sophisticated commercial offerings in the marketplace that combine the functions of a personal music player with that of a mobile phone. These products often co-opt the term *mobile music* ... While personal music players and cell phones share many qualities—they are portable devices; they are audio devices; they are highly personal devices— in the end they each serve very different social functions.
>
> (Tanaka and Gemeinboeck 2009: 174–75)

They offer a critique of the focus on ringtone and personal music player:

> The music industry, as much as it resisted the shift to downloadable music, has embraced ringtones as a significant revenue source. This represents not a new market but represents the shift of purpose of music as an *accessory* for the device, to heighten its personal uniqueness. Apple's iPod/iTunes system ... maintains the radio model of broadcast, transplanted to a download-and-synchronize mode of usage.
>
> (Tanaka and Gemeinboeck 2009: 175)

Instead, Tanaka and Gemeinboeck argue for the need for designers to reconcile 'personal and public spheres' evident in music players and mobile phones respectively, creating a 'networked interpersonal music system' (2009: 176). With their musical work *Net_Dérive*, they seek to move beyond the limits of 'market-driven' mobile media products, creating 'deeper cultural experiences' with 'an architecture of itinerant devices connected over wireless infrastructures, utilizing network-level services such as localization, to feed a dynamic audiovisual content-generation process' (Tanaka and Gemeinboeck 2009: 183). Others look at possibilities for mobile music, such as wearable music (Schroeder and Rebelo 2007). At stake is the possibility for mobile media as platforms for music, and what constraints they might put on this, or, alternatively, what affordances they possess:

Composing for such an environment is to look at the system as a kind of instrument, a musical instrument that is not an acoustic network of vibrating elements and air impulses but a human/technological network of entities and elements coming into musical interaction.

(Tanaka and Gemeinboeck 2009: 183)

Mobile music, then, is very much a phenomenon still in the making. Commercial cell phone providers and companies from music, entertainment and media industries have joined forces in various combinations, to make mobiles an important and distinctive platform for contemporary media consumption, exchange and production. Consumers have very much been involved in co-creating the meanings of mobile music. Less evident, on an organized scale, has been the efforts of various listeners, musicians and artists to experiment with and expand the possibilities of the platforms. Putting together these different, yet intimately connected, sides of mobile music as media is exactly what we need to do – to make the platforms receptive, fertile places for culture. If we manage this, the vision of mobile music is considerably enlarged, not only beyond industry visions but also dominant undertakings of music itself.

Chapter 5

The mobile invention of television
Post-broadcasting and audiovisual politics

> ... mobile TV is not yet a clearly defined media, and it has ambiguous connotations, which leaves us with many questions regarding what kinds of services could be delivered, and how actors will interact in that process.
>
> (Bria et al. 2007)

> The idea of mobile – in the sense of portable – TV, as against TV viewed via a mobile handset, is nothing new. Much hyped when first launched, it has virtually died the death commercially ... In contrast, almost everyone, at least in relatively advanced societies, already carries around a mobile device as a matter of course, so adding a TV capability is on the face of it no more or less of an issue than the addition of a camera or MP3 player.
>
> (Curwen and Whalley 2008c)

At an industrial and commercial level, television continues to be buffeted by challenges to its established business models of advertising, subscription and revenues coming from multi-platform, multi-modal media – especially evident when it comes to satellite television, digital broadcasting and the internet. The manifold changes to personal and household technology starting with VCRs, are now evidenced in personal digital video recorders, household media centres, programme downloading, DVD box sets and the customisation of television schedules through programmes such as TiVo. Into this scene comes television on the cell phone, the advent of which was accompanied by revolutionary claims (Goggin 2006). For instance, in late 2005, regarding a pilot of mobile television in Spain, a Nokia spokesperson made the following remarks:

> Television on the mobile is not going to be a traditional evolution, but a revolution that will yield new content, new hours of a maximal audience, and it will facilitate the possibility of personalizing offerings with WAP services, downloads and so on.
>
> (Bedia 2005)

There is an interesting tension evident here between 'evolution' and 'revolution' that we will encounter often in mobile television, indeed mobile media – if not technology more generally. In *Cell Phone Culture* I looked at how this discourse of mobile television layered upon many years of visions of visual communication and media at a distance – telecommunicating in pictures (Goggin 2006). It is important to think about the new kind of mobile visuality from the perspective of television histories also.

Television already has a well shaped relation to mobilities, its logics and technologies. The settings and props of television culture were shaped by the spatial arrangements of urban life, its familial, work and friendship relationships, the gendering of the household, and the transportation and communication technologies cities required, such as cars (and later planes). Indeed, there is a set of inventions, narratives, images and desires about portability and mobility that can be traced through television history. The most obvious of these is portable television. With advances in miniaturisation, electronics, reception and screen technologies, it became possible to manufacture sets that could be easily carried to different rooms of a house or building, or be watched in a workplace. Even smaller, more portable sets were made, and sets also appeared in vehicles and other forms of transportation. With the introduction of portable television in the 1960s came new ideas about 'mobile homes' (Spigel 2001; cf Schiffer 1991). This is a rich history of mobility that I can only note here, but it is worthy of further attention.

At its dawn, mobile television appeared to be a simple proposition. Woven into the industry desires for mobile television were some distinct ideas of the social. In mobile television what we have is the twinning of two extremely ubiquitous and significant technologies. As we shall see, the third technology of the internet is also deeply implicated in the evolution of mobile television – just as the internet is a much-evoked, yet surprisingly difficult to predict and specify, actor in contemporary media culture in general. In 2011, some six years on in the unfolding – in industry parlance 'roll-out' – of mobile television, what does this media form – this object – look like?

Switching on mobile television

Initially mobile television was conceived and promoted by the cell phone handset manufacturers, notably the Finnish company Nokia, in partnership with broadcasters, and programme and content providers (Christ and Pogrzeba 1999). Especially important in this early assembling of mobile television culture was the organization of 'pilots', 'trials' and the production of reports. Typically the reports released from these ventures contained findings about the promising ways people wished to consume mobile television, as summarized by Italian scholars:

> Participants in different trials carried out by telecom operators in many European countries (Germany, France, Great Britain, Italy and Finland) expect that all content from conventional television would also be available

on the mobile, even if it is not suited for mobile viewing. The viewers want to have: good picture and sound quality; value for money; right selection of channels; a single device to carry (phone); simplicity of use; service availability.

(Balbi and Prario 2009; cf. Södergard 2003)

The trials and the 'research' that accompanied them constructed particular images and rationales for the introduction of mobile television:

> Based on the findings from literature and mobile TV-trials, there exists quite some belief that mobile TV has the capability to carve out its own place as a new and distinct medium. However, much of the existing literature on mobile television is dominated by surveys conducted or financed by telecom, mobile or media players with strategic interests in the results.
>
> (Schuurman et al. 2009: 304)

While the promises of mobile television were initially enthusiastic, even utopian, much of the television delivered was not especially new, or even noticeably different from existing television programmes. In Western countries such as the US, Australia, Britain and other countries in Europe, much mobile television typically involved reworking, customizing or abbreviating well known programmes from other forms of television, especially free-to-air and subscription television. Hence the paradox of mobile TV: namely, it looks exciting, but the results so far are uninspiring. Brand has played an important role as a bridge between existing models of television, from free-to-air and subscription television, to varieties of digital television, such as mobile:

> Mobile TV is a potential playing field for any number of new media actors. In all the trials, however, the same channels that are popular for regular TV are popular for mobile TV. Viewers seem to prefer the strong brands, built up with regular TV.
>
> (Bria et al. 2007)

Reviewing mobile data innovation in the United Kingdom, another study finds: 'The brands of established video content providers are playing a more important role in the launch of mobile video services than was the case for the initial walled garden data services' (Tilson et al. 2006: 9). While we still lack studies on what is actually being offered by providers, it appears that while new specifically made for cell phone genres and programme formats have figured prominently in public discussions and media representations of mobile television, such content has formed only a minor part of what has actually been offered to consumers (Carlsson and Walden 2007; Goggin 2007b). 'The so-called *mobisodes* (short versions of serial episodes) developed for mobiles are popular,'

Urban argues, 'but this kind of content development is relatively costly' (Urban 2008: 33).

Mobile television has developed differently in at least one Asian country, namely South Korea, where it has attracted much stronger uptake and use. When first launched, mobile television in Korea was 'similar to conventional TV prior to the personal video recorder ... the user can switch channels but the pausing of content is not available' (that is, it is live mobile broadcast TV) (Cui, Chipchase and Jung 2006). An early study of Korean mobile TV consumption offered some interesting findings about it being a *personal* experience but also very often shared:

> we found TV sharing and device lending very common in Korea. That can be partially increased by collectivism culture. So we may not be expecting it happens so often in individualism cultures such as Finland or Japan ... Mobile TV use is also strongly influenced by different apartment layout, public transportation penetration, and other differences present in different regions. In cultures such as the US people are more likely to have a TV in their bedroom and in these instances Mobile TV will need to compete more directly with regular TV offerings.
>
> (Cui, Chipchase and Jung 2006)

The individual versus collective and shared, private versus public nature of mobile television has been discussed in European research. A Belgian study noted the use of mobile television, with its need for absorption, as a potential way to create a semi-private experience in a public setting (watching a programme while dining alone in a restaurant, for instance) (Vangenck *et al* 2008). While a Finnish study found that 'mobile TV service was mainly used as an individualized, personal media format' (Oksman et al. 2007: 224).

The invention of mobile television, then, in Western countries especially, owes as much to these humble, kludge-like beginnings as it does to the more recent, grander visions that have accompanied its introduction (Goggin 2006). What this story indicates is not only that third generation networks are incremental, and continuous, with their second generation networks, but also that user and viewer roles in shaping the technologies are often unexpected.

Indeed, consumers have been slow to turn to mobile television. While there has been some uptake of mobile television, especially for watching events (sports, reality programming, major national or international events), consuming short video or programme excerpts, or experimenting with made for cell phone programmes, overall the reception has fallen far short of expectations. There are various explanations offered for this lack of interest. Cost, screen size and resolution are commonly cited factors. Studies also point to problems with the quality and audibility of sound, especially in the noisy enviroments in which cell phones are often used. Mobile television is a case in point for the dashed expectations of many mobile media services overall, as a study of one of the great early adopter countries, Finland, concluded:

> Generally speaking, the market for mobile services has thus far failed to live up to the expectations industry had for a long time ... in Finland, as in other European countries, the market for 3G services is evolving very slowly. Firms are trying to understand how consumers derive value from mobile services, while practitioners and academics are struggling to predict ... mobile usage and the reasons why consumers adopt mobile services that are different from the ones they have used in the past.
>
> (Bouwman et al. 2009)

There is a further, subtle yet significant point regarding the choice of sensory modes in mobile television, that is made in a Finnish study:

> Mobile TV use was an engaging activity ... users still held the phone in their hands and most often did not do anything else while watching. In that sense, audio and text news were seen as easier channels than video: only eyes or ears, not both of them, were needed.
>
> (Oksman 2009)

Here we see a new kind of practice emerging. One recurrent idea about television is that its watching is characterized by intense absorption in a programme. While such viewing is possible, empirically many studies have established that this is not a dominant form of viewing. Rather, other forms are more common, such as those characterized by distraction – as in the case of leaving the television on for 'background' noise. This allows the interweaving of the television with the rhythms, routines, requirements and pleasures of everyday life that unfold in the vicinity of television. It does not require things to be placed on hold while watching takes pride of place. By contrast, mobile television complicates this relatively stable assembling of culture. The mobile television can be watched in places where television is not usually found. Rather than being placed in the living room, kitchen table, bedroom niche or mounted on a wall, the mobile television offers itself as a handheld device. We might recall here that in various societies, cell phones are seen as an extension of the hand (Katz and Aakhus 2002). The tableaux offered by Oksman style this new form of television as an arresting and absorbing simultaneity of hands, ears and eyes alike.

The politics of standards

The diffusion of mobile television is still in its relatively early stages, not only because of the cautiousness of providers but also, as proponents have realized since the first flush of enthusiasm, because there are a range of technical, regulatory and content issues. Håkon Ursin Steen observes:

> There is definitively a certain complexity involved in establishing a profitable market for mobile television. First, there has to be consumers willing to pay for watching mobile television (either directly, or indirectly by spending time watching advertisements). Second, there has to be licensed and available content that these consumers are interested in watching. Third, there must be handsets capable of receiving content on a given media carrier standard. Fourth, a broadband infrastructure propagating radio signals to the handsets is required ...
>
> (Steen 2009)

In most countries, mobile television has usually been delivered using the 3G network. However, the 3G network was not engineered to cope with the bandwidth and other technical issues associated with large audiences for mobile television. When cell phone carriers introduced mobile television to 3G customers, and started to promote it as *mobile television* from 2005 onwards, to provide this kind of mobile television carriers typically used the capability of 3G networks to send such content to customers who subscribe or select it – what has been called 'unicast'. The difficulty faced, however, was that 3G networks at this time had real limitations – not least of bandwidth – on how widely they could serve as a broadcasting platform (Sieber and Weck 2004). While there are only a few customers consuming mobile television in this fashion the 3G networks can cope. However, if mobile television becomes a mass form, 3G telecommunications networks will be unable to cope as the sole form of broadcast. Because of these limitations, proponents of mobile television have turned to the world of broadcasting to fashion a system that affords sufficient scalability.

Various standards have now been developed to enable the broadcasting spectrum to deliver television direct to cell phones. However, it has been difficult for broadcasters, mobile, media and entertainment companies, regulators and policymakers to agree on which standard to underpin mobile television. As well as different commercial actors in this process, particular standards have evolved from existing media forms and industry clusters – notably television broadcasting, audio and radio broadcasting, then internet and telecommunications. Further, national governments have played an important role in encouraging, mandating or backing particular standards. The fate of television on cell phones has become the fate of a fascinating babel of standards.

The Koreans and Japanese, as pioneers of mobile television, developed their own standards. South Korea was the first country to introduce mobile television on cell phones (accordingly, there is a substantial literature on mobile television in this country, such as Choi et al. 2008, Shim et al. 2006, and Shin et al. 2006). It did so using the S-DMB standard, or the satellite version of the Digital

Multimedia Broadcasting standard. This is a portable multimedia broadcasting standard that works on the back of the Digital Audio Broadcasting standard. The leading mobile carrier SK Telecom established TU Media, which received the only available licence for S-DMB from the Korean Broadcasting Commission at the end of 2004 (Lee and Kwak 2005: 6). The DMB technology had actually been developed by the German company Bosch, who exhibited it during the Hannover 2000 Expo as an in-train information system, and then demonstrated it to the Korean government in 2002 (Steen 2009: 321). The Japanese also played an important role because theirs was the first country to develop a mobile television service via satellite – with Toshiba subsidiary MBCo doing this in 1997 (Lee and Kwak 2005: 9). The Japanese were focused on mobile television in vehicles, incorporating this into the popular in-car navigation systems. Eventually SK Telecom collaborated with MBCo, even sharing a satellite – but the Japanese 'ended up with a non-cell phone DMB service' (Lee and Kwak 2005: 9). SKT asked Samsung Electronics to develop a DMB capable cell phone. TU Media launched its full service in May 2005, with 7 video and 20 audio channels (Lee and Kwak 2005: 6, 9).

South Korea also developed a second standard – Terrestrial-Digital Multimedia Broadcast (T-DMB). It is this standard that has attracted attention and been deployed internationally, with support from Korean government and industry, and also the World DMB organization. Four services launched T-DMB services in Seoul metropolitan areas in December 2005, with two further operators commencing in March 2006. Three of these operators were existing broadcasters: KBS, MBC and SBS. The other three included YTN DMB – owner of cable and satellite channels, specializing in new channels – and two new consortia, Hangkook DMB and U1 Media, bringing together IT companies, equipment manufacturers and content providers (DMB 2006). Sales of one million terminals – CDMA phones with T-DMB chipsets; terminals installed in in-car navigators; USB module receivers; T-DMB set-top boxes – were claimed by June 2006 (only seven months after launch) (DMB 2006). T-DMB was adopted by the European Telecommunications Standards Institute as an open standard in 2005 (Steen 2009), and has been used already in European countries, including France and Germany.

For their part, the Japanese developed their own standard, ISDB-T, used by the One Seg service launched in April 2006. The service is called 'One Seg' because 'the bandwidth of the single channel (6 MHz) allocated to each broadcaster is divided into 13 segments, and one of those segments is used for mobile devices' (NTT DoCoMo 2009). Just like other terrestrial digital broadcasts, the service allows data broadcast to be received at the same time as video, allowing DoCoMO customers, for instance, to:

> … watch TV programs while you are outside or commuting to and from work as well as access i-mode sites easily from data broadcasts to check program information, purchase goods introduced in programs,

receive special offer coupons, and view lots of other useful and enjoyable information.

(NTT DoCoMo 2009)

In 2009, One Seg announced the first digital television service on the iPhone.

Perhaps the most widely used – or at least clearly articulated and advocated standard – is Digital Video Broadcasting – Handheld (DVB-H) standard. DVB-H is part of the family of open digital television standards developed by an industry consortium that has developed standards for digital terrestrial television (DVB-T). So DVB-H sits firmly in the imagined futures for television co-ordinated and organized especially by the Europeans. This standard was approved early on by the European Telecommunications Standards Institute (ETSI). DVB-H is supported internationally by a number of interests in broadcasting and tele-communications (most prominently, perhaps, by the cellular mobile handset manufacturer Nokia). Europe established the European Mobile Broadcasting Council (EMBC) in 2006. In 2007, the European Commission strengthened its backing for mobile television as central to innovative wireless technologies (Redding 2006; on European innovation see Borrás 2003). It encouraged the use of DVB-H as the way to unify standards:

'Mobile broadcasting is a tremendous opportunity for Europe to maintain and expand its leadership in mobile technology and audiovisual services,'

Figure 5.1 'One Seg Digital TV on iPhone' (One Seg 2009).

said Viviane Reding, EU Commissioner for the Information Society and Media. 'Europe is today at a crossroads. We can either take the lead globally – as we did for mobile telephony based on the GSM standard developed by the European industry – or allow other regions to take the lion's share of the promising mobile TV market. "Wait-and-see" is not an option. The time has come for Europe's industry and governments to switch on to mobile TV.'

(EC 2007b)

For Commissioner Reding, Europe's triumphant move is couched in the discourse of economic national competitiveness:

Until now, the introduction and take-up of mobile TV in the EU has been slow while Europe's competitors have progressed significantly ... The Commission is strongly committed to the success of mobile TV which could be a market of up to €20 billion by 2011, reaching some 500 million customers worldwide ... 2008 is considered by the Commission as a crucial year for mobile TV take-up in the EU due to important sports events, such as the European Football Championship and the Summer Olympic Games, which will provide a unique opportunity for raising consumers' awareness and for the adoption of new services.

(EC 2007b)

The language of this exhortation is instructive. Mobile television needs to be a success for the economic benefit of Europe, thus consumers need to be made aware – in effect, taught – about its virtues. Unfortunately things did not go to plan as Commissioner Reding conceded in a 2008 interview:

The industry was not ready ... I told them very clearly that the Olympic Games and the European Football Cup were an opportunity to launch this system, but they were not ready. It is an opportunity lost. Let's wait for the next one ... If you do not have real win-win situations, things do not work. That is why if the industries [broadcasters as content providers and telecoms broadcasters as service providers] play against each other, it cannot work ... It is the same on the Internet. Online films flourish thanks to an agreement between the two parts of the economy. If they work against each other, they are going to lose.

(EurActiv 2008)

Reding redoubled her efforts – 'EU Telecoms Commissioner Viviane Reding hasn't given up pushing Mobile TV on anyone who'll listen' (Ray 2008) – and, having long urged the industry to adopt a common standard, finally forced their hand. Reding felt that Europe had a chance with a common standard to dominate this emerging industry: 'EU has a chance to become a global player just as it did with the GSM success story' (Ward 2007). Accordingly in March 2008 the EU endorsed DVH-B as its preferred technology for mobile television (EC 2008). The battle over standards for mobile television did not cease there, as, of course, it is very much a struggle for control over a crucial domain of mobile media (Braet and Ballon 2008). Thus hope springs eternal for the promoters of mobile TV, DVB-H style. In December 2009, 15 broadcaster and service provider members of the Broadcasting Mobile Council signed a letter asking vendors to update handsets with DVB-H capability. They vested hope especially in the emerging markets and the iconic media event of the 2010 World Cup:

'The FIFA football world cup 2010 may give a push to mobile TV usage across the African countries in which we operate. For that we need affordable devices with integrated DVB-H receivers,' said Francois Theron, CEO, DStv Mobile Africa.

(Dyer 2009)

While officially many industry interests were embracing DVB-H as a pan-European desideratum, soon to be adopted around the world, there were also promoters of other standards, notably the US FLO standard, continuing to argue for choice.

MediaFLO is a proprietary standard originating in 2004, devised by the North American telecommunications equipment, chipset and software company Qualcomm (best known for its now largely defunct Eudora email package, as well as the second generation digital mobile standard CDMA). FLO stands for 'Forward Link Only', or one way broadcasting from the tower to the device (something which raises interesting questions about how the technology fits into visions of users producing and distributing their own content, from the device back to the broadcasting or communications network). FLO started life as a closed standard, and has had a 'stepwise progression towards openness' (Steen 2009: 322–23). It was adopted as an open standard by the US Telecommunications Industry Association in 2006, but use of the standard involves entering into Qualcomm's licensing arrangement – felt to be discriminatory by some industry parties (EC 2007a; Steen 2009: 323). By 2009, Qualcomm was advertising FLO as a 'global open standard for broadcasting multimedia' (FLO Technologies 2009a). However, as the ardour of mobile television's backers cooled from 2007–8 onwards, FLO has enjoyed a good reception as a potential standard that could present a good, evolutionary alternative to other mobile television standards. Thus Qualcomm did not at first foreground mobile television, but rather high-quality streaming or 'clipped' multimedia – which is a better summation of what is actually being delivered over mobile networks at present. When Qualcomm launched in March 2004 it precisely targeted key concerns of the various players about network capacity and quality (mobile carriers), digital rights management (content providers) and the messy convergence of various telecommunications platforms with broadcasting and online systems (broadcasters being especially concerned about this):

> Qualcomm ... today announced the MediaFLO™ Content Distribution System ... an end-to-end product and service offering that enables secure and efficient delivery of high-quality, network-scheduled video content to a large number of subscribers for easy viewing on handsets. It can be deployed over today's unicast (point-to-point) third-generation (3G) wireless networks and will scale easily for tomorrow's multicast (one-to-many) networks.
>
> (Qualcomm 2004)

The first line of the release read: 'System Designed to Enable Operators to Exploit Off-Peak Capacity While Giving Users Immediate Access to Compelling Video Content' (Qualcomm 2004). In effect, Qualcomm's pitch grasps mobile television as a supplement and extension of other online network services and cultures. As it garnered plaudits, Qualcomm squarely pitched itself as *the* mobile television standard of choice:

> More Media. More Mobile. More You.
> MediaFLO™ technology is enabling the mobile television ecosystem with a highly scalable and open mobile entertainment platform with the highest content capacity combined with a visually compelling mobile experience.
>
> (FLO Technologies 2009c)

Thus far I have discussed the various competing efforts in digital television and digital audio and radio broadcasting. There is also the prospect of mobile broadcasting conceived on the model of internet television. As of late 2005, a suite of DVB standards was adopted for the transmission (in technical terms, datacast) of digital television using internet protocol (so-called 'IP' or 'internet' television) but via handheld mobile devices. In July 2006, ETSI approved a revision of the Digital Audio Broadcasting standard to allow transmission of mobile television via the internet. The resulting DAB-IP standard allowed Virgin Mobile to launch the UK's first mobile broadcasting service in October 2006, with its 'lobster' phone that only offered five channels and struggled for customers.

We would be remiss to concentrate too much on the manoeuvring of the various power blocs centring on Europe, the US, Japan and Korea, when less widely publicized, yet holding promise, are the efforts of China. China has its own group of competing standards, which not only represent a fascinating exercise in the politics of technology – and the assertion of China globally – but also show how China seeks to collaborate with, but also parry its European, US and Asian competitors (cf. Lee and Oh 2006). The China broadcasting regulator SARFT announced in 2006 that mobile phone service providers operating in the country would need to use a Chinese technology for broadcasting to mobile phones. However, the outcome remains unclear:

> For China several different standards compete for the mass market adoption … Multiple technologies have been developed in the last years to address the challenge of mobile TV reception. There is already disagreement in China over which standard to use, and what network will prevail, and whether cellular unicast networks or broadcast networks would be the best solution … With China's handheld TV users reaching more than 22 million by 2010 … much is at stake for producers of mobile content, handsets, chips, software, mobile network operators and China's broadcasters.
>
> (Burger et al. 2007)

In summary, then, mobile television is still in a state of flux, even more than is the case with digital broadcasting in general. Various countries in Europe and elsewhere have invested faith in the DVB-H system (consistent with choices in digital television and the technical and market developments in second and third generation mobile networks). However, the process of inventing television for portable cellular mobile and wireless devices has seen other possibilities open up and participants are actively considering other options. Despite setbacks, media players hold their faith in the version of mobile television now commercially available in a number of countries. In the face of slow take-up, mobile handset manufacturers, especially Nokia, have strongly reiterated the promise (if no longer revolutionary potential) of mobile television. Such persistence may be witnessed in the promotion of a German supporter:

> Mobile television is more than TV over your mobile phone … Digital television and digital radio, mobile data services and interactive elements merge to a new form of entertainment and information. Practically always available and with a multifunctional benefit.
>
> (Mobile 3.0 2008)

For their part, cell phone carriers have adopted a different strategy − a far more practical response to the slow uptake of mobile television. Most have moderated their claims about mobile television, even dropping any mention of it at all, preferring to just present the cellular phone as one of many ways to watch televisual and audiovisual content (the marketing strategy and advertising of global cell phone giant Vodafone is a good example of this). Other players have retreated further to the safe haven of cell phone content, building incrementally on the known quantity of messaging, downloads and premium cell phone services − rather than wading too far into the world of entertainment and broadcasting. Some telecommunications companies have moderated their enthusiasm for mobile television, instead placing a strong emphasis on Internet Protocol (IP) TV as *the* compelling direction in television. Here the tele-communications companies have explicitly evoked a vision for telecommunications convergence being about watching media anywhere, anytime, and about user choice and customization of their media experience.

What has unfolded in Europe, and indeed around the world, is a sense that, while adherents to standards would continue to push their various causes, at every opportunity, the future for mobile television would be in complementary, overlapping standards. The general possibility that mobile television still offers is using available spectrum to broadcast television signals not just to televisions in the household or in public spaces, but directly to cell phones. It is precisely this that has seen the clamorous appearance of mobile television in media policy debates. Whatever the likely outcomes would be, mobile television as a way to open up new channels was very much a project that sparked the interest of new players, content providers and cultural intermediaries. A major obstacle that arose from taking this path was that mobile television became entangled in the wider policy and regulatory debates over how spectrum is to be resumed and allocated for digital television.

Despite the promises and hype of digital television, especially the much-vaunted high-definition technologies, consumers have been slow to be convinced, and analogue phase-out has dragged. Many countries have now set firm targets for the switch over, and planning and implementation is well advanced. As well as persuading consumers of the merits of the new digital television channels and receivers – assuaging their discontent in needing to buy and adjust to new equipment, and also new services – there are a range of policy issues raised in turning off analogue television – from accessibility, affordability and reach, to licensing, programming and industrial, social and cultural goals. At the heart of many policy battles around digital broadcasting is access to spectrum.

What digital broadcasting offers is an opportunity to review how spectrum is used and allocated, and to free up spectrum for new entrants and services – the so-called 'digital dividend'. Of course, this is precisely the spectre of competition that established broadcasters have been keen to forestall, and, failing that, control on their own terms. High-definition television battles were very much about whether the new technology was indeed a quantum leap, or simply a way for existing television operators to have a compelling argument to extend their dispensation into the future by using more, not less, spectrum. Such arguments have been broadly settled, however, with governments and regulators determining that digital broadcasting will result in new spectrum being available. The details, however, are very much in the proving. High in the priorities for spectrum allocation are mobile television services.

The prospect of television being broadcast to mobile and wireless devices has been regarded as an opportunity for new kinds of television programmes and consumption, another form of post-broadcast television, as we have seen. Mobile television has also been viewed, from a media policy as well as competition policy perspective, as an opportunity to enhance diversity. In markets where terrestrial television licences have been few, and those holding them are very well entrenched as media companies, with strong, often iconic brands that are well known household names, competition has been very limited. Australia is one example of such a market: with only three free-to-air terrestrial channels nationwide, plus two public service broadcasters. In addition, Australia has sub-scription pay television operators (usually only a choice of two in capital cities), based on the fibre coaxial broadband networks (or satellite in rural areas). The fight to shape digital television has revolved around whether new television channels, owned by different interests, will be able to gain licences in the ter-restrial broadcasting networks, so adding new players to the television ecology. By contrast, mobile television promises new networks, channels, operators and new viewing possibilities. In South Korea, as just noted, licences went to three new operators. If spectrum is allocated to mobile television, operators could potentially operate whole facilities or channels themselves, or parts of such a service. Viewed in this light, the mobile television proposition seems clear – yet it has been proven difficult to gain the spectrum for the experiment to begin, as we can see in a number of jurisdictions.

Though mobile television channels have potentially been available for some years, governments, regulators and industries in many countries have been slow to finalize allocation and actually make broadcasting to mobile devices a reality. Moreover, much of the energy of the existing telecommunications and broad-casting industry has waned, as has that of potential new entrants. Mobile television no longer has the totemic quality it briefly enjoyed, as injecting new competition and new televisual possibilities into a staid broadcasting industry. Rather there is a sense that mobile television will continue to evolve, with spectrum being freed up through the 'restacking' following the closure of analogue television broadcasting.

Mobile television cultures

As we have seen, mobile television has had an unusually protracted, complex evolution, presenting difficulties on many levels – from sorting out its standards and business models, to where mobile television fits into spectrum allocation, licensing and media diversity, policy and regulation. If mobile television looks rather protean when viewed from the 'supply' side of its production, financing and industrial arrangements, it is even more fluid still when we take into our reckoning the interaction between user cultures and the affordances of technologies.

When it comes to contemporary television, established broadcasters have been slow in responding to the cumulative changes in audience expectations that have come from using technology such as video recorders, electronic programme guides and television series on DVD. These developments have been accelerated by new internet technologies and cultures, especially downloading. With the advent of file sharing peer-to-peer technologies (most famously, the video

downloading application, BitTorent) users have been able to source and config-
ure their own television experience, opening up the 'black box' of established
broadcasting (Pupillo and Noam 2008). Great user energies have been attracted
to the forging of these new do-it-yourself forms of television 'beyond broadcasting' (Meikle and Young 2008; Katz and Scannell 2009). The kind of mobile
television initially presented to potential viewers, described in this chapter
thus far, is obviously a much more circumscribed affair than these new logics
of televisual practices. This new kind of television (or televisions) does not unfold
so much in the policy deliberations on digital broadcasting, rather in the user
cultures of the internet, the computing world, but also mobile media. Most
obviously, we can observe the popular mobile television most prominently
emerging in combining the video camera and screen capabilities of the cell
phone with the new distributed do-it-yourself broadcasting architectures of the
internet such as YouTube ('broadcast yourself') (Burgess and Green 2009).

Such developments should lead us to question the idea of mobile television
itself, as it has been (albeit very recently) received. In their study of Finnish
mobile consumers from 2004–6, Bouwman et al. note that 'markets for mobile
services are very differentiated and that a careful analysis of specific clusters or
bundles of service is needed' (Bouwman et al. 2009: 314). They make the
important point that '[m]obility itself needs further conceptualization', being not
just about 'anywhere and anytime', but mobile communications in a 'specific
situation at a specific moment' (Bouwman et al. 2009: 314). Other commentators go even further, and offer support for the notion that while mobile TV will
eventually be widely available on the majority of networks around the world,
'this service is not a simple add-on to the voice and data, but comes with totally
new dimensions that challenge the present markets' (Bria et al. 2007: 1). In a
familiar refrain of versions, there is talk of 'mobile TV 2.0', emphasizing the
growing of interactivity and complexity in its development. Schatz et al. discern
three generations of mobile television: first generation, characterized by retrans-
mission and little interactivity; second generation, with peer-to-peer interaction,
and content reformatted for mobile; and third generation, with made-for-mobile
content and much more interactivity and access (Schatz, Jordan and Wagner
2007: 2). For their part, Bria et al. argue that mobile TV will 'complement
traditional TV rather than replace it':

> ... eventually it will develop into something more than just 'television
> on the move'. It will be part of a multimedia device, which emphasizes
> interactivity and enables users to produce and personalize content. Mobile
> TV is not an isolated phenomena, but one of several distribution channels
> for IP TV ...
>
> (Bria et al. 2007: 1)

They distinguish between 'TV in the mobile' – or the technical project of
sorting out standards, solutions and programme rights to make mobile television

possible – and 'TV for the mobile', which relates to 'content customised and broadcast for the mobile format' (Bria et al. 2007: 1). It is the latter category of 'TV for the mobile' that Bria et al. believe will alter the 'traditional value network around TV content', especially as cell phone carriers take an 'active role in both production and distribution' (Bria et al. 2007: 1). In the service of this line of thinking what is most interesting is their radical redefinition of mobile TV content as 'any video played on a mobile device' (Bria et al. 2007: 1). The importance of a fluid definition of mobile television, centring on video, emerges not only from analysis of industry and business models, but also from the side of user cultures. Key to such an account is a shift in post-broadcast TV to consumers wishing for – and creating – a personalized viewing experience.

In effect, video consumption, creating and sharing is central to a kind of 'unofficial' television, co-created by users with the available technologies, repurposed and user-generated content. This 'unofficial' mobile television is now taking on a larger significance in the moveable feast of mobile television (cf. 'informal media' – Seijdel and Melis 2008). Mobile television is now being regarded as part of a large development of 'social television' (Ducheneaut et al. 2008; Schatz et al. 2007). Social television is a direct challenge to the idea that television is an anti-social, privatizing, lower-class, lounge-lizard, couch surfing, domestic, household activity. Such a discourse seeks to capture, and indeed capitalize on, the various social activities that occur in, around, beside and framing television watching – the social practices associated with television that media ethnographers have highlighted for at least three decades (Lull 1990; Morley 1980). Further, social television adherents seek to highlight in a contemporary sense the social media reappropriation of television. They emphasize that television is now embedded in flows of social networking systems, distributed, ubiquitous, pervasive and mobile computing and media. The active, 'produser' audience not only shares the texts, images, sounds, words, narratives and interpretations of television, but indeed engages in peer-to-peer networking of television itself, as well as creating, redacting, and distributing content for it (Engstörm et al. 2007). Here, from the perspectives of users, mobile television is very much constituted through a media ecology in which broadcasting, internet, mobiles, people, locations and things invent a new kind of television. This is a much more throughgoing exercise than industry talk of global 'ecosystems' or multiple standards needing to co-exist, and be available, on the same devices. It stretches our ideas of mobile television much further still, more prosaic and richly unsettling all at once.

The short and long of mobile movies

From the liquid, morphing object of mobile television, I would now like to briefly discuss mobile movies and cinema. This is quite a shift perhaps, if we come from the standpoint of the relatively well established predecessor forms of television and cinema – albeit both now under great pressure and shifting shape fast. Yet mobile television and mobile movies are much closer in form that one might suspect.

There has been much talk of the cell phone as the 'fourth screen', an addition to the trinity of cinema, television and computing (Goggin 2006). On first glance, the prospects for mobile movies appear to resemble those for mobile television. There are grand expectations that cinema will be reincarnated in a pervasive new platform that will so greatly extend its reach and power. If one looks closely, however, a quite fascinating assembling of culture has been underway in this sphere of audiovisual production. Mobile film and video makers have been experimenting with the aesthetics of the small screen (issues of quality, resolution and look) and the social and cultural practices of cellular telephony (watching film on a handset in a range of new settings, such as in queues, or transit lounges, or public transport). However, rather like mobile television, mobile movies and their consumption are taking different paths than originally forecast.

Initial visions for mobile movies included the broadcast of feature-length movies to cell phones. In December 2005, Sprint became the first US carrier to offer full-length movies with its mSpot Movies, and it followed up in September 2006 with pay-per-view offerings. However, the discourse on mobile movies quickly modulated to revolve around the short or even 'micro-' movie. In February 2007, the annual 3GSM World Congress in Barcelona focused on mobile cinema, with the results of a collaboration with the Sundance Film Festival (five short films that were made available worldwide for internet and mobile download), and also with Sanjay Gupta and five other Bollywood film-makers (creating ten minute films, to be combined into a full-length cinema release entitled *Das Kahaniyaan*) (Fitchard 2007a).

While the quality and resolution of mobile moving images has greatly improved, these are still quite a way away from the standards of cinema or television broadcast. This is apparent when we move from considering movies shown on cell phones to movies shot (and perhaps also viewed) on the technology. Many film festivals now routinely offer a mobile movie competition, or a cell phone-produced short movies section (for example, the recent Stockholm and St Kilda film festivals). Many mobile movies consciously explore, and make a virtue of, the distinctive limitation and typical point of view of the cell phone camera. There has been talk of transferring cell phone-shot movies to 35 mm, or large screen formats, but as yet little has eventuated. A celebrated case is the film *SMS Sugar Man*:

> If cameraphones are becoming more sophisticated, then why not push them to their limits? That is just what South African Aryan Kaganof has done in shooting a full feature film, SMS Sugar Man, using a SonyEricsson w900i 3G handset … 'We are re-writing the book on cinema here … things will never be the same again. From now onwards, all you'll need [to make a film] is a good idea, a cell phone, a laptop and you're off. It opens up a whole world of possibilities for African filmmakers' (SMS Sugarman 2008)

In the field of mobile movies, the short film – or micro-movie – form has become especially popular. The producer community, especially in the independent and artistic sectors, has seized the mobile as a test bed for all manner of fascinating experiments in resizing, reshaping and reconceiving movies. However, this enthusiasm and openness has not been so well matched by those controlling the key nodes of distribution – whether the traditional titans of the motion picture and entertainment industries, or the new forces in the mobile equipment and telecommunications industry. Independent short film and video is being consumed across a range of digital media platforms – with brief made-for-mobile movies being watched on computer screens or iPods, as often as (or perhaps more often than) viewed using cell phones.

From the incursion of the cell phone into the cultures of cinema and movies, we find new hybrid forms that are as yet unstable, and that are activating inchoate forms and new kinds of expertise. This is suggested by Lev Manovich's interest in mobility that 'refers not to the movement of individuals and groups or accessing media from mobile devices, but to something else which so far has not been theoretically acknowledged: the movement of media objects between people, devices, and the web' (Manovich 2008: 227). In mobile movies, we find an invocation of particular kinds of social relations that are recognized from cinema – hence the interest of phone companies in full-length movies, or the fascination with filmmakers, entertainment corporations and new media companies in made-for-mobile content. Yet these alluded-to social relations cannot be recreated through mobile movies. Rather what we find is, at present at least, quite different. It is a reassembling of media cultures in which mobile movies are neither recognizably a relative of earlier archetypes of the cell phone, nor recapitulations of antecedent short or long film forms. The expertise of the user as a participatory, networked digital media producer is at play instead – and so at the heart of this reassembling of media cultures is the entwining of both the mobile and the internet in creating new networked cultures – something that is at the heart of the new social relations of participatory media.

Assembling culture

Mobile television – and associated mobile video and film – is an instructive case study. Mobile television starts out as a recognizable thing, attracting investment and commercial interest from leading companies excited by crossover of broadcasting and telecommunications. At its inception mobile television, like other varieties of mobile media, is accompanied by great excitement and fervent, if not utopian, hopes. Yet in the few short years from its appearance in 2004, hopes of ready consumer acceptance and quick profits have been dashed – or at least put on hold. It is not so much that talk of the revolution has been muted, or replaced by the reality of an evolutionary development – rather the nature of mobile television is actually proving quite elusive. This presents us with a conundrum when it comes to understanding the nature and politics of this area of mobile media.

As I have discussed, there are powerful commercial and government interests sharply engaged in the project of shaping mobile television – and the contest for its identity, audiences and spoils is fierce. Yet as mobile television moved away from a straight convergence at the interface of broadcasting and tele-communications, and instead was grafted onto and, indeed, increasingly imbri-cated into the fractal world of the internet, potential delivery platforms, service layers, applications, uses, meanings and actors proliferated. It is possible to draw a comparison between the fragmented standards of first generation mobiles, with nations and regions developing and backing their own standards with clear industry policies (Funk 2002; Steinbock 2003 and 2005), and those of mobile television. Indeed such fragmentation can be seen as a common feature of the development of technologies and markets. However, there is, on the surface at least, much more going on in mobile television that stretches traditional political and cultural economies, as well as theories of technology (cf. Feijóo et al. 2009). Here surely we have something like an assemblage – as the work of Bruno Latour would have it (2005b) – where we need to trace the contingent, complex translations and enlisting of how media cultures, and indeed the social, are put together here.

Thus in mobile television we can discern new actors entering the field of media to reassemble various sorts of cultures at play: mobile culture; television culture; national culture; transnational culture; online culture. The non-human actors implicated include: the affordances of cell phone screens; the character-istics of 3G cell phone networks, compared to broadcasting networks (hence the controversy over standards, especially the DVB-H standard); personal video recorders; the reworking of television by downloading technologies; the nature of time associated with mobile devices (hence the revisionary troping of mobile television as 'snack time'); the production of place implied by cell phones (hence advertisements showing users watching mobile TV in queues); the home and its organization (Alam and Prasad 2008), especially its gendering. While new reg-ulatory sites and policy problematics are being created here, old policy objects are also being reanimated to shore up the project of television, such as local content, media diversity, languages, free access to important television events or content.

Mobile television, then, is a terrific example of the unpredictable career of a technology. It is a failure (Latour 1996); a sleeper; likely to continue its fitful and slow development; and at some stage, apparently, it will settle in to become a natural part of global mobile media. What makes it frustrating for its industrial and governmental backers, however, is something of an adaptable, open, if patchwork quilt, platform for its users. Yet it is precisely this prospect that makes mobile television very much a coming attraction.

Chapter 6

Mobile gaming
Playing the portable

Games are an exciting way to communicate and connect with a larger community of like minded people. Rich mobile games, combined with connected near distance multiplayer gaming over Bluetooth and wide area gaming using cellular networks, opens the door for totally new gaming concepts. Mobility will add a whole new dimension to innovative and creative games concepts and will provide opportunities for the games and telecom industry alike.

(Anssi Vanjoki, Executive Vice President, Nokia Mobile Phones, quoted in Nokia 2002)

... companies are treating the cell phone like it was a second-rate game console and I don't think that's really doing it justice.

(Trip Hawkins, founder of Electronic Arts and Digital Chocolate, quoted in Chehimi et al. 2008: 19)

Introduction

Gaming is an enormous part of contemporary global media. From their inception in early computer and video games (King 2008; Wolf 2007) – building on various histories of gaming from arcade games to portable board games, to the enduring place that games have in society (Callois 2001; Huizinga 1949; Turner 1982) – games are now very big media business (Ip 2008), and a huge facet of what users do (Castronova 2006). There is a wide range of quite distinct games, game platforms, and gaming cultures and user experiences (Aarseth 2001; Consalvo 2006; Mäyrä 2007).

The place of the internet in games has grown exponentially since the mid-1990s, with many gamers taking some form of networked game architecture and interaction as a natural thing. This likely has to do with the fact that the internet is so much a taken-for-granted part of everyday life. One expects to be able to search for information, updates, modifications, fellow gamers, competitors, clubs, communities and networks for any activity online – but especially activities to do with information and communication technology. Specific games and gaming cultures have also developed around the internet since its inception. With the uneven yet widespread availability of broadband in many over-developed countries – mostly Western, but Eastern too (when one thinks of the pioneering gaming nations of South Korea and Japan) – online gaming has had a platform to develop rich, pervasive new forms.

Gaming has also been involved in distinctive crossover forms and new hybrid genres in its own right. This comes from the repurposing of game technologies: machinima – 'machine' plus 'cinema' (alluding to 'anime' too) – being perhaps the most spectacular form of the mash-up variety of this; where game 'engines' are taken from games and used to make videos that can be circulated via video-sharing and other sites on the internet. Sequences, characters, codes and engines from the phenomenally successful game World of Warcraft can be made into satirical or fan culture creations (Corneliussen and Rettberg 2008). Games conventions, genres, habitus and modes of knowledge are also finding their way into educational and cultural settings (Annetta 2008; Klopfer 2008; Leung 2006): museums, for instance, being interested in the deep cognitive, behavioural and epistemological settings of games, to provide new ways to present, and represent, cultural heritage (Ardito et al. 2009). Games are one of the most eminent cross-platform, cross-media cultural forms (Bogost 2007). For instance, games can be played across books, DVDs, internet, mobiles, spaces and pen-and-paper – distributed across all these, actually, and existing solely on no one element of these 'transfictional' instantiations (Dena 2009).

These fertile, complex trends in gaming – and its central place in media cultures – have for some years been brought to bear, and indeed quickened, by experiments and developments in mobile media. Rather like mobile music, game developers, the entertainment and media interests in global gaming, cell phone carriers and handset manufacturers, have viewed the widespread diffusion of mobile devices as a great opportunity. The technology in the pockets of billions of the world's population provides a new platform for reconceiving, designing and selling games for cell phones. In addition, cell phones are a new 'arena of innovation' (Sawhney and Lee 2005) for industrial, entrepreneurial, civic, educational and user groups interested in games. Mobile media, as we have already seen, is not just about activating the internet on mobile devices – and then harvesting the marketing and revenue streams that logically flow. Rather, mobile media have different affordances that gamers, and the ensemble of those designing and developing the game, have to grasp, play with and reconfigure (Broll and Benford 2005; Davidsson et al. 2004; Füller et al. 2005). Mobile media potentially have cameras built in, which people use for taking and sharing photos – in ways they do not use their laptops or desktop computer. With a cell phone, one can call or message, or now receive and send email, or Twitter feeds. Mobile media are portable, interwoven with new logics of mobility, in ways that are bound up with the topographies and topologies of mobile networks, but also the ways that the devices are used by people in their new reinventions of movement, spatially, economically and socially shaped as they are. Mobile media often have sensors, location, or positioning technologies built in. So games are being pieced together, or re-thought, from the intersections of these new – and old – capabilities and constraints.

It is this broad understanding of gaming's place in global media, that is setting the discussion of mobile gaming that follows. First, I sketch a history of mobile gaming, from its humble beginning with rudimentary games such as the Nokia snake game. Second, I look at the various initiatives mobile companies, entertainment providers and game developers have undertaken to offer a distinctive mobile gaming experience, and discuss the mainly lukewarm user response to date. This contrasts, third, with the many ludic uses of mobile and wireless technologies created by artists, educators and others, especially around locative media, and in hybrid and alternative reality games, that have generated a great deal of excitement.

Handset arcades

In 1997, Taneli Armanto, a Nokia engineer, created a version of the snake game for one of the company's phones. The snake game has a long history before this mobile version, going back to early arcade games (Gremlin's 'Blockade', in 1976), computers ('Worm' for the TRS-80 microcomputer in 1978, then versions of the same for Apple II) and calculators. Nokia's first snake game was designed for its then monochrome phones, launching on the N6110 (Nokia 2009). The Nokia snake game grew in complexity and quality of graphics and resolution, and was implemented for colour phones. With the advent of Nokia's specialist games handset – N-Gage – a 3D version of Snakes was designed, with a representation of a live rather than schematic snake following, as well as multiplayer options via Bluetooth:

> From the dark winter depths of the Finnish wilderness, a viral outbreak has begun, with a new generation of Snakes coming to the N-Gage platform … this latest incarnation of the world's most famous mobile game will infect N-Gage game deck users with that familiar Snakes desire to see how long you can go. Multiplayer games will quickly turn into a slippery session with support for up to 4 players via Bluetooth wireless technology. Players can start their own viral outbreak by sharing their 'infection' with other N-Gage owners …
>
> (N-Gage News 2005)

Development of Snake continued with the advent of the second generation N-Gage platform in 2008. In 2009 Nokia estimated that the snake game in its variants is available on 350 million phones (Nokia 2009). Snake has also had a lively design life in the world of smartphones, with iPhone and iTouch snake game apps – such as Star Snake, set in a galaxy – and an analogous game called SpaceBall on LG mobile phones.

Nokia's snake game still typically comes to mind as the first and most popular game on mobiles; but, as a number of scholars have noted, the history of mobile games stretches back at least some decades before this. Espen Aarspeth points to the late 1970s and early 1980s as an important starting point, with the appearance of the Sony Walkman (1979), and Nintendo's Game & Watch series (1980) followed by the same company's iconic Gameboy in 1989 (Aarseth 2001). In their useful cultural historical questioning of mobile games development, Jussi Parkikka and Jaako Suominen argue:

> that the nineteenth century experience of movement is one of the key pre-conditions behind modern day mobile entertainment. The themes of modern travel experience and the birth of modern urban space are necessary elements in understanding the user experiences behind such contemporary mobile games as Snake (1997), Playman Summer Games (2004), Racing Fever Deluxe (s.a.), or for instance pervasive games such as Botfighters (2001) and Uncle Roy All Around You (2003).
>
> (Parikka and Suominen 2006, n.p.)

Others, such as Larissa Hjorth, point out the local histories at play in shaping globally distributed, produced and consumed mobile games:

> The remediated media histories that accompany mobile and gaming discourses are multiple and divergent. In the face of global rhetoric about convergent media such as mobile gaming, the local operates as a tenacious force ... the localized nature of both play and mobility that continue to disrupt any homogeneous form of media archaeology or globalization. Play cultures mobilize the politics of the local, and localities mobilize various forms of play.
>
> (Hjorth 2007: 794; cf. Hjorth and Chan 2009)

Hjorth points to Japan and Korea, which one might expect to be leaders in the take-up of mobile games (Aoyama and Izushi 2003) – however, she notes that there is evidence to the contrary. Hence her attention to issues of location:

> mobile gaming seemed less prevalent in Asia despite the region demonstrating some of the highest broadband infrastructure in the world (as in the case of South Korea) and the pioneering of mobile technologies (as in the case of Japan with the Sony Walkman). Despite the region's burgeoning technonationalism and the growing commodification of 'Asia' globally (as is the case of Hollywood's adaptation of Asian cinema), we see distinct forms of practicing consumption and production.
>
> (Hjorth 2007: 794)

This questioning of the typical kinds of histories is very important to help us analyse the development of mobile games. Their value becomes even more apparent when we consider the multimedia and mobile media phases of mobile gaming. We will return to such discussions shortly.

The early versions of Snake and games like Siemen's Kung Fu were embedded games that shipped with cellular mobile handsets:

> The first embedded games were coded into the firmware, and powered by the extra processing abilities of devices that were not used for controlling the main functions of the phone ... These games can be specifically optimized for one platform, and take full advantage of the handset's features such as sound, vibration, or a color display ... [such] stand-alone games can provide high quality presentation, good response time for the user interface and are robust.
>
> (Bendas and Myllyaho 2002: 4)

Additional games were offered for purchase via download – an important part of a burgeoning cell phone content industry: 'the hardware evolved bringing up the possibility and interest for applications developed by third parties that can be installed by end-users' (Bendas and Myllyaho 2002: 4). In 2001, for instance, Nokia teamed up with Sanrio to offer downloadable game packs, ringtones, SMS graphics and animated screen savers for the Japanese company's 'flagship character' Hello Kitty (Nokia 2001d). For its part, Motorola featured games, as well as other cell phone content, such as themes, graphics, and ringtones, through its hellomoto portal. In 2004 carrier O2 joined with Samsung to launch Samsung Lab for games and other content, something Samsung followed up with its Fun Club portal. To advance the potential for the industry as a whole, and especially to combat difficulties posed by lack of standardization and common technologies, Ericcson, Nokia, Motorola and Siemens established the Mobile Games Interoperability Forum in 2001 (Shannon 2001; cf. Gallagher and Park 2002).

As cell phones developed, so too did the possibilities for games. Cell phones started to attract a great deal of interest, as a potentially distinctive and sophisticated platform for games. This occured at a time when the games industry internationally was consolidating its position as a vastly profitable area of consumer electronics and entertainment, and a key site of contemporary culture. Perhaps the most publicised mobile game at this time was Botfighter, developed by the Swedish company It's Alive (which later became Daydream). Botfighter was a classic first-person shooter game with a twist. Botfighter used the location capability of cell phones – namely their ability to locate a device within a cell of the GSM system – for players to interact with and shoot each other. Botfighter used a web interface also, but it was the use of the cell phone to allow players to roam a city, finding and fighting other players, that really captured the imagination of its users, and also the general public:

> In the car park of a large supermarket on the outskirts of Stockholm, Niklas Wolkert, a 31-year-old programmer, is waiting with his son for his

wife to finish shopping. Niklas looks like any other bored father until he takes his mobile phone from his jacket pocket and begins tapping out a text message. It might look innocent enough, but in a few moments, Wolkert will be stepping into a virtual world. Wolkert is about to begin a game of Botfighters – a game that uses positioning technology in the phone to turn Wolkert into a virtual assassin, fighting foes on the streets of Stockholm.

(Dodson 2002; cf Loftus 2002)

Launched in Stockholm, Botfighters was sold to cell phone operators in countries such as Turkey, Ireland, and was apparently very successful in Russia, its debut coinciding with the 2002 Moscow Theatre hostage crisis (Dennis 2003). Once a player locates an adversary, they can shoot them through a text message. Botfighter was widely discussed by scholars, as it brought together various features that we see recurring and remediated in later mobile games: the role of location in mobile media (later a feature of celebrated games such as the Japanese Mogi – Joffe 2008; Licoppe and Inada 2006, 2008 and 2009); the use of SMS to provide billing and a business model; the production of new spatial relations in an urban setting; the expansion of gaming outside the charmed circle into what becomes characterized in various ways, such as pervasive gaming (Bichard et al. 2006; Sotamaa 2002; De Souza e Silva 2006 and 2009; De Souza e Silva and Hjorth 2009; Struppek and Willis 2008).

The role of audio and sound in cell phones started to become important and an integral feature of design (Collins 2008). Cell phones also became imbricated into another area of games: television games. Games were of growing interest from those working on interactive television, who saw them as an important way to grow these long-discussed but still marginal services (Nightingale and Dwyer 2006; Quico 2003). The cell phone become important as a backchannel and interactive device for viewers to participate in quizzes, competitions, voting, and eventually contribute text messages, images or video (Goggin and Spurgeon 2007 and 2008; Spurgeon and Goggin 2007). An early example was the 2002 involvement of Nokia in incorporating the cell phone in the format of the popular quiz programme, *Who wants to be a millionare?*, the Indian version of which was famously dramatized in the 2008 movie *Slumdog Millionaire*. Television games and gaming is not my focus here, but I would note that it offers another important context for the futures – as well as the histories – of mobile games, to which we will return.

Game on: multimedia mobiles

A difficulty in developing games for cellular platforms has been the small screens, constraints on quality of graphics, battery life, the fragmented nature of mobile media and lack of standardization. Mobile gamers were, problematically, used to being casual, rather than hardcore gamers. Because of the typically short duration of use of cell phone applications, design focused on brief games, rather than deep gaming experiences:

> Typically, mobile applications are used for short episodes, possibly as one task among many. Game designers have to ensure that users can enjoy a pleasurable interaction experience under such circumstances. A common solution – seen in many current mobile games – is to create games that can be completed within a few minutes.
>
> (Geiger et al. 2004: 142)

As a games platform, cell phones compete with other mobile multimedia devices, including hand-helds and PDAs, and so while there were great expectations, the difficulties were all too apparent, as highlighted in a 2006 study:

> Limited displays of the current generation [of cell phones] ... cannot compete with the display of a PDA ... and next generation handhelds ... Another aspect is the lack of memory on the extractable RAM of the mobile phones (max 64MB). The [Sony] PSP offers a DVD device. The PDAs offer hard disks between two and four GB. The category input devices most conspicuously indicates the major lack of the mobile phones. The cellular input structure (12 buttons + special buttons based on the mobile phone type) do not support rapid movement. Next generation handhelds have the most economic design, supporting touch screens and joy-pads. Even the PDA features a better input through its larger display and the touch screen.
>
> (Fritsch, Ritter and Schiller 2006b)

This is especially apparent in the issues faced by console based game developers considering the cell phone platform – for instance, the attractiveness to gamers of 3D graphics (Chehimi, Coulton and Edwards 2008; Liarokapis 2006). Later versions of N-Gage explicitly addressed the lure of 3D graphics to gamers:

> N-Gage technology transforms Nokia handsets from simple phones into bonafide console-battling games machines. The power behind N-Gage is Nokia's 3D accelerated hardware, and while that's not present in every mobile, it's more common than you might expect ... Mainstream phones such as the N95 8GB, E75 and 5320 XpressMusic have next-generation graphics chips inside, letting them gorge on the latest games from some of the world's largest publishers. In many ways, N-Gage is smarter than portable games consoles, and certainly much more pocketable.
>
> (Nokia 2009)

There are other challenges too for mobile games developers. There are a very diverse range of mobile devices with differing capabilities, yet it is important that games applications work across these:

Mobile games (and mobile applications, in general) must adhere to strong portability requirements … in order to target more users, owning different kinds of devices, service carriers typically demand that a single application be deployed in a dozen or more platforms.

(Alves et al. 2005)

As multimedia phones became available, Nokia was again notable as a company prepared to invest heavily in dedicated mobile gaming (Martini 2007). Nokia was one of the first companies to introduce multimedia phones with its famous Communicator handset in 1996. Its heavily promoted initiative in this area was, of course, the N-Gage device, introduced in 2002. The N-Gage was designed to combine mobile communications and dedicated gaming. To make the N-Gage attractive Nokia sought to adapt and bring leading games to the cell phone through agreements in 2003 and 2004 with various leading entertainment software companies for well known games, such as Crash Nitro Kart (Vivendi Universal Games), Virtua Corp and Alien Front (SEGA), The Sims, Splintercell (Gameloft), Tomb Raider (Eidos). In promoting these 'blockbuster' adaptations, Nokia emphasized:

The Nokia N-Gage is an innovative mobile game deck device that creates an entirely new market for time, place and context sensitive game genres. Built for active and hard-core gamers, the Nokia N-Gage allows for online, mobile, multiplayer game play with today's hottest titles … Tomb Raider has been extended to include such mobile gaming services as advanced wirelessly networked gaming as well as the ability for players to direct, edit and share their own cinematic gameplay sequences over the mobile network. Tom Clancy's Splinter Cell … is the next generation blockbuster adaptation … where two players can join together in co-operative mode to solve special situations.

(Nokia 2003b)

Nokia also formed partnerships with companies such as Electronic Arts to develop dedicated titles.

Other companies sought to offer dedicated gaming phones to compete directly with Nokia. In 2005, Samsung launched two different mobile cellular handsets with 3D gaming capabilities (*Marketing Week* 2005). The same year in India, Samsung offered a new smartphone featuring Java games, as well as multilingual capabilities, internet access and 40-chord polyphonic ringtones (*India Telecom* 2005). In 2001 new joint venture Sony Ericsson viewed mobile games as an important way to further their alliance (Perez 2001), and nominated downloadable games and digital photography as the next 'killer applications' for cell phones (Collins 2002). Sony Ericcson proceeded to sign agreements with British game developer iFone and Swedish based Synergenix (*Nordic Business Report* 2002a), and the next year was engaged in multiple mobile gaming trials

(Brown-Humes 2002). Sony Ericsson claimed its T300, launched in late 2002, was the first phone able to download games (Pringle 2002). It also marketed its Z700 as a mobile gaming cell phone with large colour screen, Java, Bluetooth and 'fast GPRS connection' (*Nordic Business Report* 2002b). Sony Ericcson's avowed strategy was to target the entry level part of the market, with its T310 phone featuring an exclusive game, Tony Hawk's Pro Skater 4 (Moss 2003). In 2004, it launched five 3D-enabled handsets, including the mid-range-priced K508i, also with integrated still and video camera (Aquino 2005). As the manufacturer of the famous Play Station device, Sony, of course, enjoyed a strong base for its incursions into the mobile gaming market. The enduring popularity of console gaming, and well established handhelds – especially the dominant Nintendo (Williams 2002), but also the relatively cheap price of Play Station compared to N-Gage, at this stage at least, posed serious challenges for Nokia (Moss 2003).

For equipment manufacturers, serious investment in games has proved tricky as Nokia's N-Gage experience reveals:

> The device manufacturers such as Nokia with its NGage, take a huge risk in diversifying into the gaming business. Nokia has admitted that the sales of the Ngage have not reached the level they had hoped for. It is likely that Nokia will want to increase the installed base of the platform as the real profits in the video game industry have traditionally come from the sales of the games, not the devices.
>
> (Kontio 2004)

Nokia maintained its investment in other aspects of games. In 2001 it announced a partnership with Loki Software to distribute its Linux based games on an early 'smart home' device called the Media Terminal (Nokia 2001a; Koskela and Väänänen-Vainio-Mattila 2004). Combining digital television (DVB), streaming video (RealPlayer), full internet access, a personal video recorder and also gaming, the Media Terminal was Nokia's attempt to pitch a technology that would be the 'central device [consumers] attached to their televisions' (Nokia 2001b). Nokia doubtless experienced difficulty in establishing the unique nature of N-Gage as a gaming platform. For one thing, games manufacturers were certainly playing the field. Sega established its dedicated Sega Mobile in 2002: 'The new subsidiary sells games to mobile-service carriers, including Sprint, which is offering *Super Monkey Ball* on its new third-generation color phones. Sega's *Borakov* game is preinstalled on Motorola phones sold by Nextel Communications' (Leavitt 2003).

The approach taken by other manufacturers also struck problems. Different software solutions emerged 'trying to solve the complex problem of accommodating and running foreign application in a small and restrictive medium such as a mobile telephone's operating system' (Bendas and Myllyaho 2002: 4; cf. Rajala et al. 2005; Stenbacka 2008). A number of companies viewed games based on Sun Microsystems' Java programming language as the way forward for cell phones. A stripped down version of Java for cell phone applications was created – J2ME (Java 2 platform micro edition), now known as Java ME (Krikke 2003). In 2002, Motorola, for instance, viewed Java as 'the key to games success' and worked with 'games developers to encourage the production of more Java-based content' (Shanker et al. 2002). The ambitions of Java's backers to secure the mobile games arena, however, were thwarted. Java did not end up being the key to mobile game domination, though it has steadily developed and remained important. In late 2006, Java ME source code was made available under GNU public licence, released with the project name 'phoneME', with a brief considerably wider than games: 'Java ME technology will serve as the foundation for not only games, but for implementing core applications such as address books and messaging, or even the mobile device user interface' (Java 2007).

Pivotal to directions in mobile gaming were the possibilities of moving beyond individual or group console based play to networked gaming. This has been tackled in different ways in mobile gaming. While the downloading of games has proved popular, it has put limits on collective gaming, as observed in a Korean study:

> The mobile game industry categorizes the games into download type and network type, according to whether the game was played on-line or off-line. Download type mobile games do not charge additional fees once the mobile game has been downloaded. They are economical to use but take up a great deal of memory capacity on the mobile device. Since download type games can be played by only one gamer on a cellular phone ... the gamer is prohibited from sharing information or ideas with other gamers in a broader capacity such as an online community. In contrast, network type mobile games, such as online PC games, have functions that enable interaction and the sharing of information among players. Despite incurring higher costs ... the gamer can enjoy a more dynamic game interaction because multi-players can play together in real time.
>
> (Kim et al. 2009: 2)

The distinction drawn here between individual player downloadable mobile games and multiplayer networked games does not hold fast. Not only is downloaded game play often an experience shared with others, but an individual player often feel like it is; that is, they 'enjoy perceived copresence, even though the game may not be connected to other players' (Kim et al. 2009: 14). Nonetheless, in the move to take mobile gaming beyond basic downloading, the role of the internet has also been critical. This included various modes: whether through games devised for, or adapted for, multiplayer play on the internet; connecting game devices, such as consoles to the internet (through embedding Wi-Fi transmitters, or plugs); or through the ability of gamers to communicate via the internet, find key resources, exchange parts of games via the internet.

Much of contemporary gaming culture is strongly underwritten by internet technologies and cultures. With 3G networks – and associated moves to combine mobiles and the internet – greater attention was paid to networked gaming on cell phones (Akkawi et al. 2004). An early, cell phone-centric mode of networked gaming is possible through Bluetooth connectivity and networks. B'ngo was a console-type games player as well as a cell phone that allowed up to eight players to compete with each other via Bluetooth and GRPS (Akkawi et al. 2004: 459; Mobile Monday 2003). Bluetooth networked games were a feature of Nokia's N-Gage platform, noted above in relation to the snake game. However, Nokia too sought to create a relationship between N-Gage's mobile cellular platform and the internet's space of community and cultural formation for gaming:

> In order to support N-Gage, Nokia has developed an online arena. Inside this arena, the players can, for example, compete against each other, chat, and share images of their gaming experience ... mobile gaming communities are not expected to operate only in the mobile networks, but in the realm of the traditional Internet as well.
>
> (Siitonen 2003: 16–17)

According to Nokia:

> The N-Gage Arena will be the place where gamers meet and create virtual communities, share their experiences, find new challenges and make friends with players all over the world ... For the first time, a gamer sitting in a park in London can find another player and 'shadow race' against a player in Los Angeles or even Singapore, who has posted a shadow image of his game character in the N-Gage Arena. The London gamer can in turn post a clip of the game on the site, showing his victory and simultaneously challenge the rest of the game community.
>
> (Nokia 2003c)

Nokia promoted N-Gage through game events, such as the Nokia Game, started in 1998. Only playable on N-Gage or the Nokia 3650 phone, the 2003 Nokia Game included:

> ... the Flo Boarding game; chat with other players; as well as meet and interact with the avatar Flo, the virtual heroine of this year's story. Players can also take advantage of mobile online gaming elements to upload their high scores, download ghosts and compete against other players via Bluetooth wireless technology or mobile networks.
>
> (Nokia 2003d)

Nokia Game is an early example of mobiles featuring in pervasive games (Thomas 2006), with a strong link to brand development or communities: 'The Nokia

Game 2002 shows that support for branded product-related mobile interactions is picking up, but in terms of communities and positioning branded products as links is still in its infancy' (Heitman et al. 2004: 8).

Cellular mobile phones were not the only kind of portable terminals with connectivity. Just as cell phone manufacturers were figuring out how to add gaming capabilities to their device, console makers were experimenting with adding online capacities to their decks or controllers. To ensure consumers stay with their Xbox, PlayStation Portable or Nintendo, manufacturers sought to add wireless internet connectivity. Nintendo DS, the dual-screen handheld console released in 2004, featured Wi-Fi capability. In 2005, Nintendo launched its own Wi-Fi Connection Service, and then also offered a Wi-Fi USB connector, through which a number of users could play. In 2005, Sony attempted to dislodge Nintendo dominance of handhelds, with the launch of PlayStation Portable, which also featured Wi-Fi, and, in later models, the capability to make voice calls using Skype Voice over internet protocol software. In 2007–9 rumours abounded that Sony would finally develop a combination PSP and cell phone – a hybrid of its game division and Sony Ericcson joint venture.

To summarize, the period of multimedia mobile game development (if we can accurately characterize it in this way) spanning roughly 2001–6 saw considerable corporate investment and manoeuvring. As we have seen, the size of and revenue deriving from mobile games steadily rose. Yet the interest mobile gaming piqued was nothing on the scale desired by phone makers, carriers, game developers and media and entertainment companies. Mobile games played a critical part in the steady development and growing significance of entertainment and media on cell phones (Steinbock 2005). While games were an important and desirable feature, they were typically not the single critical 'killer app'. Nonetheless in the process the value chains – and indeed the political economy – of mobile media took on new complexities with the advent of games. As we have seen, new actors entered the world of cell phones and telecommunications from the spheres of gaming and media. This opened up new arenas of innovation, though their significance remains unclear. For instance, there was some discussion about the characteristics of mobile games – small screen, lower resolution, less computing power (Duh et al. 2008). Also of concern were the economics of purchasing and selling mobile games – how consumers paid much less for blockbuster games for consoles or online, not to mention consumers paying much less (think 'micro-payments') for the pleasure of acquiring a game. In addition, there was a debate on how these apparent characteristics of mobile gaming opened up new opportunities for the small, fledgling or even avowedly micro-enterprise game designers to be competitive. There are important implications of mobile games, then, for discussions of innovation and creativity – reflected in industry and national government discourse on mobile games (for example: Åresund 2006; IGDA 2005). Less well noticed, but actually much more profitable, was the entry of new intermediaries of various sorts, in the business of procuring, aggregating and offering games, whether to equipment suppliers (as in the Nokia, Samsung or Sony Ericcson portals); to carriers (as part of their portals, such as Vodafone Live!, or Hutchison's 3); or to service providers to market in their own right, whether via WAP or premium rate mobile data services.

In many ways, these logics continue to work themselves out in classic mobile-centric gaming developments. With the growth of mobile gaming beyond the US, Europe, Japan and Korea, in countries such as China, the circuit of gaming culture, especially in its economies of production and consumption, stands to dramatically alter. Mobile gaming has been slow to become part of China's fast growing online games industry, with 2007 revenues generated by Java and BREW mobile games estimated at only a total of RMB 777 million ($113.3 million), and only a very small proportion of cell phone users (Interfax China 2007). Interestingly in-game advertising is an important way of generating revenue in both cell phone and internet games (Interfax China 2007). I will return to these implications for mobile media at the end of this chapter, but now will turn to a set of developments that taken together vastly expand our conceptions of mobile gaming – and potentially take its politics of design and practice way out of the ken of the traditional cell phones and telecommunications industries themselves.

Ludic uses of cell phones

The development of the multimedia cell phone was only one trajectory that influenced the creation of mobile gaming. The development of the cell phone-based games market has come with considerable constraints compared to the video game market in general. The distribution of mobile games, for instance, has been dominated by carriers and large service providers, a situation underscored by the centrality of the menu on devices as a locus of control, rather like the strategic centrality of the electronic programme guide in gate keeping viewer choice in subscription and digital television (Klopfer 2008: 46). However, as we have seen, woven into mobile media – on purpose and by accident in equal parts – are an overlapping set of other developments, affordances, histories and emerging cultures of use.

This is already evident when we look at the celebrated case of Botfighters. As Sotamaa points out, the category underlying this game is the cell based nature of mobile communications, and the need of the networks to be able to identify the location of a handset within a cell: 'GSM network based locating is not as accurate as other alternatives but the advantage is that cell identification does not require any new hardware or additional cards but the games can be played by using standard GSM phones' (Sotamaa 2002: 36). Sotamaa identifies two other types of location based gaming:

> The oldest games [GPS-based treasure hunt games like *Geocaching* and *Geodashing*] are based on using Global Position System (GPS receivers that

have been in the market much longer than mobile phones or PDAs) ...
Secondly there are concepts based on local area networks (wlan etc) and
proximity sensors. The experiments produced so far are mainly outcomes of
academic and commercial research projects. These games utilize a limited
area and can make physical locations, objects, states and locations of other
players intrinsic elements of the game.

(Sotamaa 2002)

Geocaching is an outdoor game that uses GPS to hide and find containers called
'caches' or 'geocaches'. Geocaching was started in 2000, based according to
some on the old game of 'letterboxing' (clues provided in stories and texts),
and now has a large community of enthusiasts around the world (Hurd and
Schlatter 2005; O'Hara 2008). Ever since geocaching achieved wider public
notice in 2004–5 – stories regarding the nuisance and problems it allegedly
caused; publication of guides on this new recreation; the popularity of the geo-
caching.com website – the field of such mobile location activities has broadened
dramatically. There are now a widening range of mobile place-making practices.
For the present I wish to concentrate on the second area of concepts based on
wireless networks, sensors and other technologies and practices. This still remains
largely an area of academic, commercial and, I would add, artistic and community research experimentation. It is an area where innovations are burgeoning and adding much to how we understand mobile gaming.

There are now many examples of location based games, that draw upon a
combination of the available technologies but centre on cell phones. Location
based gaming features in a range of different movements within gaming generally, talked about variously as mixed reality (Cheok et al. 2002; Vogiazou et al.
2006), alternative reality or pervasive gaming (Harvey 2006; cf. Consalvo 2009).
Context and location is central to pervasive games:

> Pervasive games introduce a new emerging game genre that pushes the
> boundaries of the traditional games and enables new kinds of gaming
> experiences for players. One of the most exciting aspects in these games is
> that the context information is utilized to modify a game world or it is
> converted to game elements. In addition, gaming can be blended into the
> daily life and normal social situations of the players.
>
> (Korhonen et al. 2008: 21; cf. Grüter and Ok 2007)

As well as the challenges and opportunities of designing to take account of and
use information about context (Bell et al. 2006; Ermi and Mäyrä 2005a and b),
there are added issues to be faced with non-players, who find themselves very
much in the game space:

> the pervasive games are often played in environments inhabited by people
> who are not playing the game. The game design must ensure that the game

does not disturb too much players' social interaction outside the gameworld or disrupt nonplayers' ongoing activities. Further, since the players may be distracted from their surroundings by focusing on the game at hand, they may become a hazard for themselves or others.

(Korhonen et al. 2008: 22)

Alternative reality gaming involves interactive, participative narrative that uses the resources of places, players, media and location technologies. While debate ensues about the definition of ARGs, narrative is certainly an important quality of this form of gaming. Commentators point to the 1996 game Dreadnot as a web based precursor to famous games that are now recognized as ARGs such as The Beast (2001), Audi's The Art of the Heist (2006), and Microsoft-commissioned I Love Bees (2004).There is now also a genre of serious ARGs, funded to promote education on various topics from environmental challenges – World without Oil (2007), The Black Cloud (2009) – through war and conflict – British Red Cross's Traces of Hope (2008) (Dena 2009; Wikipedia 2008). A much discussed ARG is Perplex City, a sprawling affair, first played in London, then in different cities around the world:

Welcome to Perplex City. A city obsessed with puzzles and ciphers. A game that blurs the boundaries between fiction and reality. Begin an incredible, immersive adventure that spills out into the real world. Interrogate suspects over the phone, search police files for evidence, decipher coded emails and check newspapers for clues – working with tens of thousands of players around the world.

(http://www.perplexcity.com/, accessed on 11 May 2010; cf. Peters 2009)

Devised by social multiplayer game outfit Mind Candy, the first season of Perplex City relied heavily upon cell phones:

Using their mobile phones, players had to feed their answers and photographic evidence of their antics back to Base Camp via SMS and MMS messages, while the organisers sent out leaderboard updates, trivia questions and surprise tasks throughout the day.

(Parsons 2006)

Perplex City is but one of a dizzying array of alternative reality games. What is evident is that mobile media often plays an important role in these – as a personal, portable technology and network infrastructure that allows multimedia communication, recording and quotidian media production, that underlies and shapes the participatory structures of these nascent culture forms. Cell phones also have a set of relations to place, space and location, now proliferating with the intersection of technologies that traverse handsets and networks (Coiana et al. 2008; Nova and Girardin 2009). Yet such directions in gaming go very much beyond mobile media. Hence the question of how they relate to the global mobile media is a very interesting one.

In one sense, the relationship is incidental: just as the postal system or printed materials could be used in the game 'Letterbox', or other games relying on mail, so too text messaging, for instance, is open to enlistment in games (Flintham et al. 2007) – just as phoneboxes might be used to ring and give players information, as in the game I Love Bees. Further, as some of the often discussed pervasive, alternative reality and other games reveal, there are a wide range of corporate actors involved. Indeed one of the interesting things is that such mixed or alternative reality gaming attracts large corporations, from car makers to software companies, as a branding, marketing exercise. Presumably the appeal lies in new architectures of persuasion and rhetoric that go beyond existing models of advertising, and require non-trivial investment from audiences. Most of these large, transnationational corporations will have little problem obtaining and putting together the necessary technology, skills, expertise and participants (whether paid, or willing customers or bystanders) to assemble such a logistical feat in gaming (on co-operation in gaming see Crabtree et al. 2007). This is not so, however, to many users and citizens, who, for a mix of non-commercial or potential small-scale commercial reasons, might wish to enter into this new kind of gaming (for an interesting attempt to put pervasive games in the hands of their users, to create communities around 'mods', see Wetzel et al. 2009). Here the questions raised for the political and cultural economies of mobile media are really about the affordances of the infrastructure, who may have access to them, for what purposes and on what terms and conditions.

Conclusion

In a little over a decade, mobile gaming has been established as a significant part of contemporary gaming cultures. It has not proven as lucrative as hoped, but in various forms it is firmly established as a central part of cell phone culture – whether as embedded games on a handset, downloadable games from a portal or premium rate number, or apps. Social, multiplayer gaming is now part of the mobile experience vying with solely internet based alternatives (Hadenius 2003). Perhaps mobile gaming's greatest contribution has been to challenge dominant, gendered preconceptions of console and online gaming, about the duration, genre and type of practice that characterizes 'real gaming', or genuine gamers and their communities and cultures (Barkhuus et al. 2005). Mobile gaming tends to the episodic, or fragmentary; to reconfigure the large screen, embodied experiences of many gaming locales; and, instead, to encourage awareness of context – indeed through location technologies allowing incorporation of place into gameplay.

Games, then, are an important aspect of global mobile media. There is an obvious set of engagements, and new arrangements, which see cell phones recognized as an important part of the gaming business. As yet games companies have not exerted much influence in how mobile media has been shaped – with little investment into cell phones from games companies or their entertainment owners. This is different from the investments of other media companies, notably music, television or movie companies discussed in Chapters 4 and 5, or internet companies discussed in Chapter 7. Nonetheless, the investments have certainly been serious, and the revenues steadily increasing. Where we might think of directing attention is in the evolving structures of control and participation that govern and construct mobile gaming – at the intersection of its cultural and political economies. If cell phones are near ubitiquous infrastructures with billions of users worldwide, what kind of games appear upon these handsets? How open are cell phone carriers to offering their platform for innovation? These questions get pushed even further when we contemplate the vistas of mobile gaming that claim to be almost co-terminous with our everyday lives, its places and materials. What are the relationships among the different kinds of technologies, mobile media and others, that constitute the architecture of such pervasive, immersive gaming? What are the kinds of participation, and its politics, that this phenomenon, complex as it is, entails?

Chapter 7

Mobile internet
New social technologies

> Imagine a future in which individuals use mobile computers to maintain constant contact with a vast information network that unites everyone into a single community. Is this future a utopia or a social abomination? ... If pervasive computers are to be successful, they need to support human social lives.
>
> (Dryer, Eisbach and Ark 1999: 652, 674)

> As the first generation to be raised with the Internet, Gen Y has an intuitive ability to use ICT as a means to foster, support, discuss and explore new ideas ... Recognizing the growing connection between mobile media and youth, the popular social networking community MySpace has teamed with Helio to provide a mobile version that includes access to Yahoo! Mail, Yahoo! Messenger, and various Yahoo! services.
>
> (*Barking Robot* 2006)

> A mobile phone – or whatever device we carry around which uses GSM technology and its successors – is going to be everywhere, and everyone will have one. It has do be designed to be universal. So that everyone can use it. So that you can do anything with it ... I personally believe that it is important to humanity to connect peoples across the world as widely as possible. I think we must preserve the diversity of cultures and ideas. But also I think we must connect people to give more global harmony. We should not add connectivity to the long list that the richer countries have and the poorer ones do not, a list which of course has clean water, health care and peace pretty near the top.
>
> (Berners-Lee 2007)

That the future of the internet is mobile is an idea that dates at least from the mid-1990s. This was roughly the point in time when both the internet itself and cellular phones were headed on parallel trajectories of dizzying popularity. Early attempts to marry the two technologies in the form of Wireless Access Protocol in the late 1990s were unsuccessful (Funk 2001; Goggin 2006; Hass 2006). For most of the first decade of the new century, Japan remained the one country where the internet was distinctively a mobile experience – with the celebrated i-Mode, mobile data and internet system, that was not really able to be replicated elsewhere (Funk 2001 and 2004). Things quickly changed from 2006–7 onwards; cell phones really did become the future, and for some countries, the present of the internet. Thus mobile internet now really is a multifarious development with enormous significance for how we understand global mobile media. It also raises significant challenges for our understanding and theorization that I will aim to elucidate in this chapter.

Mobile internet has tended to refer to the accessing of internet via a cellular mobile device, and this will be my focus in what follows. Nonetheless it is worth noting two important developments in access technologies, discussed in Chapter 2, that complicate this story. First, dual-mode devices that allow cell phones to access Wi-Fi networks now make up a high proportion of all devices. They are also being widely used where Wi-Fi networks are available, as Wi-Fi is often cheaper than mobile data charges (and licensing requirements for operators are much less onerous – Lemstra and Hayes 2009). Apple's iTouch is an example of a device that does not use the mobile cellular network, but otherwise has the look, feel and capability of the kindred device in the form of the iPhone. The proximity and interchangeability – though often still awkward – between cellular mobile and WiFi networks suggests a certain hybridity to how mobile media is developed. The cultures of use associated with WiFi are also interweaving with those of mobile cultures, though at the time of writing they remain largely distinct. It is in the still evolving, yet likely to be widely implemented technology of Wi-Max, where the fusion, or at least juxtaposition of mobile and wireless, will come to the fore. Second, mobile broadband has enjoyed a phenomenal rise in the 2006–10 period to become the most common way for the mobile network to be used to access the internet.

Mobile social software: MoSoSo

Social networking systems are now widely used on the internet, and are felt by many to be the contemporary internet's central identity (Alemán and Wartman 2009). There are now a bewildering array of big and small, commercial and not-for-profit, public, private and governmental social networking systems. Well known social networking systems include Cyworld, Friendster (Boyd 2004), Orkut, Mixi, Bebo, Baidu, QQ, MySpace, LinkedIn and, the current behemoth of all, Facebook. The origins of social networking systems in their recognizable forms go back at least a decade (Boyd and Ellison 2007).

Less well known are the many mobile social software (or MoSoSo) systems. These have not enjoyed as much popularity to date as their internet counterparts. Yet they have been avidly used by significant groups of users and have been the subject of significant investment and research by developers and researchers (Bilandzic and Foth 2009). The early impulse behind mobile computing was especially driven by research in artificial intelligence, and ideas about 'mobile agents', or entities that could mediate computer-to-human interaction (Dryer, Eisbach and Ark 1999). Then a confluence of two important shifts – from desktop to mobile computing, and from individual to social software – encouraged development of applications that made possible informal contact among people in the same proximity, whether friends, friends of friends, strangers or colleagues, capitalizing on serendipity, which was indeed the name of one early application (Eagle 2004; Eagle and Pentland 2005).

Perhaps the first popular mobile social software was the Japanese Lovegety technology:

> Young lovers are letting Lovegety do the talking for them ... 'In the two and a half months since the product entered markets, we've already shipped 350,000 Lovegetys. Right now we can't produce enough of them to meet demand,' says Takeya Takafuji, executive of Erfolg, the company that manufactures Tamagotchi and Lovegety. Affectionately called the 'Lovege,' the oval device has three buttons the user sets according to the kind of activity she or he has in mind: 'talk', 'karaoke' and 'get2'. (The latter is a wildcard – but perhaps could mean 'get to it.') Once the holder selects a mode, the device searches for Lovegety holders of the opposite sex in a five meter radius. If it locates a holder with the same mode, the 'get' light flashes and the device beeps, so the pair can find each other. If there is a holder in the vicinity with a different mode, then the 'find' light flashes and a different sound goes off, alerting the user of a near get.
>
> (Iwatani 1998)

Before the decade was out, the Lovegety fad passed, but it has been a touchstone to discussions of match-making, location, social software and cell phones ever since:

> After a flurry of attention in the business press and technology pages, and sales estimated at around a half-million devices, the Lovegety faded from view. Perhaps toting around a device designated solely to finding dates just felt too desperate in the end, or perhaps the shallow program modes made the 'matching' function seem rather futile, once the initial thrill of the bleeping and flashing lights wore off.
>
> (Crawford 2008: 79–80)

The first widely used mobile social software in the US was Dodgeball. Dodgeball allowed a user to broadcast her or his information to others in their location. The original Dodgeball was launched in April 2000, and it was an early WAP application. An innovative feature of Dodgeball was 'friendfinder'. An archived page from April 2003 states:

> Welcome! Dodgeball.com is aimed at helping people find places to eat and drink in New York City. Sign up to start adding your own restaurant & bar reviews. The New York City edition now features 2587 bars & restaurants with 5036 reviews written by our 1681 editors.
>
> (Dodgeball 2003)

In August 2006, Dodgeball was featured by *Time* magazine as one of its top seven cool websites.

> I'm 24 years old, have a good job, friends ... Every morning, before I brush my teeth, I sign in to my Instant Messenger to let everyone know I'm awake. I check for new e-mail ... comments on my blog or mentions of me or my blog on my friends' blogs. Next I flip open my phone and check for last night's Dodgeball messages. Dodgeball is the most intimate and invasive network I belong to. It links my online community to my cellphone, so when I send a text message to 36343 (Dodge), the program pings out a message with my location to all the people in my Dodgeball network. Acceptance into another person's Dodgeball network is a very personal way to say you want to hang out. I scroll through the messages to see where my friends went last night, and when, tracking their progress through various bars and noting the crossed paths ... I note how close Christopher and Tom were last night, only a block away, but see that they never met up.
>
> (Stites 2006)

Dodgeball was but one of many mobile social software applications that were to follow (for a list of 20 or so active or in protoype stage in that year, see Arnaldi 2004). A briefly popular UK application was Playtxt, which allowed users to key in their postcode, and see which of their friends was available in that area:

> Dodgeball and England's Playtxt are two examples of mobile social-software services ... They help users find old friends, or potential new ones, on the go. Typically, users set up a profile listing interests, hobbies and romantic availability. They also state what kind of people they'd like to meet ... Not surprisingly, MoSoSos are ideal for hooking up young, active professionals tied to their mobile phones or laptops, and they're starting to take off.
>
> (Terdiman 2005)

Some of these applications are now relatively well established, interoperable across carrier networks, and attracting a steady band of adherents.

In the US, the mobile social mapping application, Loopt, claims to be the first service since SMS to work across most major mobile networks (perhaps more an indictment of US interconnection arrangements than a claim to fame!). With the motto 'Discover the World Around You', Loopt promises to 'turn your phone into a social compass':

> Loopt shows users where friends are located and what they are doing via detailed, interactive maps on their mobile phones. Loopt helps friends connect on the fly and navigate their social lives by orienting them to people, places and events. Users can also share location updates, geo-tagged photos

and comments with friends in their mobile address book or on online social networks, communities and blogs.

(Loopt 2009)

Loopt is a classic start-up, founded by three computer science majors from Stanford University. Based in Silicon Valley, Loopt is backed by venture capital from Sequoia Capital and New Enterprise Associates (and also featuring former CEO and co-founder of TiVO as a board director). Loopt puts a premium on privacy and security, and highlights the work it does with leading organizations concerned with these issues. Another mobile social software that is attracting users is Whrrl. Developed by the Seattle based company Pelago, founded in 2006, Whrrl is described as a

> ... location-based application that leverages your social network to help you discover new adventures in the real world. Whrrl shows you where your friends are right now, what they're doing, and where they have been.
>
> (Pelago 2009b)

As well as the original Whrrl, there is the storytelling application Whrrl 2.0 ('What's your story?') for web and cell phone (especially iPhone) that

> ... lets people share and remember their real-world experiences as they happen. Everyone – whether physically present or not – can contribute to the experience. Stories can be published to Facebook and Twitter, and the storyteller controls who can view and participate.
>
> (Pelago 2009b)

Not content with developing, and presumably spinning off, mobile social media applications, Pelago also wishes to change the world:

> Pelago's mission is to remove all barriers to information, inspiration and human connection. We believe the intersection of pervasive location technology and rapid democratization of media creates a platform to inspire, connect and inform people in ways the world has never seen. We at Pelago think this is huge – entirely new classes of applications become possible in this vast new playground for innovators. We foresee a world in which human behavior in the physical world is digitized, like human behavior on the Web is today.
>
> (Pelago 2009a)

Brightkite is yet another US mobile social software application, aiming to be accessible and non-technical:

> ... we know nothing beats the simple act of meeting up with friends and sharing a drink ... So we created Brightkite to make it easier to do

just that. Brightkite is a simple way to keep up with friends and places. We created a product that lets you instantly see what's going on with the people who matter most to you, your friends. So check out what they're up to, meet new friends along the way and get out and enjoy your neighborhoods.

(Brightkite 2009a)

Brightkite offers capability to post information to other social networking systems such as Twitter, Facebook and Flickr ('simplify your life'). It also seeks to create a community, encouraging 'kiteups', social media organized meet-ups, whether in Kansas or Tokyo (Brightkite 2009b).

Centrl, a 'location-based social network for the web and mobile phones' (centrl.com, accessed on 11 May 2010), also integrates with and publishes content across popular social networking platforms – like other new applications seeking to seamlessly interwork with users' existing and preferred applications, rather than requiring them to learn or seriously commit to another system. One can log in to Centrl from one's own current social network, clicking through to third party apps developed to make this as easy as possible. Centrl is commercially and retail focused, highlighting recommendations and offers. Mobile social software is apparently endless at this moment, but the final application I will briefly note is 'Foursquare', co-founded by Dennis Crowley (who previously started dodgeball.com). Like Centrl, Foursquare is a combination of social networking systems, location-aware media and customer loyalty and marketing schemes: 'Foursquare on your phone gives you & your friends new ways of exploring your city. Earn points & unlock badges for discovering new things' (Foursquare 2009).

While there are a wide range of mobile social software initiatives, of which I have only discussed a few, clearly there are recurrent themes about how people connect to each, where they do so and with what meanings. Thus there is an important debate to have about the nature of mobile social software, and the extent to which the main way it has been imagined thus far has been about reproducing people that look, feel and act like us (Thom-Santelli 2007). Alice Crawford offers an important critique of the 'pattern-matching' and implicit visions of social sorting that typically have characterized mobile social software such as Serendipity, Dodgeball and the more recent applications just discussed:

social software at this point is all about matches: about finding sameness in a sea of otherness and connecting like with like—or the friend of like with like ... so much profile-building in social software takes the form of elaborating a constellation of media/commodities one has an affinity for: favorite movies, television shows, sports teams, bands, lifestyle-affiliations, and the like ... Accordingly, the nature of affinity is defined in large part as sharing similarly shaped constellations of commodity likes and dislikes. To my knowledge, there is no available option in which a user can choose 'Opposites Attract'.

(Crawford 2008: 89)

Given the close – though certainly not necessary – association between mobile social software and the urban, there are important questions to consider about how we imagine cities (Choi 2010), which are, after all, where the majority of the world's population now live:

> Where the erotic and our relationship to difference are already ambivalent affairs, mososo seems poised to further marginalize difference from the experience of urban space ... The use of mososo does not guarantee that one will limit one's encounters to electronically facilitated matchmaking and social engagements in public space ... However, the increasingly pervasive nature of mobile interfaces that provide easy-action affordances for homophilic social sorting should be the subject of lively critical debate amongst those who value a vibrant, diverse mode of urban life.
>
> (Crawford 2008: 89, 95)

Critical to this discussion is recognition of the different approaches being taken to mobile social software (Licoppe and Guillot 2006; Lugano 2008). Lee Humphreys compares Dodgeball with two other applications, BEDD (which connects people in close proximity using Bluetooth) and SMS.ac (connecting people via text message within or across countries) (Humphreys 2008). She notes that people 'will use these services based on their lives and personal contexts', but that 'spatial practices' also will be decisive (Humphreys 2008: 129). BEDD was taken up by users in Indonesia, initially as a matchmaking and dating service, but became a technology for building community in paradoxical ways – an example of how the cell phone in that country developed into 'a mode of interaction but also a platform through which to explore other current issues and debates related to dating, sexuality and media' (Humphreys and Barker 2007).

While commentators debate the relationship among technology, affordances, practices of place and space, relationships and cultures of use, many of the enterprises and applications spearheading mobile social software in its first decade simply have not survived. SMS.ac, for instance, was launched in 2002, claiming six million users in its first six months, but by 2005–6 was starting to be dogged by claims of spam, billing complaints and unfair practice (Wikipedia 2009, 'SMS.ac'):

> SMS.ac is one of those right-place, right-time, right-technology companies that has nearly all the elements for colossal success. But it also has hovering over it a big red flag that could wrong-foot it at any moment ... At least a handful of consumers ... have complained on the Internet and in the

mainstream press that SMS.ac has charged them for services they never asked for, making that billing relationship into potentially its greatest liability.

(Shannon 2006)

At this stage, SMS.ac's management claimed more than 50 million members in 187 countries (Shannon 2006). In 2007 it was fined by the British premium rate service regulator PhonePayPlus for selling mobile message services without adequate pricing information. Then in 2009 employee allegations of unfair labour practices emerged. The company created a spin-off mobile site, Fanbox, which eventually subsumed SMS.ac: 'Profit from your passion: tools to share and monetize your thoughts' (Fanbox 2009c). The self-styled 'world's largest mobile community', Fanbox offers a business model for users who are creating content, but not being directly paid:

> Unlike other companies that publish members' music and video without paying the creators of user-generated content, FanBox's unique community-driven economy ensures that there's an upside for everyone. At FanBox, everybody gets paid.
>
> (Fanbox 2009a)

FanBox's own depiction of its company culture is empowering all members of its team, through open communication, hard work and fun:

> Core Values … To show respect, squash fear, eliminate politics, help each other improve, and for faster decision making … We work extremely hard, but at FanBox we also have incredible amounts of fun. We have weekly social events on Fridays, the very competitive FanBox Olympics (including bowling, dodgeball, tug-of-war, costume contests and scavengers hunts), company retreats, quarter ending parties and company picnics.
>
> (FanBox 2009b)

While many mobile social software start-ups have just died out, or, like FanBox, engaged in aggressive commercial practices towards their customers, others have been taken over. The founder of Dodgeball recalls how he went to graduate school with his friend Alex:

> Resurrected dodgeball again in Fall 2003 (post Friendster, pre Myspace). Launched it as 'mobile social software'. It became our thesis. Graduated … in May 2004. Gave ourselves 6 months to work on dodgeball ('maybe this can become our job!'). We sold dodgeball to Google in May 2005. 18 months later we're told 'there's no future for dodgeball at Google'.
>
> (Crowley 2008)

Figure 7.1 Dodgeball close-down party (note logo under surfing image). (Source: Crowley 2008)

In October 2007 Google also acquired the Finnish software venture Jaiku, also the next best thing, and competitor to Twitter. Like Dodgeball, Google never really put much effort into nurturing Jaiku – instead apparently absorbing its code, and then farewelling it, at the same time it shut down Dodgeball:

> As we mentioned last April, we are in the process of porting Jaiku over to Google App Engine ... With the open source Jaiku Engine project, organizations, groups and individuals will be able to roll-their-own microblogging services and deploy them on Google App Engine ... Some of you may also be familiar with Dodgeball.com, a mobile social networking service that lets you share your location with friends via text message. We have decided to

discontinue Dodgeball.com in the next couple of months, after which this service will no longer be available.

(Gundotra 2009)

Shortly thereafter Jaiku co-founder Jyri Engeström took his leave of Google, seeking to 'make meaning' (Siegler 2009).

A number of mobile social software companies, like Dodgeball or Jaiku, have been purchased by large corporations, and – whether because of this, or simply because of lack of momentum – have floundered. Not so – or at least as yet – for the short message broadcasting service Twitter. A fascinating aspect of cell phone culture has been the resilience and ductility of text messaging. Twitter combines text messaging with the instant messaging cultures of the PC and internet, as well as blogging and social networking, to produce something variously called 'micro-blogging', update culture, micro-journalism, or even a new form of locative media (Crawford 2009a and b). Devised by Jack Dorsey, in the San Francisco 'creative environment' company Obvious, in March 2006, Twitter was launched publicly in August 2006 (Twitter 2009). It quickly gained rave reviews, and it spun off as Twitter Inc. in May 2007, with its other co-founder Biz Stone prominent in promoting the technology to new audiences.

Twitter's genius appears to be two-fold. It cleverly extends the affordances of cell phone text messaging, especially popularizing this, and intensifying it, for the slow-adopting North American market. Like the internet, it works across different platforms:

> ... Twitter has grown into a real-time short messaging service that works over multiple networks and devices ... Twitter's core technology is a device agnostic message routing system with rudimentary social networking features. By accepting messages from sms, web, mobile web, instant message, or from third party API projects, Twitter makes it easy for folks to stay connected.

(Twitter 2009)

Twitter is still a start-up, with investment from micro-capital funds – and, perhaps wisely, in early 2009 it was still coy about its future business model and commercialization:

> Twitter has many appealing opportunities for generating revenue but we are holding off on implementation for now because we don't want to distract ourselves from the more important work at hand which is to create a compelling service and great user experience for millions of people around the world. While our business model is in a research phase, we spend more money than we make.

(Twitter 2009)

This is a recurrent difficulty for small, innovative businesses creating new internet or mobile technologies, especially those that very much rely on the interest and cultural investment of users – and indeed old-fashioned network externalities. Many small, new companies have been snaffled up by large media companies, wishing to incorporate their new service or angle into an incorporated, cross-platform enterprise. While Twitter has maintained a focus on being 'a service for friends, family, and co–workers to communicate and stay connected through the exchange of quick, frequent answers to one simple question: What are you doing?' (Twitter 2009b), Jaiku styled itself as 'Your Conversation', and promised: 'Text Jaikus from any phone. Share your availability, location, and calendar from your smartphone' (see www.jaiku.com, last accessed 25 May 2010). Unfortunately, as we have seen, this was a conversation that was absorbed into the reaches of Google's store of code (Battelle 2005).

Mobile social software: the Facebook moment

With the advent of smartphones, mobile email on mobile and handheld devices has become increasingly prevalent in Western countries, epitomized in devices like Sidekick, Nokia Communicator, Pre and the BlackBerry. Internet browsing has become more prevalent, with redesigned WAP, with better handsets and faster GPRS, EDGE and 3G networks offering improved user experience. The compelling applications, however, are coming from the phenomenon of social media. As we have seen, mobile social software was a rich and fascinating phenomenon in its own right, and a social and technical laboratory of networking possibilities. However, mobile social software did not become a pervasive user phenomenon until social media had been well established on computers – and then software was reconfigured for mobile platforms.

In the West, social networking systems have been developed around desktop Internet platforms. In Asian countries, especially Japan and Korea, cell phones have long been important in internet access and use (Jung 2009) – especially in their pioneering of social software. In Japan the dominant social networking system has been Mixi, launched in February 2004: 'It lets users create profiles, make friends with other users, post diaries, discuss in communities, share pictures and music with friends' (Tanaka 2009). In August 2007, mobile page views (an indicator of usage) – surpassed PC page views for the first time (Breuer 2009). Misa Matsuda charts this increase in accessing social networking systems via *keitai* (Japanese mobile phone):

> The accessing of SNS via keitai has also increased among university students and young people in their twenties who have entered the workforce. In particular, mixi, which is the most popular SNS accessed via PC, has seen a rapid increase in access via keitai by this youth group.
>
> (Matsuda 2010: 33)

With an estimated 17 million users in late 2009, it was releasing mixi apps, on the 'open social' model (Tanaka 2009).

In South Korea, Cyworld's Mini-hompy has been a phenomenon in its own right, with accelerating rates of cell phone ownership and usage adding to its importance for the transaction of everyday life and shaping of identity (Hjorth 2009a).

In 2010, Facebook had established itself as the leading social networking system in the West. In the process, it has become a platform adopted, and reshaped, by users in non-Western countries also. Started by Harvard under-graduate students Eduardo Saverin and Mark Zuckerberg in 2002 (Mezrich 2009), Facebook attracted investment from venture capital, and quickly evolved to claim 300 million users worldwide by September 2009 (Johnson 2009), something that co-founder Zuckerberg glossed as Facebook 'just getting started on our goal of connecting everyone' (Zuckerberg 2009). In October 2007, the corporation announced its Facebook Platform for Mobiles (Facebook 2007). At the same time Research in Motion (RIM) launched its Facebook® for Black-Berry® Smartphones (RIM 2007):

> Facebook users can wirelessly send and view messages, photos, pokes and Wall posts. The rich, native application goes beyond browser-based access, automatically pushing notifications to the user's BlackBerry smartphone … The application allows users to take a photo, upload it to the site with captions and tags; quickly and easily invite friends; manage events; manage photo albums; and manage their status while on the go.
>
> (RIM 2007)

RIM's Facebook product was the first successful Facebook application custo-mized for a cellular mobile handset. Other vendors also developed native or streamlined Facebook applications, with the advent of the Facebook app on the iPhone representing a high point in its development. By late 2009, Facebook was

Figure 7.2 Mixi ad (http://mixi.jp/, accessed on 11 May 2010).

claiming to have 65 million users on cell phones, and continuing to deal with ongoing issues such as the contradictions between 'connecting everyone' and the politics of harvesting and circulating their information (Boyd 2008).

A difficulty in Facebook's internationalization and diffusion in emerging markets and developing countries lay especially in the bandwidth still required for mobile internet and mobile data applications. In August 2009, it announced Facebook Lite, 'a faster, simpler way to keep in touch with your friends'. No doubt developed with one eye on the fast growing, bandwidth-light Twitter, Facebook Lite was also aimed at low-broadband users in developing countries and emerging markets, especially in its fastest growing markets in Asia, for instance, in Indonesia and the Philippines (Alampay 2008):

> ... Asian countries also have many well-established social networks, and in those with good internet connections, mobile phones are often key to that connectivity. Being able to produce a version of Facebook that loads quickly on mobile phones is thus essential to its wider growth.
>
> (Arthur 2009)

What we might call the Facebook moment represented the turning point for Western countries. However, although Facebook was also popular in Asian countries, as the case of Indonesia reveals, there was a sense in which it assumed more significance in North America and Europe. Such developments in social media technologies for cell phones fed into a new discourse about 'mobile web 2.0' (Jaokar and Fish 2006). If web 2.0 barely offers a kernel of sense, and we are just beginnning to unpack its politics of participation (Bassett 2008; Goggin & Hjorth 2009), then mobile web 2.0 is in many ways even conceptually more bereft. What is really at stake in mobile internet developments goes well beyond the web 2.0 appellation. The scene is a much more disorienting, and less liberating or amenable one than web 2.0 acolytes concede. This emerges in the most systematic effort to fashion mobile web, undertaken by the internet community.

Mobile web: connecting the world

The mobile internet has been famously slow to materialize. With the popularity of the web and its characteristics – ease of use, linking the resources of the internet, working across devices, platforms, applications and screen, it was an obvious facet of the internet upon which to concentrate efforts. Thus, the appearance and popularity of the web led to concerted attempts in the second half of the 1990s for mobile internet to be implemented successfully. Broadly there were two groups involved in this process: the telecommunications and cell phone industry, and the internet community. On the part of the internet community, it was the newer group around the development of the web that played a leading role – and was visibly involved in building bridges with the cell phone

Figure 7.3 'Receive your status update in the queue': Facebook mobile advertisement, Bali, Indonesia.

vendors and carriers. This group was the World Wide Standards Consortium, led by the most famous inventor of the web itself, Sir Tim Berners-Lee.

It is probably more accurate to see the history of mobile internet as an evolutionary process, but it is certainly possible to discern two periods of intense development and activity. There is the period I have just characterised in the late 1990s and early 2000s, the beginning of focused, co-ordinated activity – seeking to harmonize, for instance, the mark-up language for mobile web developed by the industry (such as the Japanese language), and that devised as part of the W3C official standards, building on the web's Hypertext Markup Language (HTML). Then there is a resurgence of efforts in the middle of the first decade of the 2000s. The continuing, wide diffusion of cell phones across the world, combined with growing numbers of smartphones and deployment of 3G networks, offered an even more ubiquitous platform for internet via cell phones – not to mention advanced handsets, greater data capacity and faster speeds. Developments were also afoot in the neighbouring world of internet.

Internet usage and access was also continuing to rise. Broadband internet was available in much of the developed world, despite real gaps in access and perceived problems with speed. The internet was finding its way even deeper into the nooks and crannies of everyday life. Innovation continued apace, especially in the transformation of media and its cultures, making convergent media a reality. The user has emerged as a key feature of contemporary internet, as thematized by the discourse of web 2.0.

In May 2005, the W3C launched its mobile web initiative, to make 'browsing the web from mobile devices a reality':

> Many of today's mobile devices already feature Web browsers and the demand for mobile devices continues to grow. Despite these trends, browsing the Web from a mobile device – for example, to find product information, consult timetables, check email, transfer money – has not become as convenient as expected. Users often find that their favorite Web sites are not accessible or not as easy to use on their mobile phone as on their desktop computer. Content providers have difficulties building Web sites that work well on all types and configurations of mobile phones offering Web access.
>
> (W3C 2005)

'Mobile access to the Web has been a second class experience for far too long,' said Berners-Lee, suggesting that the initiative would recognize 'the mobile device as a first class participant, and will produce materials to help developers make the mobile Web experience worthwhile' (W3C 2005). To achieve this, Berners-Lee and his colleagues hoped for a co-ordinated development of standards across the internet community and cell phone groups such as Open Mobile Alliance and 3GPP. Work followed on technical standards development through the mobile web initiative, resulting in useful advances. However, it appears that there was not the support from the cell phones industry anticipated at the initiative's launch. In late 2009, Vodafone continued as one of the few sponsors, and certainly the most powerful one. However, the action in mobile web was to come from another direction: the developing world.

In December 2006, a workshop was held in Bangalore, India, the epicentre of the country's information technology industries. As well as W3C staff, the organizers included Nokia, academics, NGOs (including the new Mobile Active organization) and Jataayu Software (specializing in mobile applications); and the programme was funded by the European Commission. The white paper developed from the event put the question of the developing world's need and uses for cell phones squarely on the agenda of those developing the technology, including the W3C:

> While more and more people are using the Web, a significant number of people still do not have regular, effective access and ability to use digital technologies ... An important step in the direction of filling this gap has

been the deployment of mobile networks all around the world ... However, even if accessing phone services is very important, the gap will be more completely filled when access to a higher level of information technologies will be widespread. Now, with the availability of high speed mobile data networks, and the appearance of increasingly-affordable Web-enabled phones, one can imagine that the potential to help bridge the digital divide has increased, in that people with access to a mobile phone would be able to access the Internet and the Web. But, it is fundamental to understand the needs and the expectations of the people, and the specific challenges and issues of accessing the Web from a mobile phone as a primary and often sole platform, so that the potential of resolving the gap becomes reality.

(Boyera 2006)

At the heart of the mobile web, for such supporters, is its potential to improve the lives of people in developing countries:

It is very important not to forget the real goal of providing ICT in developing countries. The point is to use Web technologies as a mean to provide services (health, banking, government services, education, business, etc.) which would improve the life of the under-privileged populations. Using mobile phones as the support for services is considered the right way to go. However, using the Web and Web technologies as the software platform for developing those services is not yet a reality.

(Boyera 2006)

The problems cited include: no web-browser availability on low-end phones; configuration; user interface; cost. Against this perceived advantages included 'large scope and wide audience', and 'easy availability and discoverability of existing services (e.g. through search engines, portals ...)' (Boyera 2006). The workshop provided a warrant for W3C to undertake the necessary work, organized around some very interesting themes:

- understanding regional commonalities and differences in terms of needs, context, culture, availabilities of mobile network and devices;
- gathering data on characteristics of cell phones available in the developing world;
- developing guidelines on how to write web content or develop mobile web based e-services aimed at underprivileged populations or rural communities;
- cooperating with all players from the mobile industry (operators, handset manufacturers, browser makers) and related international bodies like OMA or GSMA to make low-cost handsets web-enabled.

(Boyera 2006)

A further desideratum was the 'internationalization of content: being able to enter data and view content in local languages' (Boyera 2006). The participants pointed to a 'business interest in developing lightweight Web access on ultra low-cost handsets' for operators, handset manufacturers, browser makers, service providers, and users alike (Boyera 2006). To focus the minds of the carriers, for instance, the great potential of these developing markets was underlined:

> ... history shows that voice services always reach a saturation point, and this will happen in developing countries like it happened in the developed world. ARPU [average revenue per user] will only increase with data-services, and value-added solutions on 2/3G networks. If 5 billions of people are just using voice services and SMS, the business may quickly reach a saturation point.
>
> (Boyera 2006)

The upshot was the formation of the 'Mobile Web for Social Development' interest group, as a joint project of W3C and the European Digital World Forum, which in late 2009 released its roadmap. This roadmap contains important recommendations to promote use of mobiles for development applications, and to lower barriers and cost. Interestingly it is predicated on existing knowledge, so very much on SMS, which it describes as 'clearly today the leading platform for delivering content and services to people' (Boyera 2009). It does not investigate the 'possible mid/long-term future when mobile broadband and smart phones will be widely available' (Boyera 2009) – very interesting given the massive investment being put into both of these technologies in wealthier countries, with real potential to make these the default mobile media technologies.

Mobile internet in the global South: 'join the evolution'

As we can see, the renewed interest in mobile internet, under the rubric of mobile web, and even mobile web 2.0, has also become a site for engagement with the developing world. What it accentuates is a contradictory moment in the development of both the internet and the cell phone – it is another face of mobile internet, just emerging, and not well recognized or understood. Consider for a moment the argument that the high bandwidth, web 2.0, smartphone-bedazzled view of mobile internet – that arguably the Facebook mobile moment exemplifies – is a phenomenon of the global North. That is, the wealthy countries in the West and in Asia, and then the middle-class and upper-class users in a range of developing countries. This is likely the case still, even in the genuine efforts just discussed of the internet community to acknowledge and design for the great majority of future users, who would be based in the developing countries and accessing the internet on mobile platforms.

As I have identified there are considerable tensions in the reworking of the vision of the web for all on cell phones to accommodate these realities. What it underlines is that there is a certain path dependency – what one might in another vocabulary call a social imaginary (Flichy 2007a; Taylor 2004) – of mobile internet, that is deeply structured by the specific experience of particular high internet diffused countries in the 1999–2007 period. We have deeply cherished, or at least deeply held, ideas of technology – what we can call imaginaries – that are in fact not universal or general. Rather, such imaginaries are based on particular, historically and culturally specific experiences and encounters with technologies. I would argue that this was the case with the mobile internet, as I have briefly traced here. Its histories lie in the early efforts of both the telecommunications industries and the emergent internet industries and communities, especially through those involved in the web such as W3C. Then there are the different histories of wireless internet (especially Wi-Fi) that play a role, and the development of mobile broadband. Finally, there are the various technologies that bridge cell phones and internet, especially the social networking systems I note here.

What becomes apparent from 2007 is that mobile internet is taking shape in rather different ways from a combination of user, design, cultural, pricing and political economy reasons in a number of other countries, for the internet was being predominantly accessed via the cell phone. These included countries in South America, Africa and elsewhere, but also countries in Eastern Europe. Here we can observe the creation of new forms of digital culture, with some resemblance to practices first associated with North American, European and Western internet, such as chat, messaging and file-sharing. Yet often these were locally devised and originated. While focused on and generated by mobile devices, software and applications, they departed from text messaging as much as other forms of mobile internet predicated on recasting, resizing and recoding internet protocols and technologies (whether the web or social networking systems) for mobile platforms.

One fascinating case in point is that of South Africa.[1] While the South African cell phone industry has tried to introduce a range of mobile internet applications (Benn and Kachieng'a 2005), the one that first attracted significant numbers of users was quite unforeseen. The instant messaging (IM) software MXit combines messaging, conversation, contact lists, file-sharing, photo-sharing, and is also compatible with other IM services and Facebook. MXit works across different cell phone (Windows Mobile, iPhone, Android, mobile, BlackBerry) and computer (PC, Mac) platforms. It also offers music, movies, fantasy and fun, and MXit Forum 'debate'. In late 2009, MXit claimed 15 million registered users, principally in South Africa, but also Indonesia, and a smaller group of users spread across the world. MXit uses a currency called 'moola', with one moola the equivalent of one South African cent. Perhaps the most successful devised-for-mobile homegrown social software outside Asian countries, MXit has achieved such a following due to its cheap price, compared to SMS. What is also paramount is that MXit offers a package of internet applications that work effectively on a cell phone. While the user needs a GPRS or 3G mobile, this still brings the internet into the ken of the many South African users who cannot afford a computer and internet access, and do not otherwise have easy access to internet through public access points, kiosks or internet cafés.

The origins of MXit lie in a game devised by the South African company Swist Group Technologies. The game included a SMS feature that did not take off due to lack of mobile capability. In 2003 it was revised and released as the first version of MXit. Since this time, MXit has attracted many users and also, as befits a widely used technology, its share of anxiety and opprobrium due to perceptions it is leading to obssessive use and disturbance of youth (Chigona and Chigona 2009). In August 2009, media reports appeared of 'MXit schoolgirl missing' – a fourteen-year-old schoolgirl, Nabeela Omar, from Johannesburg, of whom 'it is believed that she may have struck up a relationship with a man she met on MXit' (Gifford 2009). Commentators called for a ban on MXit: 'I think its time our mobile network regulater [sic] to do something about this network MXit, i suggest if possible it can be suspended for now before its too late cos our children are so obsessed with Mxit' (Gifford 2009). Although the girl returned home unharmed two days later, the case focused attention on education, regulation and even banning of MXit.

While marketed as a fun communication and entertainment tool, MXit has also played a very interesting role in creating a forum for political and social discussion, as Marion Walton and Jonathan Donner argue in their fascinating paper on South Africa's 2009 elections (Walton and Donner 2009). Walton and Donner's focus is upon understanding emerging political participation in the global South, especially through the 'mobile social software platforms [which]

Figure 7.4 MXit mobile instant messaging software (source: http://www.mxitlifestyle.com/, accessed on 11 May 2010).

are emerging that suit the low-bandwidth environments and cost-constraints of millions of mobile-centric internet users in the developing world' (Walton and Donner 2009: 1). They look at four examples of mobile mediated communication in the South African elections. The first two of these fall into more easily recognized examples of mobile culture and media: the polemics and controversies emanating in 'SMS wars', and the use of specially designed internet sites for mobile (.mobi sites) by the political parties. The second two cases relate to mobile social software, and the way political content was included or excluded from these. Here Walton and Donner contrast the Mig33 mobile social software – where political content was encouraged, yet users were relatively nonplussed by this potential political culture – with that of MXit. MXit's operators discouraged political content, but users engaged in political discussion nonetheless. What emerges from the analysis is the importance of these mobile spaces for political culture and participation, yet the ways that these are being shaped by their operators and owners especially – with recognition, discussion or debate of the implications of this:

> Whether policy interventions are needed to open up bounded mobile social media systems, or otherwise encourage owners of mobile social software systems to develop spaces for public discourse is a matter for further discussion ... Perhaps the rapid pace of technological change and the pressure of competing systems such as The Grid, Noknok, Facebook and Mig33 will ensure that soon all citizens can find spaces that afford them writing-rights for public participation online. Deepening mobile access to the networked publics promised by Web2.0 would allow mobile centric users to place their issues on record, to mobilize others and potentially to influence the broader public agenda.
>
> (Walton and Donner 2009: 9)

The issues that Walton and Donner presciently raise are part of a wider, detailed agenda of issues raised by global mobile media that as yet have received little sustained, critical attention. It is the exploration of policies, participation, publics and power that are the subject of the remainder of the book.

Note

1 Regarding mobile internet in South Africa, and indeed other developing countries, I have been very much influenced by the pioneering work of Jonathan Donner. My interest in the application MXit, and South African media and political culture, was piqued by Donner's excellent paper with Marion Walton (Walton and Donner 2009).

Part III

Politics of mobile media networks

Chapter 8

The computer, the internet, and the cell phone

The case of the iPhone

It was the biggest launch since the Apollo program. How did Apple's smartphone – which slickly packages features already available in other handsets – become such a highly anticipated phenomenon? The answer lies not in Steve Jobs' (undisputed) marketing prowess but in the abject failure of other handset manufacturers to deliver a portable Internet device with mass appeal. So the iPhone has ascended, and its liftoff was a rousing success.

(Geekipedia 2007)

The thing is hard to type on. It's too slow. It's too big. It doesn't have instant messaging. It's too expensive. (Or, no, wait, it's too cheap!) It doesn't support my work e-mail. It's locked to AT&T. Steve Jobs secretly hates puppies. And – all together now – we're sick of hearing about it! Yes, there's been a lot of hype written about the iPhone, and a lot of guff too. So much so that it seems weird to add more, after Danny Fanboy and Bobby McBlogger have had their day. But when that day is over, Apple's iPhone is still the best thing invented this year.

(Grossman 2007)

The iPhone cracked open the carrier-centric structure of the wireless industry and unlocked a host of benefits for consumers, developers, manufacturers – and potentially the carriers themselves. Consumers get an easy-to-use handheld computer. And, as with the advent of the PC, the iPhone has sparked a wave of development that will make it even more powerful … Manufacturers will have more control over what they produce; users – not the usual cabal of complacent juggernauts – will have more influence over what gets built.

(Vogelstein 2008)

Since its launch in mid-2007, the Apple iPhone has become the mobile media form par excellence. It is a very interesting – and now strategically crucial – case for many reasons. What is fascinating about the iPhone to start with is that Apple presents it as something that represents a great break, or paradigm shift, from the cell phone. I tend to think that the iPhone actually shares more with previous cell phones than Apple concedes. Indeed that the iPhone is actually a fascinating case of what can be called 'cultural adaptation' (Moran and Keane 2010).

First, the kind of adaptation the iPhone represents is about adapting the cell phone for the internet. It is about adapting the mobile to – finally – put it at the centre of computing, the internet and digital culture. For instance, the iPhone is very much a platform for, and creature of, its applications. Its 'Apps Store' allows a wide range of programs and applications for the iPhone to be readily purchased and downloaded, bringing the affordances of computing to the cell phone in a form that previously has not been possible. Second, the iPhone is very much a haptic adaption. The cell phone very much emerged as a haptic technology, rather than primarily an aural, listening or speaking technology, especially with the popularity of text messaging – underscored by the emphasis on the cell phone as a 'hand' (or 'handy') technology, and especially through the text messaging 'thumb' culture. Third, the iPhone promises to make the cell phone even more customizable and adaptable – identity on the move, made to order. For instance, the iPhone menus can be configured to a much greater extent than previously in line with the user's wishes: thus each iPhone screen can look quite different.

I would argue that the iPhone is indeed an important adaptation of the cell phone – though not quite in the terms that Apple presents it – and as such is enormously revealing for understanding the politics of mobile media. The iPhone does draw from the grammar of cell phone design, and recombine a number of well established affordances, elements and technologies. It also borrows from the well established, distinctive traits of Apple 'i' technologies: the hardware of the iPod, and the software, intellectual property and digital rights management regime of the iTunes application. In doing so, it does push the cell phone much more towards the world of computers and the internet. However, and this moves into my second argument, the iPhone sets in train a new logic of adaptation that Apple cannot license. With the iPhone, Apple sets out to take the control of adaptation from the hands of cell phone carriers and manufacturers. Also to allow new flexibility, third-party applications, programming and data exchange. Apple tries to control, circumscribe and manage the way in which it puts new powers of adaptation in the user's hand: to allow the user to get under the bonnet, to borrow a motoring metaphor. What Apple does not reckon on, or at least cannot hold at bay, is the warp-speed way that unauthorized modification of the iPhone occurs – thanks to enthusiastic hackers, and the immediate, sweeping dissemination of hacking tools via the internet (something already presaged by user frustration with the controls associated with the iPod; Consentino 2006). Certainly the bulk of users may still find such do-it-yourself adaptation of the iPhone too difficult, but a larger than usual group of users did avail themselves of the iPhone hacks. All of which probably just added further to the aura of the iPhone.

Enter the iPhone

The first time a technology came to be called the iPhone was actually in the mid-1990s, when it meant the 'internet phone'. With the rapidly growing mass consumption of the internet, developers were hard at work to devise a form of telephony that could work via the new network of networks. This form of internet telephony was called the iPhone. This has now developed into a relatively easy-to-use household technology called Voice over Internet Protocol, with its best known proponent being Skype. In the 1999–2000 period, a different class of cell phone devices were marketed, also bearing the name of the iPhone. Key to these was a claim that the cell phone would now become a prime device for accessing the internet.

For its part, Apple started work on its iPhone in 2005, with a prototype finally emerging in mid-2006 (Vogelstein 2008). Previously Apple had already created one cell phone, aimed at preserving its hold on the digital music market. This was the ROKR, released in September 2005. The ROKR was a joint venture between Motorola and Apple. Motorola had responsibility for the phone (in conjunction with the cell phone carrier Cingular), while Apple focused on the music software (Vogelstein 2008). Unlike Motorola's sleek, popular RAZR phone, the first version of the ROKR looked a lot like a classic, rather clunky, cell phone. It only held one hundred songs, and did not allow music to be directly downloaded. However, the ROKR was the first cell phone to feature the Apple iTunes application.

The latest version, ROKR E8, launched in April 2008, does much more closely resemble the RAZR. Nonetheless its reputation was dismal – the apogee of its reception being *Wired Magazine*'s cover, with its headline, 'You call *this* the phone of the future?' (Vogelstein 2008).

At the time that the ROKR was invented, the talk was of the 'music phone'. However, a key problem with the collaboration between Apple and Motorola in devising the ROKR was over the computer giant's approach to intellectual property and digital rights management:

> A key part of the iTunes package, for example, is FairPlay, Apple's digital rights management software … FairPlay would set limits on the new phone: It couldn't play music from any major online store but iTunes. It couldn't hold more than 100 songs. 'It's obvious why Apple is doing this,' says Patrick Parodi, head of the Mobile Entertainment Forum, an industry trade group. 'They don't want to cannibalize the iPod.'
>
> (Rose 2005)

As the ROKR went to market, the iPhone was in development – allowing Apple tighter control over music and other content. Clearly Apple's strength lay in computers, operating systems and integrated suites of applications. For instance, its engineers rewrote the Apple OSX operating system for the iPhone. Apple also shone in the area of design, with its iPhone building on the shape and look of its classic iPod device. However, Apple showed less proficiency with the other features of cell phones. The much heralded iPhone ran initially on the 2.5

generation digital cell phone network, with the third generation (3G) iPhone following roughly a year later, in mid-2008.

The iPhone fever

Perhaps what most distinguished the iPhone from many other adaptations of cell phones was its rapturous reception, and, hand-in-hand with this, Apple's phenomenally successful marketing campaign. Herein lies the paradox of adaptation that the iPhone represents. The iPhone is clearly an adaptation of the cell phone. As *Wired* magazine's Geekipedia points out, the iPhone is an obvious descendant of the smartphone – the multimedia cell phone that combines various computer programs with entertainment options. Yet the 'biggest launch since the Apollo' rebadges this evolution as a revolution. Clearly design values, chic and usability, all features of the Apple world of iMac and iPods, are key to this; so too is the careful crafting of the iPhone's reception by its makers.

The arrival of the iPhone was much anticipated, and featured long queues of afficionados, who were prepared to wait out in all conditions for the privilege of being the first to hold and try the new device. The iPhone queues started with the first launch in the US. Then Apple staged the launch, complete with queues, in many other countries – each launch not only featuring as a local media event, but often with an international flavour too.

In July 2008, I happened to be in Wellington, New Zealand, when one morning the arrival of the iPhone, complete with now customary queues, was announced. Not only did this signal the arrival of the iPhone in Aeteroa, it also marked the launch of the first 3G iPhone worldwide. The news of the launch in Wellington was quickly updated with the relevation that the young student at the head of the queue, who was the first person to obtain an iPhone, was actually paid to do so. It has now been acknowledged officially elsewhere by at least one operator that the iPhone queues were a key marketing ploy, and that extras were paid to participate:

> Poland's biggest telecoms operator, Telekomunikacja Polska, acknowledged last week that it had paid young, hip-looking film extras to stand in queues for the national launch of Apple's iPhone. 'It was a marketing move. We thought it was a pretty interesting strategy,' TP spokesman Wojciech Jabczynski said. 'The aim was to attract attention. The people in the queues told passers-by about the iPhone.'
>
> (*The Australian* 2008)

The marketing hype notwithstanding, the iPhone was named as the invention of the year by *Time* magazine in 2007. *Time*'s Larry Grossman gives five reasons for his verdict: the iPhone is 'pretty', 'touchy-feely', 'it will make other phones better', 'it's not a phone, it's a platform', and it 'is but the ghost of iPhones yet to come' (Grossman, 2007). The accompanying photo of the device is captioned: 'It's a genuine handheld computer, the first device that really deserves the name.'

Touch politics

In early 2009, the reception accorded the iPhone has led to various efforts to copy, clone and cope with its success (Fung 2004). Manufacturers from Samsung through to LG ('Touch Phones') and Motorola ('Krave' touch-screen phone), to the newer competitor HTC ('Touch Diamond' and 'Touch Pro') took a haptic turn in 2008. The politics of touch in which the iPhone, and global mobile media generally, are imbricated, and indeed shape, is tellingly illustrated by the case of disability and accessibility.

Cell phones are widely used by people with disabilities, and we have much evidence of their benefits as well as the distinctive cultures of use of cell phones by various groups of people with disabilities, notably, for instance, by deaf users, blind users and users with physical disabilities (Goggin and Newell 2006, 2007a; Goggin and Noonan 2006). However, the rise of the cell phone has also been accompanied by new kinds of exclusion, a disabling power relations of technology (Goggin and Newell, 2003, 2006). With the rise of cell phones and the minaturization of components, advances in processing and design, and also the growing reliance of networks and devices on software operating systems and applications, cell phones became progressively smaller – making handsets difficult for many people to press, hold and manipulate.

There has been a substantial body of design activism around cell phones since the early 1990s (ACCAN 2009; Goggin and Newell 2003). Phone companies and handset manufacturers have often been sympathetic to user concerns; however, designing for accessibility, under the mantle of universal design for instance, has remained a fraught and still marginal exercise (Annable, Goggin and Stienstra 2007). There is quite some complexity to the challenge of designing for accessibility, requiring: a range of suitable handsets to be widely available; pricing and affordability issues to be addressed; trade-offs between potential features and capabilities; complex issues about profitability and market size (NCD 2004). One important initiative by the cell phone industry internationally has been the development and release of the Global Accessibility Reporting Initiative (GARI), undertaken by the Mobile Manufacturers Forum and the Australian Mobile Telecommunications Association. This is a publicly available database on accessibility features on second and third generation cell phones (Garrett and Astbrink 2010). Despite this and other important initiatives by industry and regulators, new mobile technologies continue to be released onto the market, without manufacturers appearing to feel the need to incorporate accessibility features. A notable example is the celebrated Apple iPhone.

Key to the marketing of the iPhone was its claim to be well designed, intuitive and easy to use, especially in using touch for navigation. Surprisingly, there were large areas of accessibility the iPhone did not address – affordances that the status quo of second generation digital cell phones now largely took for granted:

> ... it includes no accessibility features for people who are totally blind. It also has no meaningful access for people with low vision. While the iPhone does allow modest enlargement of certain images and text—like maps, web pages, and e-mails—it does not allow for icons to be enlarged or rearranged in a more accessible manner ... Apple acknowledges that the iPhone doesn't work for blind people in their accessibility report ... the nature of this phone, a perfectly flat screen with only one button, makes it hard for us to imagine how it could be accessed by someone needing tactile feedback and tactually identifiable controls. We wonder how a company that says it prides itself on cutting-edge innovation can create something that is so completely unusable for people with vision loss. We strongly encourage Apple to work with the blindness community to create a truly innovative and accessible iPhone. And while they're at it, why not do the same for the iPod?
>
> (Augusto 2007)

Around the world, other disability technology bloggers joined the chorus:

> While millions swooned over the iPhone, a number of people, especially those with visual impairments and some with physical disabilities, felt either left out of the hoopla or angered by Apple's apparent lack of consideration for universal design in the state-of-the-art cell phone ... For users with blindness, the touch screen interface offers no tactile feedback. Furthermore, the flat buttons can only be activated through contact with human skin, so those with physical disabilities cannot use a stylus or other pointing devices to make calls or access music and movies on an iPhone.
>
> (Lance 2008)

Remarkably the Apple iPhone took accessibility for many users with disability, especially blind users, backwards. After the ensuing outcry about the exclusionary nature of the iPhone, Apple slowly responded.

In June 2009, Apple launched a new, accessible version of the iPhone, making up for lost time by claiming it as a breakthrough, revolutionary no less:

> What makes VoiceOver on iPhone truly remarkable is that you control it using simple gestures that let you physically interact with items on screen ... Instead of memorizing hundreds of keyboard commands, or endlessly pressing tiny arrow keys to find what you're looking for, with VoiceOver, you simply touch the screen to hear a description of the item under your finger, then gesture with a double-tap, drag, or flick to control the phone.

VoiceOver delivers an experience unlike any screen reader you've ever used before. Traditional screen readers describe individual elements on the screen, but struggle to communicate where each element is located or provide information about adjoining objects ... But with VoiceOver on iPhone 3G S, you'll experience something entirely new.

(Apple 2009a)

Apple incorporated the software Voiceover and Zoom into its user interface, and greatly improved the accessibility of its in-built applications. Shortly after the launch of these new features, the implications of such engagement with accessibility technologies were not clear. Nonetheless, many blind users, who had been very disappointed at Apple's seemingly complete lack of interest in making the iPhone accessible, were impressed. The potential competitive advantage for Apple in designing its iPhone for blind users is that it could attract customers who currently may need to pay a substantial amount for cell phones (such as Nokia, for instance), as well as the screenreader and GPS software. Early user responses identified the prospect of purchasing a phone 'off the shelf' (that is, with the software already installed in, and shipped with, the iPhone) as an attractive proposition. Apple have publicized to user communities that they are working with third party developers to help make applications more accessible. Others feel that problems still remain. Veteran US technology expert and audio blogger, Jonathan Mosen delivered a balanced but telling assessment:

Apple should be congratulated for taking a device that clearly breached Section 255 of the US Telecommunications Act, and having a go and making it compliant ... Whether it can compete with well established offerings in terms of productive, efficient access, I am not convinced. I still ask, what have we gained in terms of efficient access to the exchange of information. Had Apple come out with the same offering today, but with the addition of a version of the iPhone with a qwerty keyboard, I think they would have been right on the money.

(Mosen 2009)

The limitation regarding the input device is a crucial point for Mosen, in rebutting Apple's promotion of its screen reader, and touch and voice interfaces:

... are arrow keys and a keyboard or number pad really so bad? It would appear to me to be an optimal interface for a blind person to use ... [T]he really interesting philosophical point for me relates to their comment about knowing where information appears on the screen ... who says that where information appears on the screen of a phone is important? Not many, if any, blind people ... Irrespective of where it appears, I want a foolproof, 100 per cent guaranteed way of hearing that information without fuss.

> The description on the Apple site simply seeks to turn what is a negative for us, the lack of arrow keys and a real keyboard, into a positive.
>
> (Mosen 2009)

The case of the iPhone, then, is a very interesting development in disability and technology. It is still unclear what motivated Apple to finally modify the iPhone, to create the affordances already well established in cell phones for users such as blind people. Clearly, Apple did not welcome the adverse publicity from the now vocal disability and accessible technology communities around the world, using the very online technologies closed off to them in the iPhone. Presumably Apple feared further negative publicity, as well as legal action, that might be taken by advocacy groups, such as the US National Federation of the Blind and American Council of the Blind, which have a strong track record in doing so (for instance, tackling AOL in the late 1990s for its inaccessible interfaces). In responding positively, if tardily, Apple in some respects went a little beyond the accessibility norms regarded as standard by blind communities, if still not generally put into place by companies, nor enforced by governments and regulators. In other key respects, however, Apple is still unwilling to comprehend and embrace the culture of blind users, let alone address outstanding issues for other groups of people with disabilities, such as those with physical disabilities or mobility impairments.

iPhone apps: new forms of mobile consumption

Cell phones, even the application-rich smartphone, have been difficult devices for many to manipulate, and to reprogramme in the way that users of computers, and especially users of the internet, expect to be able to do. There is an irony in this. As mentioned, cell phones have actually been an eminently customisable device in other ways. Users have adorned them with their favorite keepsakes. They have changed the faces and colours of their cell phone. They regularly change the ringtone, screensaver or desktop. They care intensely about the cell phone, as a signifier of fashion and identity.

However, thinking about and using the cell phone as something that can be programmed and networked, according to the user preference, has been a difficult proposition. Moreover, there has been little of an open market in cell phone applications at the consumer level. The typical scenario is that applications – notably games – can be downloaded via mobile internet (WAP) sites, or via premium mobile content, and then can run on the device (memory permitting). There are also many internet websites that offer applications for cell. Certainly there are some cell phone users who regularly download such applications (evidence of a burgeoning mobile content industry) – but the process is not especially user friendly.

Enter the iPhone 'Apps store'. Using the iTune interface and user experience, the Apps store does make it much easier to be aware of, choose, pay for and download applications for iPhone. As *Wired* journalist Charlie Sorrel notes, a major attraction of the iPhone apps stores was making it so much easier for consumers to find and buy apps:

> Until the iPhone came along, it was difficult to find, buy and install an application that wasn't made available on a phone's preprogrammed menus. It went like this: Find app (using Google). Find out who sells it. Buy it (entering your credit card details every time). Download to PC. Find cable or setup Bluetooth. Transfer from PC. Find in phone file browser. Install. Gah!
> (Sorrel 2009)

Apple's pitch is 'Applications unlike anything you've seen on a phone before':

> Applications designed for iPhone are nothing short of amazing. That's because they leverage the groundbreaking technology in iPhone – like the Multi-Touch interface, the accelerometer, GPS, real-time 3D graphics, and 3D positional audio. Just tap into the App Store and choose from thousands of applications ready to download now.
> (Apple Apps store, www.apple.com, accessed on 15 October 2008)

Both via the internet and using the iPhone itself, the experience of finding applications is much enhanced. Not only is the iPhone a signal adaptation of the internet and cell phones, it itself is highly adaptable by its users. The applications and programming options of the iPhone themselves feature very visibly in iPhone culture, as the Apple promotion suggests – as users try, swap and discuss applications. It has also meant that the iPhone is an important new platform for developers, a community who have often found the experience of developing applications for cell phones a frustrating experience. Indeed the iPhone has faced serious criticisms from developers. In the first place, Apple launched the iPhone without allowing access to third party developers. This allowed it to announce the release of a software development kit with some fanfare. The basic terms upon which Apple engages with iPhone application developers are still quite controversial, and seen by many as too restrictive, and slanted in Apple's favour. There have been a number of celebrated examples in which Apple has cracked down on developers.

With Apple's easing of the restrictions on developers, the applications available include novel uses of a cell phone. A number of these revolve around the iPhone's three-element accelerometer (cf. Baek et al. 2006). The iPhone's accelerometer is a sensing device that is able to gauge the orientation of the phone, and make appropriate changes in the screen. For instance, someone viewing photos of their iPhone can rotate the device 90 degrees, from portrait to landscape layout and the display will detect the movement and change accordingly (Apple 2008). The iPhone is equipped with two other sensors also: a proximity sensor and an ambient light sensor.

Rich Ling opens his book *New tech, new ties* with a story of a plumber who knocks on his door, distractedly talking on the phone (Ling 2008). When Ling opens the door, the plumber without so much as a by your leave, walks in, avidly continuing his conversation, and begins measuring up for the job. With the iPhone, the mobile phone is not only the great communication and business tool of the tradesperson, it is literally a tool they can use in their work. With the application 'Level', the iPhone becomes a spirit level (or carpenter's level), which can be used to see if a surface is flat or plumb. There are now a myriad of uses of the iPhone's new adaptation of sensing technology, including applications that allow you to play games swinging the phone, such as iBowl ('Simply swing your iPhone like a bowling ball and see how many strikes you can get'). Here the iPhone is clearly an adaptation of the gaming practices and moves familiar from Nintendo's Wii remote, the wireless controller for the popular video game console (Johnson 2008).

There is much more to say about the burgeoning culture of the iPhone centring upon its great potential for adaptability with downloading of apps, flexible configuration, and new logic of sensing, motion and touch. The iPhone is a novel *combinatoire* at the least, for melding mobile, computing and internet cultures. But what are the limits and politics of adaptation that its architecture, code and design allow and constrain?

'It will make other phones better': iPhone innovation

If we discount the most overblown claims for the iPhone – the 'Jesus' phone, the most awaited launch since Apollo 11, and so on – then one of the remaining grand claims concerning the iPhone is that it strikes a fatal blow to the locked down cell phone platforms. In the words of *Wired*'s Fred Vogelstein, the iPhone 'blew up the wireless industry'. Whether in these terms, or others, this is the central claim about the magnitude and meaning of the iPhone's killer adaptation. While conceding various shortcomings of the iPhone, Vogelstein submits that:

> wireless carriers begin to show signs of abandoning their walled-garden approach to snaring consumers … Eventually this will result in a completely new wireless experience, in which applications work on any device and over any network …
>
> (Vogelstein 2008)

On this view, the benefits of the iPhone stand not only to accrue to Apple and to iPhone application developers, but to the cell phone industry itself (what in the US is typically referred to as 'wireless'):

> It may appear that the carriers' nightmares have been realized, that the iPhone has given all the power to consumers, developers and manufacturers,

while turning wireless networks into dumb pipes. But by fostering more innovation, carriers' networks could get *more* valuable, not less. Consumers will spend more time on devices, and thus on networks, racking up bigger bills and generating more revenue for everyone.

(Vogelstein, 2008)

The iPhone, then, is an adaptation of the cell phone highly suited to the master themes of its time: end-to-end digital innovation.

There is some truth to this account. Apple was able to negotiate unusually favourable terms with carriers, regarding the split of revenues. This was one reason why Apple also struck exclusive deals with carriers: such as its deal with AT&T when it first launched in the US. While few details are in the public domain, it does appear that Apple managed to gain a better deal than that typically struck with other mobile content providers (the bargaining power of the carriers being a great bug-bear in the industry). However, it is important not to overstate this achievement. The political economy of mobile media is still very much structured and controlled by the cellular mobile carriers, which by virtue of their control of the networks, custody of the customer databases and long established sunk capital and pervasive presence, still command what is otherwise a maelstrom of media convergence.

It is important to view the emergence of the iPhone and Apple as a significant player in the cultural and political economies of mobile media, from the consumer's perspective. Apple is a peculiar kind of cell phone manufacturer, enjoying compelling and desirable horizontal integration. Thus it may be able to extract better gains from negotiation with mobile carriers. Even so, there is no reason to think that Apple will pass on these gains holus-bolus to the consumer or end user. To the contrary, there is a lively discussion and considerable literature on the strangleholds that Apple places on consumers of its computers, software and digital content. These strictures might be different from the suffocating embrace of cell phone carriers, and the norms of use and standard contracts obtained there – and it is heartening to see cell phone carriers' systems of control challenged by the iPhone. However, Apple has its own well defined interests in not opening things up too much; indeed the company consistently seeks to circumscribe use and circulation of digital materials, and to demarcate the arena of digital culture in new ways that serve its own interests. It is this aspect of the iPhone's adaptation of cell phones that goes squarely to the raging battles in digital cultures that I will now consider in some depth.

The cultural politics of iPhone modification

The flipside of the iPhone fever, and its Jesus-phone status, has been the clamorous role that hackers, with their devilish intentions, have played in its reception. Here unseen and undesired adaptations have eventuated, despite the company's best wishes and attempts to control unauthorized uses. Recall that when first launched the iPhone was very much a 'closed' device at a number of levels: locked to one network provider; its applications only provided by Apple, and not open to the wider developer community; its content safeguarded by the digital rights management regime well established through iTunes. Yet no sooner had the iPhone launched than it was hacked, with modifications and instructions freely available on blogs and websites.

While there was talk, and some evidence, that Apple did take legal or corporate action to stop or at least deter users from unlocking or modifying the iPhone, it could be argued that these unauthorized adaptations, displaying such keen interest in laying it bare, played into the mythos of the device. While many devices and software are now routinely cracked and modified, there was a visibility to the hacking of the iPhone that made the usually more underground tools and downloads much easier to find. Many users in countries in which the iPhone had not been launched were able to buy the device, activate and connect it with a provider of their choice – so adding to the advance praise of the technology. In China, as we saw in Chapter 2, the Shanhzai, copycat culture, has meant that the iPhone has been speedily and spectacularly re-assembled with a profitable yield for the informal economies of the street.

By 2010 the iPhone was a more open platform, with a strong set of controls but also great availability for developers. Apple could claim credit for have catalysed a thriving user culture, which itself has some ability to modify software and hardware. However, the iPhone does still remain quite a 'closed' platform. Jonathan Zittrain's early critique in his *The Future of the Internet and How to Stop It* remain the most systematic to date, if now a little outdated. Zittrain argues that the iPhone and similar moves amount to 'tethered applicances'. Zittrain opens with an image of Steve Job's January 2007 Macworld launch of the iPhone. Like Jobs, Zittrain himself draws a comparison between the launch of the iPhone and that of the Apple II computer 30 years before:

> Though these two inventions—iPhone and Apple II—were launched by the same man, the revolutions that they inaugurated are radically different. For the technology that each inaugurated is radically different. The Apple II was quintessentially generative technology. It was a platform. It invited people to tinker with it ... The iPhone is the opposite. It is sterile. Rather than a platform that invites innovation, the iPhone comes preprogrammed. You are not allowed to add programs to the all-in-one device that Steve Jobs sells you. Its functionality is locked in, though Apple can change it through remote updates. Indeed, to those who managed to tinker with the code to enable the iPhone to support more or different applications, Apple threatened (and then delivered on the threat) to transform the iPhone into an iBrick ... Whereas the world would innovate for the Apple II, only Apple would innovate for the iPhone.
>
> (Zittrain 2008: 2)

For Zittrain, the iPod is an example par excellence of the 'tethered appliance' that now threatens to change the shape of the internet:

> People now have the opportunity to respond to these problems [of PC and internet failures brought on by bad code] by moving away from the PC and toward more centrally controlled – 'tethered' – information appliances like mobile phones, video game consoles, TiVos, iPods, iPhones, and BlackBerries.
>
> (Zittrain 2008: 101)

According to Zittrain, 'tethered devices' fail to be generative platforms and, what's more, they are configured to be actively inimical to user experimentation and co-creation:

> These tethered appliances receive remote updates from the manufacturer, but they generally are not configured to allow anyone else to tinker with them ... Indeed, recall that some recent devices, like the iPhone, are up- dated in ways that actively seek out and erase any user modifications.
>
> (Zittrain 2008: 106)

Some of Zittrain's criticisms of the iPhone has less force, given that Apple has now released a software developer kit – and that the device can be activated on a wide range of cell phone networks. Yet Zittrain's critique still carries force, given the dialectics of 'open' and 'closed' in the iPhone as device and platform (see Clapperton and Corones 2007; Defeo 2008; Haubenreich 2008).

The interesting thing about Zittrain's account is that having invoked the iPhone as problematic he does not follow through to analyse the politics of the cell phone. Rather his focus is on the internet and computing devices as gen- erative, with Wikipedia and classic internet decentralized participatory forms, such as the Request For Comment (RFC), as examples of good practice. In Zittrain's thinking, the cell phone is used as a contrast to such generative internet possibilities. The cell phone is the foil, the 'bad object', that shows the dystopian future of digital culture. In his discussion of Nicholas Negroponte's controversial 'one laptop per child' project – with its giveaway of one hundred million laptops (the so-called XOs) to each child in the world – Zittrain likes its spirit of gen- erativity, while critizing its lack of attention to education, and also its tethered aspects. With these caveats, Zittrain much prefers the XO project rather than its cell phone alternative:

> The easier and more risk-averse path is to distribute mobile phones and other basic Net appliances to the developing world just as those devices are becoming more central in the developed one, bridging the digital divide in one sense – providing useful technology – while leaving out the generative

elements most important to the digital space's success: the integration of people as participants in it rather than only consumers of it.

(Zittrain 2008: 240)

What Zittrain overlooks here is that, actually, the cell phone is already widely used in the developed world – in generative and innovative ways, despite its limitations, as discussed in Chapter 7. In fact, the story of the cell phone's low-tech, user adaptations in developing countries, as we have seen, is now becoming an important part of the media cultural dynamics of the rest of the world (Donner 2009a and b).

Zittrain's position on the cell phone, which is shared by other theorists too (Benkler 2006), draws our attention to the control architectures inscribed in coveted devices such as the iPhone. However, rather than following through the intricate struggles over mobile media, such a position vests all too much hope in the participatory culture centring on the internet – and so both over- and under-reads the politics of adaptation occurring with the iPhone. If the iPhone is a highly significant, if controversial adaptation of the cell phone, that at the same time draws attention to, and intervenes with, the cultural politics of adaptation, it is not the only makeover in town. There is much, much more going on, in the world of cell phones and mobile internet.

Open source and cell phones

The entry of the iPhone has redrawn the terrain upon which the future of the cell phone, and indeed mobile and wireless internet, will play out. It is an open question, as I have been arguing, to what extent the iPhone is a revolutionary force in these politics of smartphones, or whether it is adding another vector and power bloc into a messy geopolitics of mobile technologies and networks. As well as the handset designs, there are a set of skirmishes, now fully fledged campaigns, if not battles, that have opened up, which involve operating systems and software – struggles that have been played out extensively in relation to software, computers and the internet (Chopra and Dexter 2008). As set out in Chapter 2, software and operating systems have been important constitutive features of cell phones since their computing power and network capabilities exponentially grew in the 1990s. What the iPhone has done is to cast the capabilities of computing, software, applications and internet on mobile devices – and the large question of the potential affordances of mobile platforms – in stark relief. Ranged against Apple and the tour de force of its operating systems and applications is a shifting alliance of mobile carriers, handset manufacturers and computer giants centring on open source software developments.

For some years now, a number of powerful corporate interests have made strategic investments in open source systems and software. Nokia, with its purchase of Symbian, then turning it into an open source venture, as well as other partners and consortia, have also seen open source as a valuable element of its competitive development strategies, sitting alongside, and interacting with, its proprietary or open standards developments (cf. DeNardis 2009).

Take, for instance, another much publicized adaptation of the cell phone: Google's Android. In September 2008, T-Mobile launched its G1, the first Android phone. The gambit of the Android is its reliance on an open source model. Like the iPhone, the Android seeks to inaugurate a new kind of mobile phone, with a vision, set of affordances and assumptions that principally come from computing and internet cultures. Rather than 'just being a phone', it also aspires to be an alternative platform. In the case of Android, it is a project of the Open Handset Alliance, a consortium of several companies: Google, Intel and Qualcomm, along with Motorola, T-Mobile, Sprint Nextel and China Mobile (Helft and Markoff 2007).

> What would it take to build a better mobile phone?
>
> A commitment to openness, a shared vision for the future, and concrete plans to make the vision a reality.
>
> Welcome to the Open Handset Alliance™, a group of 47 technology and mobile companies who have come together to accelerate innovation in mobile and offer consumers a richer, less expensive, and better mobile experience. Together we have developed Android™, the first complete, open, and free mobile platform.
>
> (OHA 2009a)

Suggesting that '[b]uilding a better mobile phone would enrich the lives of countless people across the globe', Open Handset Alliance puts an emphasis on 'innovating in the open':

> Each member of the Open Handset Alliance is strongly committed to greater openness in the mobile ecosystem. Increased openness will enable everyone in our industry to innovate more rapidly and respond better to consumers' demands ... Android was built from the ground up with the explicit goal to be the first open, complete, and free platform created specifically for mobile devices.
>
> (OHA 2009b)

On the Open Handset Alliance website is a short video, hosted on YouTube, entitled 'If I had a magic phone', featuring several young children: 'Kids talk about what their dream phone would do. Learn more about the Open Handset Alliance's plans to build a better phone ... What will your magic phone do?' (OHA 2009b). After various scenes of children imagining their phone would take them to the moon, make cupcakes, pizza and cookies, turn into underpants, help animals feel better, fit into their pocket and have a keyboard, a child finally says 'give me anything I want' (which is figured as ice-cream).

Claiming to bring 'Internet-style innovation and openness to mobile phones', Android is built upon the open Linux kernel. Android includes an operating system, middleware and mobile applications. It allows applications to use any of the phone's core functionality, and claims not to 'differentiate between the phone's core applications and third-party applications' – all having 'equal access' to the phone capabilities (Android 2009d). Other key selling points are user customization – 'users are able to fully tailor the phone to their interests' – and the breaking down of barriers between internet and mobile phone, enabling, for instance, developers to 'combine information from the web with data on an individual's mobile phone ... to provide a more relevant user experience' (such as knowing when a friend is in the vicinity and being able to connect with them) (Android 2009d). Android also offers its alternative to iPhone apps – the Android Market, with its own developer and content control policies (Android 2009a, b and c) that appear less restrictive than those of iPhone apps (Apple 2009b).

Shortly after launch, AT&T, one of the two US carriers not to join the Open Handset Alliance (the other being Verizon), raised questions about security, privacy, access to other email platforms than Google's Gmail and what applications would be uniquely available (Gardiner 2007a). Underlying these issues, clearly, is a dominant carrier wishing to preserve its existing, extensive subscriber base, and its sweet deal with iPhone: 'AT&T is in no hurry to join an upstart open source alliance whose very existence may or may not threaten the company's core business mode' (Gardiner 2007a). Other companies were nonplussed, or at least dallying, with Open Handset Alliance included the leading processor manufacturer ARM (Gardiner 2008) For its part, Nokia made a show of welcome to the advent of a new open source platform:

> 'It's great to see a new comer to the market,' said Bill Plummer, Nokia's head of multimedia for North America. 'Google's entry to the space is also a validation of our own vision of a truly open market.'
>
> (Gardiner 2007b)

Pundits immediately queried Nokia's own conception of openness, something I'll explore in a much more expanded form below, and in Chapter 9. Interestingly Motorola, Nokia's great competitor, did cast its lot in with Open Handset Alliance, as a way to develop new handset models more quickly, hoping to regain profitability (Ganapati 2008).

Android was slower to develop than expected. By mid-2009, only HTC's G1 phone was available, with the company planning others for release later that year (Ganapati 2009). Samsung was also planning to release Android based phones in 2009, with LG still considering the system. New entrants into the cellular mobile handset market, Garmin and Asus, had developed phones based on Android, but were experiencing difficulty attracting carriers to these (Ganapati 2009). Like other new entrants seeking to build upon their strengths, and muscle into the mobile media arena by displacing the cell phone giants, Garmin proposed a GPS phone in early 2008:

> If nothing else, the Nuviphone marks part two of an emergent trend: new players from outside the clique bringing their own beer. Apple brought the mobile industry's first pleasurable user interface and the genuine technological innovation that makes it work. Garmin hopes to bring GPS that's more than a disabled afterthought.
>
> (Beschizza 2008)

Google's meteoric rise has been widely disssected, especially for its dominance of the contemporary internet search and its moves to strategically position itself as central to the future of culture – with its digitization project with libraries. Google now joins Apple as yet one more computer and internet behemoth seeking to shape the future of mobile media also. The politics of the deployment of open source by corporations such as Google, Nokia and others will be interesting to observe – to see where they diverge over time from the kinds of closed networks that corporations typically favour (for an instructive discussion, see Sawhney 2009: 113–14).

Not that the large corporations can rest easily as yet: there are many other open source cell phone projects underway, such as the Neo Freerunner Linux-based smartphone running the Openmoko platform (Beschizza 2007b). The Neo Freerunner phone went on sale in mid-2008, but is still restricted to developers, rather than general consumers (Openmoko 2008). Harmeet Sawhney has discussed such developments as mobile extensions of the internet, looking at their potential for creating what he calls 'arenas of innovation'. According to Sawhney:

> For open-cell-phone enthusiasts, present-day cell phones are like mainframes. The users have little flexibility. They have to function pretty much within the tight parameters set by the system design. The open-cell-phone enthusiasts hope to do to this paradigm what the Jobs and Woz generation did to the mainframes. In effect, they want to make the cell phones as flexible as the personal computers.
>
> (Sawhney 2009: 113)

This would be presumably the vision of cell phones, after Zittrain. It goes to the heart of the fantasy of the iPhone too. But as well as migration of innovation from the internet (or computing) to the mobile, Sawhney suggests we should pay attention to the possibility of migration the other way – namely from cell phones to internet and computing (Sawnhey 2009: 114–15).

Conclusion

How might we understanding these teeming, legion adaptations of the cell phone? The smartphones, iPhone, Android, BlackBerry, open source and other phones that seek to modify the cell phone to better take account of the things users expect from internet cultures? In the first place, more research is needed to chart the detailed adaptation of the iPhone across the various places where it has been launched. It will be especially interesting to hear how the iPhone has fared in countries where mobile media has been much more advanced than, say, the US – for instance, in Japan, where mobile internet was so much a part of both cell phone and internet experience, and where the cell phone has proven so protean and culturally significant, to an extent that the iPhone has seemed so 2007; or in China, where the varieties of cell phones, including iPhone copies, are legion. Here the iPhone could be placed in at least two histories of new media adaptation – that of the histories of the cell phone and its consumption, and that of the internet also.

As well as the critical vocabulary of cultural adaptation we might borrow from other areas of media, such as television and film, we also need to think about the concepts that are associated with technology. To understand the double movement of adaptation in the case of the iPhone, for instance, we need to engage with the new lexicon of copying, modification, authorized and unauthorized use, versioning and so on, that comes from computer, internet and digital cultures. What emerge here are new considerations for understanding both the processes of adaptation in mobile media, and the dynamics of culture that subtends them. Critically important to this is the role of 'software platforms' (Evans et al. 2006) in the burgeoning field of smartphones – but also, inescapably, across the various domains of mobile media, and their networks and cultures. Software and hardware platforms in mobile media, and what they open up, constrain, allow or produce, and in whose's interests, are the subject to which we shall now turn.

Chapter 9

The mobile commons?

Open networked cultures beyond the politics of code

[The] central question is whether there will, or will not, be a core common infrastructure that is governed as a commons and therefore available to anyone who wishes to participate in the networked information environment outside of the market-based proprietary framework.

(Benkler 2006: 23)

The politics of spectrum have always underpinned questions about the media, and while spectrum policy is as important as ever for television and radio stations, the 2000s have presented the world with a chance to seize new capacity through digital systems. This chance is only open to developing countries if the law permits at least some unlicensed access to spectrum – access without a fee and without advance permission.

(Sandvig 2006: 54)

Dear Inhabitants of the 'legal' Commons,

Greetings! This missive arrives at your threshold from the proverbial Asiatic street, located in the shadow of an improvised bazaar, where all manner of oriental pirates and other dodgy characters gather to trade in what many amongst you consider to be stolen goods. We call them 'borrowed' goods. But a difference in the language in which one talks about things ('stolen' vs, 'borrowed') is also a measure of the distance between two different worlds … what you call a 'pirated' DVD is what we would call a DVD 'borrowed' from the street, and the price we pay for it is equivalent, or at least analogous to an incremental subscription to the great circulating public library of the Asiatic street. We address this, written in the precincts of that library, to all you who enjoy the salubrious comfort of the legal commons, especially the one that calls itself 'creative'. We have occasionally stepped into your enclosures, and have fond memories of our forays. However, our sojourns in your world have of necessity had to be brief. Before long, we have been asked about our provenance, our intent, our documents. There has rarely been enough paper for us to prove that we had the right of way. We appreciate and admire the determination with which you nurture your garden of licences. The proliferation and variety of flowering contracts and clauses in your hothouses is astounding. But we find the paradox of a space that is called a commons and yet so fenced in, and in so many ways, somewhat intriguing.

(Sengupta 2006: 19)

The commons debate has served to constellate a set of crucial propositions about value, democracy and openness regarding the emergent platforms of contemporary culture. The contemporary reinvigoration of the doctrine of the commons, especially led by the work of a number of legal scholars, notably Lawrence Lessig (2001), has also seen the engagement of audiences outside specialist academic and policy settings – not least in work of the creative commons movement (http://creativecommons.org/ accessed on 12 May 2010). Thus the different accounts of the commons provide an important set of reflections upon the nature of digital technologies, their economies, and social and cultural relations. Perhaps the most important reason for the influence of the commons is that its contemporary correlate has been taken to be the internet. Particular aspects of internet technologies, platforms, applications, cultures and layers are valorized by proponents of the commons – and these exemplary cases taken from the internet serve to underpin the normative claims a number of commons theorists make for general notions of society, economics, ethics and justice. The commons has enjoyed a great influence, and indeed a concrete model, for conceiving alternative visions of the internet. The commons has also been applied far more widely to digital technology, culture and networks in general, and indeed even more broadly to information, biotechnology, agriculture and all manner of spheres of contemporary life (Bardhan and Ray 2008; Dasgupta et al. 1997). Surprisingly, though, the commons has rarely been applied to mobile communication and media.

First, commons theorists have not really grasped or grappled with mobile networks. If they do discuss mobile networks, these are seen as leading exhibits of 'enclosed', proprietary networks, locked down for non-market, public or creative use by telecommunications companies and handset and device manufacturers. Second, when commons theorists – or indeed theorists with coeval accounts of the importance of internet culture, co-creation, creative innovation – consider mobile networks, they see the real possibilities of openness coming from the ability of mobile devices to access wireless technologies, such as Wi-Fi or Wi-Max. In another move mobile devices gain their meaning and possibilities for openness by being placed in the universe of the social, collaborative media of Web 2.0. Third, the idea of the internet that many of the leading commons theorists use is based on a quite specific experience of the internet in North America, oriented around fast bandwidth, the wide availability and affordability of PCs, and the particular educational, work, home and public settings of computing, internet, and cell phone use. Despite the fact that the internet is taken to be the eminently global medium, and indeed is now a place where languages other than English dominate its users, the dominant understandings of the internet in the Anglophone world do not reflect this (Danet and Herring 2007; Goggin and McLelland 2009). In addition, the internet is a mobile experience for many users – Japan and Korea being two quite different countries where this is clearly so (for instance, see Ito, Okabe and Matsuda 2005), as are many countries now in what used to be called the second and third world. Much of the world's population has access to television, and now cell phones – but personal computers and reliable, comprehensive internet access are not so widely diffused. I am not suggesting that we now valorize cell phones over internet, but rather that we recognize, as we are often exhorted to do, the interrelations of these two technological systems, and also place these in general ecologies of media, communications and technologies.

So, one impulse behind this chapter is to propose and elaborate the idea of the mobile commons – to see what light it casts on the politics of mobile networks, and ideals of open network cultures in which mobile media play a leading role. However, as I shall argue, drawing on the work of a range of thinkers, the idea of the commons has significant problems – centring on the place that property, contracts and a particular idea of law play in it. Hence having sketched an idea of mobile commons, I shall nip it in the bud with a proleptic critique. My contention is that we need to move well beyond commons, to draw upon ideas in the heritage of telecommunications as well as unfolding cultures of mobile media, to develop an unconstrained idea of open, mobile, networked cultures.

Wireless and internet versus mobile commons

What the considerable literature on, and activity in pursuit of, the commons highlights with great clarity and urgency are the struggles underway about the shape and characteristics of the digital environment; which is to say – especially once the denotative and connotative power of the digital fades away – the future of media. We can see this clearly in perhaps the most elaborated and lucid account of the commons, Yochai Benkler's *The Wealth of Networks* (Benkler 2006).

Benkler argues that recent transformations have 'created new opportunities for how we make and exchange information, knowledge, and culture', and have 'increased the role of nonmarket and non-proprietary production, both by individuals alone and by cooperative efforts in a wide range of loosely or tightly woven collaborations' (Benkler 2006: 2). For Benkler, software, video, new kinds of investigative reporting and multiplayer online games are leading examples. While these possibilities will hopefully yield an 'open, diverse, liberal equilibrium' (Benkler 2006: 22), Benkler is also concerned about a dystopian outcome from the lack of the core, commonly owned and shared infrastructure. Benkler singles out two particular threats (or 'enclosure' movements) to a commons, the 'enclosure movement' around intellectual property and digital rights management, and the concentration of market structure for broadband wires and connections. In the case of broadband, there have been some countervailing forces, according to Benkler:

> The emergence of open wireless networks, based on 'spectrum commons', counteracts this trend to some extent, as does the current apparent business

practice of broadband owners not to use their ownership to control the flow of information over their networks.

(2006: 25)

Benkler valorizes open wireless networks, underscoring their ability to create alternative communication and computational structure, and so offers a real alternative to 'enclosed' broadband networks (Goggin 2007a). What is exemplary about Benkler's utopian rendering of wireless communication is its contrast with mobile cellular technologies:

> The development of open wireless networks, owned by their users and focused on sophisticated general-purpose devices at their edges also offers a counterpoint to the emerging trend among mobile telephony providers to offer a relatively limited and controlled version of the Internet over the phones they sell.
>
> (Benkler 2006: 404)

Benkler sees a conflict between the open, wireless networks and closed mobile ones, in which the only hope for a vision of a commons lies in the extent to which phone vendors 'build into the mobile telephones the ability to tap into open wireless networks, and use them as general-purpose access points to the Internet' (Benkler 2006: 405). The outcome of this friction between wireless and mobiles and their inscription in devices, along with the question of whether users will be prepared to carry another wireless device alongside their mobile phone 'will determine the extent to which the benefits of open wireless networks will be transposed into the mobile domain' (Benkler 2006: 405).

Benkler's intriguing if problematic account here extends the account of the wireless commons. A methodical and relatively straightforward application of classic commons theory to wireless commons opens thus:

> As wireless access needs increase with the rapid proliferation of mobile handheld computing devices, wireless commons are expected to play an indispensable role for communications and commerce in coming years. Thus it becomes important to understand: How do these wireless commons create common good? How can the participants who consume the freely available resources cause an eventual demise of the commons? What countermeasures will allow the commons to continue to flourish?
>
> (Damsgaard et al. 2006: 105–6)

To forestall the tragedy of the commons (Burke 2001; Feeny et al. 1990; Hardin 1968), Damsgaard et al. suggest that 'some technological solutions are available to reduce misuse of the available resources, but the commons primarily depend on the cooperative behavior of the users' (Damsgaard et al. 2006: 109). The concept of the wireless commons arose from the growth in wireless technologies, and the debates about spectrum. There was a lively debate about the virtues of spectrum commons models (Buck 2002), as opposed to other models of conceiving and managing spectrum such as purely property based models, or the earlier public administration (Ting et al. 2005; cf. Hwang and Yoon 2009's proposal for a mixed regime in Korea; Ballon and Delaere 2009). At stake was the use of unlicensed spectrum – important for allowing the unconstrained use of various wireless technologies. Such open approaches to spectrum were especially significant in the rise of the 802.11x Wi-Fi standards, their implementation and the socio-technical innovations and co-operative models associated with these. While such visions of open wireless have pivoted on spectrum, and proposals for spectrum commons, there are potentially much wider and more thoroughgoing implications, some of which Benkler opens up. The rich complexities and possibilities of wirelessness, especially around Wi-Fi (Goggin and Gregg 2007), have been the subject of important work by various scholars, including Adrian Mackenzie (2005 and 2009) and Christian Sandvig (2004 and 2006).

Before I consider cell phones from a commons perspective, I would note the quite different tradition and concepts telecommunications carries with it that still have a strong influence on how mobile media is modelled. Surprisingly, while there have been many attempts to theorize the internet from the perspective of a commons (indeed, as I have noted, the internet has not only been seen as a prized instance of the commons, but it has served to model the commons itself), the idea of mobile commons has still not often been raised. Of the rare exceptions, Rich Ling, the pre-eminent thinker on mobiles and society, has an interesting discussion of mobile communication and its potential to contribute to the 'tragedy of the commons':

> If we consider the public sphere as a type of commons, the mobile telephone brings up two issues ... The first is what we might call a type of audio pollution of the public sphere because of the increasing number of mobile telephone calls ... Here it seems that the sense of the commons is being reasserted through various adjustments. The other is the withdrawal from the public sphere. As Jane Jacobs noted, the thing that makes the public sphere vibrant is the continual contact with unexpected forms of interactions ... There is the possibility that ICTs and mobile communication will take a small bite out of the already minimal sociability that is available in this sphere.
>
> (Ling 2005: 193)

This is a useful way to reframe a recurrent debate in mobile communication; however, what I am interested in here is proposing what a commons particular to mobile media might look like.

There are few writers or participants in mobile media who deal specifically with the question of the commons. In her study of mobile media, Valerie

Feldmann ends with an argument for an 'innovation commons', and directs our attention to the open question of 'how to design policies for mobile media in a way that frees innovation, promotes competition and allows people to adopt, appropriate, transform and reshape new media' (Feldmann 2005: 224). Another project that affiliates itself with the concept of the commons is the very interesting Canadian mobile digital commons network. This is a network which broadly aligned itself with commons movements across digital culture (Longford 2006), and aims to explore 'the connections between human beings, urban and wilderness settings, and mobile technologies' (Longford 2007). When initiated, its journal *Wi* aimed to publish results of 'two years of collaboration amongst designers, theorists, artists, engineers, software developers as a research network in mobile, wireless and gaming technologies' (Crow and Sawchuk 2006). *Wi* has now been re-badged as a 'journal of mobile media', and while it does not contain an explicit theorization on mobile commons it offers rich cognate work aiming to open up mobile platforms.

While there is little explicit discussion of mobile commons, there have been a few critiques of the closed nature of mobile platforms. Many of these do counterpose the open, public internet, with the comparatively highly controlled nature of mobile platforms (Rheingold 2002). I discussed such a critique in Chapter 8 – Jonathon Zittrain's critique of 'tethered devices'. There are quite a number of critiques of 'walled gardens' in mobile data – questioning the growth of mobile portals, in which cell phone carriers and service providers offer content for sale (especially premium rate content). Perhaps the most suggestive work to date has been that of Harmeet Sawhney, who, rather than simply counterposing 'open' internet (or wireless internet) to 'closed' mobile platforms, theorizes cell phones as 'arenas of innovation' (Sawhney 2005).

In many ways, the movement around open mobiles has come from practitioners of various sorts and hues. For instance, there has been important work underway to develop concepts and tools for mobile platforms as cultural platforms in the open source and free software movements, and in artistic circles. An early effort to open up mobile technologies, making them available for user experimentation, was undertaken by the Manchester based art collective, the-phone-book that offered workshops on how users could program cell phones. Those involved in mobile music, such as Atau Tanaka and collaborators, discussed in Chapter 4, have extended such work, with explicit, programmatic ideas about the need to open up mobile networks. The same is true of a range of designers, artists, developers and users in locative media, evoked by the phrase 'locative commons' (Tuters 2004; see also Tuters and Varnelis 2006).

Open source software for cell phones has received a fillip in recent years. As discussed in Chapter 8, the iPhone has crystallized and made much more visible a set of developments around mobile media – that promise to open up the platforms and technologies for a greater range of commercial and non-commercial uses. As well as the role of open source systems in the commercial wars over the future of the cell phone, the promise of open source is of opening cell phones up for consumers and developers, as a *Wired* journalist makes plain:

> Open-source, free as a bird and ready to make calls, this crop of current and forthcoming Linux-based smartphones wants to wean you off the proprietary teat. Some are for tinkerers, others (allegedly) for actual consumers, but if you've had enough trying to get Windows Mobile and Palm to do what you want them to do, this is where you can get your nix kicks.
>
> (Beschizza 2007b)

As well as the use of open source by quite large companies, there are also other, smaller, if not fledgling open source initiatives in mobiles.

A prominent example is the Openmoko project, and its flagship Neo 1973 smartphone, first offered for sale in mid-2007. The phone is named after the year in which Martin Cooper, the inventor of the cell phone, made the first call. There are other groups of enthusiasts, seeking to do to cell phones what mythical pioneers in home computing did. Thus the 'Silicon Valley Mobile Homebrew Group':

> We're a collection of entrepreneurs, engineers and innovators looking to do cool things with mobile platforms. Despite what you might have heard in the media, we're not trying to hack mobile phone networks, displace the network operators or compete toe to toe with the commercial handset manufacturers. If anything, we're just impatient that the industry hasn't caught up with us, and we're inventing our own future.
>
> (http://hbmobile.org/, accessed 1 September 2009)

As one tech blog observed, 'the whole point of HomeBrew Mobile is to make everything customizable, even down to the case design' (Gast 2007).

The sardonic Homebrew Mobile logo carries the recital: 'One phone to rule them all, one ringtone to find them, one carrier to find them all, and to the service plan bind them' (HB MobileWiki, http://wiki.hbmobile.org/, accessed 1 September 2009). While the Homebrew Mobile crew seemed to have vanished without a trace, their efforts and musing reveal something about popular desire to reshape cell phones and mobile platforms. Take, for instance, their brainstorming exercise 'What is a mobile phone?':

> A mobile phone isn't just a mobile phone, it's lots of things … This is a high-level 'features' list, some are provided by pure software (such as an address book) and some by hardware, usually driven by some software. So, a mobile phone is a … Regular Phone!; VoIP Phone; Video Phone; 'Headless' Phone; Instant Messenger; Clock; Audio Player; Video Player; Mapping Device; Personal Information Manager; Medical Recorder; Calculator; Camera/Camcorder; E-Mail Client; News Reader; Encyclopedia; Web Browser;

E-Book Reader; Games Console; File Storage Device; Torch/Flashlight; TV Remote Control.

(HomeBrew Mobile 2008)

Another place where there is now considerable work in developing open source for mobiles is in the twin spheres of cell phones for development and mobile activism (Mudhai 2006). The World Wide Web consortium mobile internet for development work incorporates and emphasizes open source in cell phones. Mobile activism is a burgeoning area, forming part of the resistant energies of the broader social and political movements around democracy and digital media (Boler 2008). The well known international group Mobile Active – 'a global network of people using mobile technology for social impact' (mobileactive.org accessed on 12 May 2010) – has been leading the discussion, promotion and development of open source and open mobile applications as an integral part of its aims to:

> help organizations make use of the most ubiquitous communications tech-nology in the world with data, tools, and how-to resources; build a network of practitioners and technologists in a supportive community of practice.
>
> (MobileActive 2009)

To summarize my argument so far: the commons has provided an influential model for new media, especially in North America, but it has been also been used around the world, precisely and loosely, to imagine the digital environment, its struggles and politics. Cell phones and mobile media have been seen as a blockage or dystopian instance, where the commons is very far from applying. Typically we can observe two conceptual moves. First, mobile data protocols and applications are contrasted disapprovingly with the open, public internet. Second, cellular mobile networks are contrasted unfavourably with wireless net-works, based on the Wi-Fi (802.11) or Wi-Max standards. These two conceptual moves have not, in my estimation, led to focused attention upon contesting forms of control, and opening up, of mobile platforms – in the same way we see with the various commons movements in the internet, though clearly concepts and tools from, say, creative commons, apply to cell phones. Where there has been work on the politics of mobile code, as I have suggested, is in a range of activity from open source and free software movements, to artistic and inde-pendent cultural production communities.

Modelling a mobile commons

What would a mobile commons look like? If there is an actual, or looming, enclosure of mobile platforms, what forms does this take exactly? There are various ways of conceptualising the layers or levels of technology, but I would suggest that, regarding mobiles, there are at least five loci of control.

Handsets and devices

Broadly speaking mobiles comprise a handset or device and a Subscriber Information Management (SIM) card. SIM cards carry information on the address (phone number) of the device, as well as account information (Vedder 2001). In theory, as we know, a SIM card can be taken from one device, and inserted into another to switch an account and user identity across devices. Clearly the SIM card is something under the control of the phone company or service provider, and is difficult for a user to modify, as it articulates the user into two important systems in which security is key. First, there is connection to the telecommunications network. Here addressing is provided by telephone numbers, instead of, or as well as, internet protocol addresses. Secondly, the SIM card connects the device to the account, subscriber management and billing systems of the mobile operator. In most cases, it is only possible to use one SIM card with each device. There are, of course, marvellous examples of the technology being appropriated by low end modification. In the Philippines, for instance, the small cell phone vendors and do-it-yourself repairers who have tiny shops in most towns, can affix an additional SIM card holder on the inside of the case of the phone. This allows the insertion of an additional SIM card, so the user can switch between two network providers, depending on location or preference.

If the SIM card is a crucial gateway to the activation of the device and access to mobile networks, so too can controls be applied at the level of the device. The most obvious such control is the locking of the phone to a particular network provider. A user who purchases a phone on a low cost plan from a provider often has their phone 'locked' to the original provider's network. It cannot be modified and used on another network without the payment of a fee (or the unauthorized modification and removal of the lock).

While the user is free to use many functions of the device offline, whether clock functions, camera, games, music, radio, storage or programme functions, the activation of the device onto the network lies significantly in the gift of the cell phone operator. The systems of access and control that govern the connection of the phone, or mobile device to the network, bear the hallmarks of the regimes of telecommunications. Now many mobile devices also have Wi-Fi capability, and so are able to connect to the internet directly, through wireless hotspots. In the future, devices are likely to incorporate other network access capabilities, notably Wi-Max.

The other major way that the user can connect to a network is using the Bluetooth protocol. The Bluetooth protocol allows the user to connect their phone to other Bluetooth-equipped devices, including computers, cameras and printers, and to exchange and share files. The Bluetooth protocol only works over a relatively short range. However, it has emerged as a significant force in new cultures of use and user innovation, as discussed earlier in this book. (Of course, Bluetooth is also being used by commercial forces to hail or connect to users, as in the phenomenon of advertising that uses the protocol to interact with mobile phone users when they are in the vinicity of a billboard or shop.) The interesting thing about Bluetooth networks, of course, is that they are very casual, short term, opportunistic, and formed from contacts in close promixity – an unstable and felicitous performance of network and space. Bluetooth networks are also quite unregulated, in contrast to cellular mobile networks and the internet (something that has raised concerns, as the use of Bluetooth via cell phones is becoming visible as an activity, especially in teenagers and young people).

The domestication of mobiles that Bluetooth highlights is a general framing of the technology. Despite the relatively closed nature of handsets and access that I have just mentioned, there has been considerable user innovation, most obvious in the phenomenon of customization and personalization of phones through ornaments, changeable faces on phones, wallpapers and ringtones (Hjorth 2005). This kind of innovation is a classic instance of consumer culture, where users rely on commercial availability of objects, products, or services to domesticate their devices. It is important to acknowledge this creative force in mobile consumption because it may contribute to the achievement of a commons – but might also point to a different kind of model of mobile media, as it does the iPhone – with the fascinating thing about the reception of the iPhone being the rapidity, fluency and enthusiasm with which users have hacked the device. The hacking of the iPhone is a phenomenon in its own right, which has advanced the cause, and raised the stakes, of openness in mobile media.

Network installation and interoperability

People in rural areas have often installed their own telephone lines to connect to the phone system, for instance in Australia, the US and in many countries in the developing world. However, the particular technical characteristics and affordances of mobile network transmission, switching and digital encoding make it difficult for individuals or loosely coordinated communities to set up their own mobile cellular networks – in the way, for instance, that activist and community enthusiasts of Wi-Fi do. While there do exist community networks around cellular mobiles, these require a deal of co-ordination, capital and collaboration with wholesale network providers and operators to be successful.

Operating systems and software

Like computers, cell phones use operating systems and software. The operating systems have mostly been proprietary, notably the Symbian operating system. It is fair to say that there has been less awareness of, and less resistance to proprietary operating systems, and development of alternatives, than we see in the open source software movements around computing and internet. Similarly, most software used on cell phones is proprietary; for instance, licensed versions of popular computing software, such as Microsoft Office or Acrobat Reader, developed for handheld and mobile devices such as smartphones, Portable Digital Assistants, and BlackBerries. There is a range of software commercially developed and available for cell phones, ranging from the expected office and business applications to new private sphere opportunities such as surveillance of children or employees:

'Mobile Spy: Reveal the Truth in Real Time'
Are your children or employees abusing the privileges of your Windows Mobile based smartphone? Are you worried they are using the phone for unallowed or inappropriate activities? Mobile Spy will reveal the truth for any company or family. You will finally learn the truth about their call, mobile web and text message activities by logging into your Mobile Spy account from any computer.
(http://www.mobile-spy.com/spy_features.htm, accessed 3 July 2008)

Recently, there has been growing interest in the use of Linux systems for cell phones, with the first international conference held in November 2006 on the business case and technology choice for all open source in mobiles, but especially Linux and open source Java. There are quite successful software initiatives for cell phones, notably Opie (Open Palmtop Integrated Environment), developed by Trolltech. Opie forms part of Trolltech's comprehensive Qtopia Phone Edition applications platform. In addition, there are now organizations dedicated to promoting and developing open source software for handhelds, such as handhelds.org (accessed on 12 May 2010, which also has a concentration on wearable computers). As is evident, much of the initial activity has centred upon handheld computing devices and PDAs, rather than classic cell phones, though now with the advent of smartphones and mobile media the open software community (Bitzer and Schröder 2006) is tackling cell phones.

Control of channels and content

Cell phones have been critical to the development of open markets in telecommunications carriers, and competition is well advanced in many countries. However, powerful commercial players, as we have seen, still play a dominant role in controlling access to mobile platforms. Notable here are the carriers.

Despite interconnect agreements and competition rules, carriers are still able to restrict options for service providers to offer commercial content (videos, downloads and so on, being areas where clearly third party content providers and aggregators do have a viable and lucrative business). Thus with the emergence of mobile data services, and new third party operators (indeed some specialists in mobile services internationally such as Mobile Interactive Group or MIG; http://www.migcan.com/, accessed on 12 May 2010), there have been fierce battles fought between the carriers seeking to develop and promote their 'portal' (or proprietary mobile premium services) versus the content and service providers wishing either to sell products to the carriers or to access mobile platforms to sell services direct to consumers (Goggin and Spurgeon 2005 and 2007).

As well as the industry struggles over cell phone operators, new entrants (premium rate content and service providers) and traditional broadcast interests over the shape and operation of mobile networks, there has also been considerable, if belated, governmental interest discussed in Chapter 5. In these debates, there has been little discussion of the place of these new mobile data channels and services and user-generated content (Feijóo et al. 2007). Theoretically, access to mobile data services, including premium mobile messaging or video services, is open to anyone with sufficient funds. For instance, the non-profit, charity and non-government organization sector has been an innovative user of cell phones, as evidenced in the use by organizations such as Médicins san Frontierès of text messaging for contacting their supporters or the enlisting of messaging by organizations in the youth sector, or by organizations working in HIV-AIDs and sexually transmitted diseases.

What is striking, however, is that mobile networks are rarely, if ever, conceptualized as distribution platforms that might be open to community, citizen, alternative, cultural producer or artistic expression. Compare this to the world movement around community media, which has been successful in having channels, spectrum and resources set aside for radio and television broadcasting. Such arguments have been raised in regulatory discussions on mobile television – but there has been little development of concrete proposals about what programmes or channels viewers should be able to watch or listen to, let alone what access users should have as producers and creators of material.

An important source of contest to the mobile operator's control of cellular mobiles comes from the potential uses of the internet protocol. As mobile internet becomes more widely used, then a greater proportion of internet applications and technologies can theoretically be used via mobile devices. An early example is the use of VoIP (voice over internet protocol) applications over cell phones. Here there are new ways for users to fashion telephony, messaging and data connection to other individual users or groups, overriding to some extent the controls of circuit switching mobile telecommunications networks, at least within the limitations of VoIP software, which, for instance, allows conferencing, but with a practical limit on the number of users. Some cell phone carriers and service providers try to limit or stop use of mobile VoIP applications, but with the advent of apps for smartphones this has become much easier for users to circumvent.

Intellectual property

In the realm of the internet, and digital culture generally, there is a strong trend in intellectual property towards greater claims and regimes of control, extending the theoretical and practical rights of copyright holders. Because of the stronger controls afforded to cellular mobiles, as outlined above, it is arguable that intellectual property extensions, such as digital rights management and anti-circumvention measures, could well find greater support on mobile networks, as they are currently configured, than the internet in general.

Initiatives on copyright on mobile content are in their infancy, with the Open Mobile Alliance releasing a digital rights management standard in 2002, followed by version 2.0 in 2004 (OMA 2004; see discussion in de Zwart, Lindsay and Rodrick 2007). While the copyright issues – and, one might add, the user and cultural citizenship issues – are apparently clearer with mobile premium services, as a species of the 'walled garden', the rapid growth of peer-to-peer, user-generated content and content sharing, via cell phones poses a dilemma. Examples of such user-generated content include photos or video either distributed via cell phones or internet (especially via the new distributed applications such as YouTube or MySpace), or images with a significant news value provided to mainstream newspapers, magazines or television. As de Zwart, Lindsay and Rodrick argue, advanced digital rights management risks alienating users and copyright owners alike (Netanel 2007). Instead they call for a balanced approach, suggesting that there are ways of using current developments in intellectual property and copyright systems to better address the interests of all parties in mobile networks. It is fair to say that such approaches would still not go far enough for a vision of mobile commons. Two measures are probably needed here: an extension of current initiatives on commons to incorporate mobile platforms, and an identification of the intellectual property and copyright issues specific to cell phones that hinder the creation and maintenance of a commons.

To summarize: I have attempted a preliminary discussion of the different layers, and loci of control, of mobile networks. I think it is entirely feasible, indeed quite useful, to develop this into a full argument for a mobile commons, and also to develop a specific vision of what this might look like. One further impetus for such an argument is the movement reworking core landline telecommunications networks as well as next generation mobile networks to be substantially based on IP networks.

Limits of the Commons: other ways of opening up networks

As I have sought to show in this book, mobile media is quite a complicated, hybrid object, under transformation, unstable, and very much subject to different constructions from different standpoints and observers. While mobile media has developed from precursors, notably the telephone, telecommunications and cellular phone, it amounts to a complex, contingent, fractal model that cannot simply be equated to that of internet – or at least the dominant representations and thematics of internet and digital culture. The project of imagining a mobile commons is an instructive one. However, I wish to pause at this point in order to recall the limits and problems with the concept of the commons.

Construed in its broadest, most radical form, the commons is an attractive one. It about the right and ability of all to share in the resources, aspirations and wealth of a society. The near and present danger to such a vision of a commonwealth in the contemporary world is the power that a few private corporations hold over the technologies so central to our lives. This is a widely shared critique, in its best known form made by Lawrence Lessig in successive books (2000, 2001, 2004 and 2008). Lessig is concerned to highlight the stakes for 'free culture' of such a movement to lock up a society's means of expression and circulation of ideas. The countervailing logic he proposes is the commons. This is operationalized in the 'creative commons' movement. Creative Commons is an organization founded in 2001 that launched its first and best known project a year later. These are free copyright licences that 'help you license your works freely for certain uses, on certain conditions; or dedicate your works to the public domain' (Creative Commons 2009). Creative Commons licences are used in 50 jurisdictions, and there were an estimated 130 million works so licensed by 2008 (Creative Commons 2009). While a widespread, significant and sharply focused undertaking, it also has its problems. First, it is very much bound up with legal perspectives, and creates a new approach to the law governing copyright. The understanding of culture Creative Commons reveals is a narrow one, as one especially ascerbic critique has it:

> the Creative Commons network provides only a simulacrum of a commons. *It is a commons without commonalty* [authors' emphasis]. Under the name of the commons, we actually have a privatised, individuated and dispersed collection of objects and resources that subsist in a technical-legal space of confusing and differential legal restrictions, ownership rights and permissions. The Creative Commons network might enable sharing of culture goods and resources amongst possessive individuals and groups. But these goods are neither really shared in common, nor owned in common, nor accountable to the common itself. It is left to the whims of private individuals and groups to permit reuse.
>
> (Berry and Moss 2005)

Berry and Moss call for a different political imaginary to envision and activate a free culture that is radically democratic and draws different relations between individuals and collectivities (Berry and Moss 2005; see also Berry 2008 and 2009). A number of others criticize two underpinning notions of the commons movement. First, its reliance on the economically rational individual, for instance, conceived along the lines of rational choice theory. This is most evident in the pessimistic strain of Hardin's 'tragedy of the commons', for which public use of a resource most likely leads to overuse and its demise. Second, the desire of its proponents, notably Lessig when it comes to digital commons, to accommodate and improve capitalism – rather than to seek to find fundamentally different economic, social and cultural models. This is a tension in Valerie

Feldmann's idea of an innovation commons in mobile media, which is very much about creating conditions for competition, and persuading companies that they will benefit from allowing 'open access to and free use of mobile media content and services' (2005: 224). Here we might recall that telecommunications during the twentieth century in most of the world was actually something owned and controlled by citizens, through their sovereign governments and the posts-telegraph-telephone administrations they superintended. This was a public character shaping the idea of the telephone, and then telecommunications, that now has been disavowed – that comes back to haunt the neo-liberal dispensation in any case.

There are various other important critiques of the commons, not least that originate from the global South – that has real force when it comes to digital technology, at a time when the intellectual property vested interests in the global North are seeking to extend and enforce their rights, especially in the new geo-political sources of power and markets such as China. As we have seen, mobile media is an area where there is much commercial and non-commercial contest about technology and intellectual property. This is revealed by the example of copycat culture and rapidly cloned handsets in China. It is also indicated by the teeming area of everyday appropriation and invention of mobile media by users across the world, whether in the informal businesses and ways that cell phones are repaired, modified, shared, adorned, hacked or generally used in ways that fly under the radar of their inventors, deployers, merchants or controllers.

Space does not permit a full discussion of commons and its critiques, but hopefully this suffices to indicate why it is not enough to predicate a mobile commons in order to fully open up mobile networks in the service of cultural freedom. Certainly it would be useful to operationalizing creative commons instruments, practices and repositories in mobile media. However, this is only one possible starting point and trajectory for conjuring up new socio-technical futures in this realm. To further explore the stakes of opening up mobile net-works, I want to take another tack and consider mobile publics.

Mobile publics

In the discussion of the possibilities of the commons to advance a better under-standing of open mobile networks, we struck a problem with the relationship between commons and those people and things that might constitute it. There is a missing sense of commonality, but also a lack of attention to discerning and recognizing the relations of the common. The problematic here is about who has a stake in, belongs to, uses, desires, is controlled by, mobile media. We could think about this through discussions of communities, and indeed there is quite a literature on how cell phones are placed into, and effect, communities: a slim literature on mobile communities, or entities congregating through cell phones. Instead I would like to consider the public. In shorthand, 'public' is a concept that gathers together strangers, or people who do not know each other, or do not wish to be strongly and intimately affiliated. 'Community', by contrast, often has a normative sense that citizens need to be brought together in relations of identification and connection that can overcome anomie and the fate of the monad (Goggin and Crawford 2010). Now this is certainly arguable, as there is considerable, and indeed fruitful, slippage, between notions of 'public' and 'community'.

The meaning of the public and how publics historically emerge have long been important to understanding media. How do things move from being actions pertaining to, or transactions among, private individuals to becoming things that affect a greater group – that we might term the public? The North American journalist and thinker Walter Lippmann proposed a theory of the public, as a sequel to his book on public opinion. Casting a long shadow over twentieth-century media and its understanding, Lippmann was sceptical of how individuals conjoined, hence its title *The Phantom Public* (Lippmann 1925). In response, the philosopher of education and democracy, John Dewey, penned a book entitled *The Public and its Problems* (1927). Dewey suggested that publics come into interest when a group of individuals, or an interest group, have a stake in trying to control or regulate a problem – and wish to appoint and enlist officials, as a government, to use the common resources, or wealth, to adequately organize the community.

Since the 1920s, an important part of the constitution of such publics has occurred through the burgeoning media. Thus publics have emerged in relation to media forms and technologies, such as books and other artefacts of print culture, in relation to television or the internet. There has been a substantial body of work on media and publics, that seeks to develop alternatives to what is seen as the impasse of available notions, especially of the public sphere (Bennett and Carter 2001; Bohman 2004; Iveson 2007; Kolko 2003; Livingstone 2005; Warner 2005). Such work is a reprise of the debates of Lippmann and Dewey, and others, via the work of later theorists, such as James Carey, Michel Foucault and Bruno Latour (Bergman 2008; Latour 2005a; Robbins 1993; Russill 2005 and 2006). With the advent of cellular phones, there has been much debate about how this technology, and its communicative and cultural architectures and practices, participates in the redrawing of the boundaries between private and public spheres. Research into and debate on this topic continues to flourish, contending with the multiplication of both private and publics spheres (Sheller and Urry 2003), but as yet there has been little work explicitly addressing mobile publics. The most elaborated idea comes from mobilities researches (Sheller 2004; Urry 2007). Here the emphasis is on understanding how publics are now formed in more contingent, evanescent, and shifting ways than previously understood. In approaching mobile publics, we should certainly learn from the burgeoning and suggestive body of work on networked, digital publics (Boler 2008). Theorists of networked publics have been keen to recognize the place of cell phones in contemporary media. However, while there has been much work on the shape of publics in other facets of new media, especially the internet

(Boyd 2007), there has been little inquiry into cell phones. Cellular phones have often been mentioned in such discussion, indeed often featured as the emblem of new publics. However, the basic task enunciated by Mizuko Ito remains – namely to 'trace the contours of an emerging set of networked publics, describing their historical evolution and ... current controversies that are likely to shape their future' (Ito 2008: 13).

It is beyond the scope of this book to offer a full account of mobile publics, but I do propose key directions for this important project. First, there is a need for concrete studies of how publics are coming into being through mobile media (such as Nyre 2008: 66–80). Not as part of a vague, digitally converged public, but as quite distinct publics with demonstrable connections to other media cultures and publics (such as Christopher M. Kelty's 'recursive publics'; Kelty 2008). Such formations have important cultural and political implications. Through this we can also glimpse the kind of problems, demands and conditions such publics generate (Galloway 2004 and 2007; Kelty 2008). How can participants have a conversation? How can they have an argument? How are such exchanges and interactions archived – that is, what is the relationship among such mobile media and institutions of memory? What are the powers and rights of members of such publics – to use cell phones for communication, participation, cultural production, expression and exchange (as raised, for instance, by Walton and Donner 2009)? What are the responsibilities of private or public organizations providing this now valuable and publicly significant mobile media? When Google, Facebook, Twitter or Apple change their policies or practices regarding their technologies and applications, there is now immediate, clamorous debate about the changes to affordances and the implications for media cultures, and how it might cut across or threaten the activities of such publics. In contrast, there is little such debate or serious consideration of impacts of changes to mobile media upon their still only part visible publics.

Second, there is much research and discussion needed about how mobile media changes, indeed enlarges, our understanding of what publics are. Consider for instance two potential new kinds of publics, centring on mobile media: tactical assemblies formed through text messaging, camera phones; the new urban publics constituted by locative media and mobile gaming practices (Ananny and Strohecker 2009; Greenfield and Shepard 2007; Hudson and Zimmermann 2009; Townsend 2000 and 2006; Tuulos et al. 2007); the combination of sensors, data and city-dwelling and practices represented in 'participatory urbanism' (Satchell 2009).

Text messaging has drawn much attention because of its use in activism, protest and dissent. The celebrated example is the overthrow of Philippines President Joseph Estrada in 2001, brought down by popular protest in which text messaging played a key role. For Howard Rheingold, this feeds into the phenomena of 'smart mobs' (Rheingold 2002), whereas for others care needs to be taken to eschew the technological sublime, to instead understand the precise role of cell phones and messaging in social organising (Pertierra et al. 2002;

Rafael 2003). Heeding such cautionary notes, it is still possible to view the rich phenomenon of text messaging as being associated with new mobile publics. There are new kinds of assemblies, related to the use of text messaging and cell phones for gathering people together and acting in concert – whether the Madrid bombing of 11 March 2004 ('M-11') (Castells 2009: 349–61), the Sydney Cronulla riots of late 2005 (Goggin 2006), the protests in Oaxaca, Mexico, in 2006 (Martínez 2008: 125–28), the 'Green Revolution' uprising in Iran in mid-2009, or the use of text messaging in the subaltern political cultures of a number of countries – not least China (Yu 2004) – as an alternative channel for the circulation of news, gossip and satire. Then there are the ways that mobile messaging is implicated in the reworking of media cultures via participation television, and new variations on existing formats of reality and quiz television – controversial developments for many as the debate on the significance and cultural politics of China's *Super Girl* programme shows (Jian and Liu 2009; Meng 2009; Weber and Jia 2007).

A second example may be found in the new modes of urban citizenship, belonging and engagement that can be seen in the entwining of mobile media technologies, locative media, positioning technologies, mobile social software and also the urban screens movement (Boeder et al. 2006). Here mobile media are playing an important role as a technology of everyday urban life. However, their significance lies in the affordances and shaping of mobile media to participate in the emergence of a new shifting public. This mobile public is networked yet clearly located; involved in communication with intimates via cell phones, but also manifest (sometimes simultaneously) in emergent communicative architectures (such as SMS projection, installation of screens, and use of mobile media modes of interactivity); interested in gaming, but across platforms, environments and private and public lives. It can be designed and planned for, but can be unpredictable too: 'These environments avail us of the possibility for chance, indeterminacy, and random happenings to take place that may at times usurp our carefully pre-programmed events' (Crow et al. 2009: 174).

Conclusion

I would argue that the commons engages a different account of politics, and different traditions of political theory (soundly liberal, democratic and free market), than that of accounts of the publics (especially recent ones). While the commons is a very useful way to diagnose some aspects of the politics of cell phones, and also to activate measures towards addressing these (as the creative commons movements show), it does not adequately engage with other dimensions of digital culture and new media – notably in the case of cell phones, the new framing of these technologies as media.

The model of 'phone' is also problematic, if still powerful. In the co-production of the telephone and the social, I would argue that notions of community were uppermost as this talking technology developed through the twentieth century (for example, see Fischer 1992). Yet at the beginnings of the telephone, famously in the example of the Hungarian use of the telephone for broadcasting news – the celebrated Telefon Hirmondó of the 1920s – these technologies were imagined, and shaped, as media (Marvin 1988; cf. early Italian telephone history discussed in Balbi and Prario 2009). The other interesting thing about the telephone, especially as it shifts into the model of telecommunications, is that it is associated with a very strong sense of the public, bound up with specific, clearly defined notions of the nation-state, its boundaries and citizens. Mobile media creates other kinds of publics now, both transnationally and through the national and local too.

Along these lines, another way to model mobile media and to find ways to open up its networks lies in a critique of the commons, and an associated recuperation and revision of the notion of public associated with the telephone. In my mind, such an undertaking is consistent with the enlargment of media I have sought to discuss in this book; where in the case of mobile music, television, games and iInternet, cell phones are being reshaped in a way that obviously connects them with problematics of publics (and audience), familiar from other traditions of media, even the favoured new media of the present such as the internet.

Chapter 10

Culture garden
For mobile media futures

The claim of cellular mobiles to be a genuinely global technology is not in any doubt, underscored by the dizzying and still mounting numbers of cell phone subscribers, the size and scale of investment, capital and revenues in the industry, and the significance of the technology in the everyday lives of so many. The cell phone is a sufficient pliable, flexible, even ductible technology to be domesticated in very different ways by those interested in cell phones around the world. In this book, I have sought to approach cell phones as a global *media*. Naturally, I have encountered a few challenges, and pitfalls, in seeking to do this, not least in only scratching the surface of the topic. Hopefully, though, I have succeeded in showing that such a thing as global mobile media exists, and that, while still nascent, it holds quite some significance for media, culture and society; that it both resembles, and departs dramatically from, other kinds of global media; and that we have a long way to go before global mobile media is given the attention it deserves – at least in our debates over the future of our culture.

Network bases and infrastructures

I have only looked at a few areas of mobile media – music, television, games and internet – and then really only sketching some aspects of the dynamics of these. Of course, there are many others: mobile news; mobile advertising; mobile cinema; mobile learning. Nonetheless, it is possible to discern a structure of ownership and control; industry consortium, peak lobbying bodies; a set of new genres, forms and narratives; regulatory and policy institutions and discourses; imaginaries, metaphors, myths, identities and representations – associated with, and indeed making, mobile media. Like existing, or at least better established, more clearly identifiable, forms of media, mobile media is organized at a global level.

There is a concentration of power, especially in the hands of capital – as represented by the massive corporations that dominate stock exchanges and bourses worldwide, as well as the mobiles and telecommunications industry. These include carriers such as Verizon, AT&T, British Telecom, Vodafone, 3,

NTT DoCoMo, KTT and others. China Mobile is, of course, a pre-eminent player among the corporations that hold sway, but interestingly it is substantially controlled by a sovereign government (as is, for instance, SingTel Optus, owned by the Singapore government). Thus already we find a demonstration of the interplay between private capital and state wealth and control, which complicates the pure versions of neoliberalism. When it comes to mobile media, the unarguable power of such corporations plays out unevenly at the global level. For instance, while in the global media literature there are often villains of the piece, corporations that emerge as the Leviathans, exercising undemocratic sway over large swathes of the world, we find in mobile media that there are actually few pervasive, widely distributed global operations. France Télécom, Vodafone and 3 are among these, but even here we find that transnational corporations do very much work through the level of the regional and national. We need to build up a picture of global mobile media, then, from a detailed understanding of its national, regional and international parts and co-ordinates. In specific countries (Mexico, Nigeria), or regions (South America, Africa), we find new entrants helping to consolidate the fortunes and power of rich elites and bourgeoisie in these area – and, in so doing, building international alliances and blocs. Fortunately such arrangements around mobile media cannot be taken for granted. Fortunately, I say, because this means such power can be resisted and combated. As well as strong, sharply defined centres and nodes of power, we also find tensions, contradiction, even destruction.

There are struggles around the control of the current cellular mobile networks, principally in the hands of the old, or at least somewhat reformed, telecommunications carriers, and the new, if relatively concentrated and often oligopolistic mobile carriers. There has been a battle royal underway between the old dispensation of telecommunications and mobile networks, and the new barons of broadband – offering wireless internet (fast and faster), new mobile and wireless networks (mapping, positioning, sensor), internet protocol networks, digital television, IP television networks and 4G networks. Mobile companies have increasingly been challenged, or partnered, with the big mainstream media interests, as well as the new giants borne from computing or internet (Intel, Google).

Then there are the conflicts over which companies profit from offering services to customers. Here the carriers are torn between owning and operating the networks (the old business of common and private carriage) and selling services, programmes and capabilities to customers (the new business of content). In mobile media, first the premium rate service and content providers, and then all manner of service providers, media and entertainment companies, games and applications developers, mobile commerce operators, advertisers and many others, are asserting their rights to use network infrastructure and capabilities, and to compete with each other and the carriers to gain relationships with customers. Many of the regulation and policy debates since the beginning of the liberalization of telecommunications, and certainly since the inception of markets in mobile communications, have been responding to these underlying structural tensions, giving birth to mobile media.

An important part of mobile media is the role played by the technology at the edges of the network: phones, basic and smart; handhelds and wireless technologies; embedded wireless and mobile chips in all manner of new devices. The established handset, and network, equipment manufacturers such as Nokia, Samsung, LG, SonyEricsson and Motorola have long contended for the stakes over mobile networks with the carriers and service providers. With the revived interest in smartphones, especially the new entrants represented by the iPhone (Apple) and BlackBerry (RIM), vendors are in a stronger position to influence the shape of mobile media. So too are the software companies and application developers and owners, as mobile media is being opened up to much more than a computing and public internet platform.

As we can see with the various areas of mobile media discussed in this book, other interests attach to mobile media, depending on whether it is an adaptation and transformation of television, rather than games, navigation compared to music. In mobile television, we have the entry of the mobile into the field of television. Here mobile companies are a new force, with specific objectives, in how television is organized, regulated and controlled – and what forms culture in this domain takes. Mobile media here is an open question, in which new interests from the world of cellular mobile contend with the existing, if stressed, regimes of broadcasters, producers and various actors and intermediaries. Like all other media, television is an entity, once recognizable, still recognizable perhaps, but very much in the process of revision. New actors and interests come into being, neither envisaged from the side of cell phones, nor the part of television: those interested in, and invested in, social TV, for instance. Each sphere of mobile media, then, involves a reckoning with these particular entrepôts of the old media and mobile interests, and the new hybrid mobile media interests peculiar to each.

To make matters worse, or at least to make the flows and structures of power in global mobile media even more difficult to comprehend and conjure with, there are cross-hatching connections across emergent mobile media forms that are unique to this media. Navigation, location based technologies and the geospatial web (Scharl and Tochtermann 2007). Navigation and music. Games and locative media. Social software and television. Many of these rich seams are shared with other areas of new media – most obviously, the internet figures in many, if not most, of them. There is something peculiar in the nature of mobile media, as it has evolved, that makes this at least a fertile test-bed for the scrambling of many media forms, young and old; even if it is yet to be seen how this assemblage achieves a finished, 'black-box' form (at least, if only, if ever, provisionally). If mobile media is in the process of creation, and proving, crisscrossing these affordances, capabilities and forms, there is even more experimentation to be had if we factor in the local contexts for all of this; the role of particular technology development paths, cultures, languages, social and economic circumstances, in what kind of mobile media technology is supplied where, and what the range of actors, not least users, make of it.

Mapping and regulating global mobile media

The emerging political and cultural economies of global mobile media pose some obvious challenges for the analyst, industry participant or investor, developer, artist or media producer, audiences, prosumers and plain users and consumers alike.

First, there is the challenge of adequately understanding the varieties of mobile media, and how it is emerging and being organized, at a global level. While there is now already a very large literature – dispersed across economics, business and management; scientific and technological disciplines; law and policy; social psychology, anthropology and social sciences; and, to a much lesser extent, communications, media and cultural studies and humanities disciplines; not to mention a voluminous private and public discourse on mobile media in press, blogs, social media and everyday conversation – there is still much we do not know about the basic use, consumption, production, audiences, media forms and emergent institutions of mobile media, especially in countries where mobile media is only now developing, or in countries where the forms of mobile media – for example, low-tech mobile media in developing countries – have not been well recognized or understood until very recently.

Second, global mobile media, despite its predicted appearance, has largely confounded regulators and policymakers. For example, policymakers around the world – anticipating the concerns of citizenry and electorates – have wrung their hands very publicly around the perceived threat of inappropriate, sexual or anti-social content on mobile media handsets and platforms. International discussions on mobile content regulation have very heavily focused on what might be termed 'negative' content regulation. Negative content regulation stems from the need to manage, restrict, authorize, govern and regulate certain types of cultural materials. 'Negative' regulation, of course, is very productive with respect to power. At stake in debates about making mobiles – as with the internet – safe for 'families' and 'children' are very normative notions of citizens and their families. There are important links between narrow notions of regulation as the province of the state and the expanded sense of the scope and reach of regulation of society, culture and everyday life (something theorized in du Gay et al's 'circuit of culture' model; du Gay et al. 1997). This caveat aside, perceptions of what needs to be so regulated vary across cultures, social arrangements, nations and population groups. In quite a few Western countries, access of pornographic and sexual material on cell phones for minors is a priority issue for regulation. The safety of cell phones for children in the face of paedophilia, or now 'sexting' (exchange of nude or erotic pictures via mobile text by teenagers), is also very often the subject of moral panics. Yet it is important to be quite specific about which issues are most thematized in various countries, as the experience of the internet bears out – where in some countries political expression and dissent provoke much anxiety (China or Singapore, for instance), or the threat of terrorism after the New York bombings of 11 September 2001, Madrid in 2004 or Mumbai in 2008.

Despite the ostensible concerns about negative content, few countries have in place sensible, consolidated communications and media laws to deal with regulating mobile content (let alone the cross-platform media ecology, where content is reconfigured, abbreviated or adapted for a range of media, not least internet applications). Around the world, the prevalent mode of regulation in relation to many aspects of cell phones has been self-regulation. This has largely left industry in the box seat to shape important features of cell phones as cultural technologies and platforms. Self-regulation is in most cases closely bound up with forms of co-regulation. It is imperative, in my view, that those actors with an interest (especially governments entrusted with serving their publics) eschew the rhetorics of self-regulation, and as democratically as possible debate the new forms of co-regulation that frame self-regulatory schemes. In these contexts, some important concerns and groups of users are being marginalized in the current regulatory arena and effort. The combination of the focus on 'negative' aspects of mobile content and the structures of self- and co-regulation has meant that the much more economically serious impacts of predatory behaviour by companies towards their customers in mobile media are only now being taken seriously. Matters of consumer protection, in relation to accurate information on pricing, terms and conditions of contracts, customers complaints and so on, have attracted little industry or government action, and scant public or policy interest, despite their potential impact on many millions of consumers. What underlies this, I think, is a lack of interest in new forms of consumption in which cell phones are fundamentally involved.

Less prominent also in public discussion and governmental or industry policy have been 'positive' aspects of mobile content regulation, such as objectives of promoting certain sorts of desired genres, formats or national content. Canada is a very interesting example here, but it is a country in which discussions of national content have been an important part of mobile content regulation debates, as part of a general rethinking of cultural regulation of convergent media in a world where national boundaries are evidently porous in the face of such technologies.

The cell phone industry – especially the carriers as large, often cross-border companies with concerns of 'brand damage' foremost in their calculations – has not been prepared in any serious form to defend cell phones as an important space of self-expression, though smaller entities, such as content providers, have done this in practice. Further, advocates of free speech and cultural expression on the internet have not been active in mobile regulation debates, nor argued for cell phones as an open platform. Thus questions of what cultural rights citizens have with respect to commercial mobile spaces, or even public internet over mobiles, have been mostly unexplored, and indeed policies made and enacted with little public involvement or debate. It is this cultural politics of global mobile media with which the last third of this book has been concerned.

Open mobile networks

Mobile technologies are becoming important for cultural expression and production, and by extension, it might be argued, for concepts of cultural citizenship. Yet, as I have observed, cultural citizenship concerns have rarely been raised to date in mobile content regulation. There are signs of this changing as mobiles shift into the heartland of media, and so impinge on traditional rights and expectations felt to arise when discussing newspapers, radio or television. Indeed debates about mobile television have shown signs of cell phones being taken seriously as a cultural, as much as communications, technology. However, the area where cultural citizenship concerns, and indeed cultural political issues have been raised, is in the brave new world of smartphones and apps that the 'iPhone moment' represents. As I have argued, the iPhone and the apps phenomenon highlight the possibilities and potential of mobile media platforms – and their importance. Smartphones are not new, nor are applications. The iPhone has, however, galvanized users, developers, industry, policy makers and a range of publics alike, to articulate their concerns and desires regarding mobile media.

It is a good time to elaborate an agenda and usher in an urgent debate about open mobile networks, their affordances, conditions, models, users, audiences, publics and implications. There have been isolated and fitful attempts to do this, of course. There have also been gestures towards incorporating cell phones into the passionate general debates about access, connectivity, representation, resources, legibility, audibility and visibility in digital cultures; however, as I have suggested, typically cell phones have been added, or annexed, to accounts largely modelled on a narrow understanding of the internet. It is not simply a matter of decrying cell phones for their 'walled gardens', as compared to the untethered internet that needs nurturing. Rather, the interplay of commercial and non-commercial forces, spaces and facilities for culture on mobile platforms needs to be understood, and tended. Global mobile media could indeed be, to coin a phrase, a fertile garden for culture. Thus we sorely need a detailed, grounded set of analyses, maps and debates on how mobile media are unfolding, what their cultural politics are, as well as some vivid, materially attuned yet utopian imaginings of what kinds of cultural futures might be possible with mobiles, and how we could bring this about.

Bibliography

3rd Generation Partnership Projects (3GPP) (2009) 'LTE', 3GPP, http://www.3gpp.org/article/lte (accessed 1 November 2009).

Aarseth, E. (2001) 'Allegories of space: the question of spatiality in computer games', in M. Eskelinen and R. Koskimaa (eds) *CyberText Yearbook 2000*, Jyväskylä: Research Centre for Contemporary Culture, University of Jyväskylä.

Adegoke, Y. (2002) 'The relationship between the fan and the artist', *Financial Times*, 26 November, 20.

Adesope, O., Olubunmi, S. and McCracken, J. (2007) 'Implementing mobile learning in developing countries: Prospects and challenges', in C. Montgomerie and J. Seale (eds) *Proceedings of world conference on educational multimedia, hypermedia and telecommunications 2007*, Chesapeake, VA: AACE.

Advertising Standards Authority (ASA) (2009) 'A Frog's Tale that spawned viewer outrage', http://www.asa.org/ (accessed 16 December 2009).

Age (1960) 'Telephone ring maybe bird whistle', *The Age* (Melbourne), 24 September, 4.

Aitken, R. (2007) *Performing Capital: toward a cultural economy of popular and global finance*, Basingstoke: Palgrave Macmillan.

Akkawi, A., Schaller, S., Wellnitz, O. and Wolf, L. (2004) 'Networked mobile gaming for 3G-networks', in M. Rauterberg (ed.) *Entertainment Computing – ICEC 2004*, Berlin: Springer, 457–67.

Alam, M. and Prasad, N. (2008) 'Convergence transforms digital home: techno-economic impact', *Wireless Personal Communication*, 44: 75–93.

Alampay, E. A. (2008) 'Filipino entrepreneurs on the Internet: when social networking websites meet mobile commerce', *Science Technology & Society*, 13: 211–31.

Albarran, A. B. and Chan-Olmsted, S. M. (eds) (1998) *Global Media Economics: commercialization, concentration and integration of world media markets*, Ames, IA: Iowa State University Press.

Alemán, A. M. Martínez and Wartman, K. L. (2009) *Online Social Networking on Campus: understanding what matters in student culture*, New York: Routledge.

Allan, Stuart (2006) *Online News: Journalism and the Internet*, Maidenhead and New York: Open University Press.

Allan, S. and Thorsen, E. (eds) (2009) *Citizen Journalism: Global Perspectives*, New York: Peter Lang, 2009.

Alleman, J. and Rappoport, P. (2009) 'Next generation networks: the demand side issues', in P. Curwen, J. Haucap and B. Preissl (eds) *Telecommunications Markets: drivers and impediments*, Berlin: Springer, 396–414.

Allen, K. (2009) 'Hints of deal with Apple lift software firm', *Guardian.co.uk*, http://www.guardian.co.uk/business/2009/aug/20/katie-allen-market-forces-column, 20 August (accessed 4 September 2009).

Alves, V., Matos Jr., P., Cole, L., Borba, P. and Ramalho, G. (2005) 'Extracting and evolving mobile games product lines', in H. Obbink and K. Pohl (eds) *Proceedings of 9th International Software Product Line conference*, Rennes, France, 26–29 September, 70–81.

América Móvil (2008) *Annual Report*, http://www.americamovil.com/ (accessed 15 July 2010).

Ananny, M. and Strohecker, C. (2009) 'TexTales: creating interactive forums with urban publics', in M. Foth (ed.) *Handbook of Research on Urban Informatics: the practice and promise of the real-time city*, Hershey, PA: Information Science Reference, 68–86.

Anderson, C. (2006) *The Long Tail: why the future of business is selling less of more*, New York: Hyperion.

——(2009) *Free: the future of a radical price*, New York: Hyperion.

Andersson, P. and Rosenqvist, C. (2006) 'Mobile music, customer value, and changing market needs', *International Journal on Media Management*, 8: 92–103.

Andrews, R. (2009) 'Li Ka-Shing confirms Spotify stake, will tie up with 3, INQ', PDA: The Digital Content Blog, *Guardian.co.uk*, http://www.guardian.co.uk/media/pda/2009/aug/21/spotify-mobilephones, 21 August (accessed 4 September 2009).

Android (2009a) 'Android Market Content Policy for Developers', http://www.android.com/market/terms/developer-content-policy.html (accessed 28 August 2009).

——(2009b) 'Market Developer Distribution Agreement', http://www.android.com/us/developer-distribution-agreement.html (accessed 28 August 2009).

——(2009c) 'Publishing on Android Market', http://developer.android.com/guide/publishing/publishing.html#market (accessed 28 August 2009).

——(2009d) 'What is Android?', http://www.android.com/about/ (accessed 28 August 2009).

Anheier, H., Isar, Y. R, Paul, A. and Cunningham, S. (eds) (2008) *The Cultural Economy*, Thousand Oaks, CA and London: Sage.

Annable, G., Goggin, G. and Stienstra, D. (eds) (2007) 'Accessibility and inclusion in information technologies,' special issue of *The Information Society*, 23.

Annetta, L. A. (ed.) (2008) *Serious Educational Games: from theory to practice*, Rotterdam, Taipei: Sense Publishers.

Anwar, S. T. (2002) 'NTT DoCoMo and M-Commerce: a case study in market expansion and global strategy', *Thunderbird International Business Review*, 44: 139–64.

——(2003) 'Vodafone and the wireless industry: a case in market expansion and global strategy', *Journal of Business & Industrial Marketing*, 18: 270–88.

Aoyama, Y. and Izushi, H. (2003) 'Hardware gimmick or cultural innovation? technological, cultural, and social foundations of the Japanese video game industry', *Research Policy*, 32: 423–44.

Apple (2008) 'Accelerometer: Made to move', http://www.apple.com/iphone/features/accelerometer.html (accessed 13 May 2010).

——(2009a) 'Vision', http://www.apple.com/accessibility/iphone/vision.html (accessed 15 July 2009).

——(2009b) 'App submission', iPhone Developer Program Support, http://developer.apple.com/support/iphone/appsubmission/ (accessed 28 August 2009).

Aquino, N. P. (2005) 'Mobile games open up new revenue channel', *Businessworld*, February, 1.

Ardito, C., Buono, P., Costabile, M. F., Lanzilotti, R. and Piccinno, A. (2009) 'Enabling interactive exploration of cultural heritage: an experience of designing systems for mobile devices', *Knowledge, Technology & Policy*, 22: 79–86.

Åresund, M. (2006) *Nordic Playground*, Oslo: Nordic Innovation Centre, http://www. nordicinnovation.net/_img/042464_nordic_playground_final_report.pdf (accessed 14 November 2009).

Arnaldi, T. (2004) 'Mobile social software applications', http://www.elasticspace.com/ 2004/06/mobile-social-software (accessed 8 December 2009).

Arthur, C. (2009) 'Facebook prepares "Facebook Lite" for mobile and dialup abroad', 12 August, *Guardian*, http://www.guardian.co.uk/technology/2009/aug/12/facebook- lite-india-china-russia-asia (accessed 15 October 2009).

Ash, A. and Thrift, N. (eds) (2004) *The Blackwell Cultural Economy Reader*, Malden, MA: Blackwell.

Augusto, C. (2007) 'Hope for iPhone access?!', 27 July, www.afb.org/blog/blog_ comments.asp?TopicID=3030 (accessed 15 July 2009).

Australian Communications Consumer Action Network (ACCAN) (2009) *Future Consumer: emerging consumer issues in telecommunications, convergent communication and media*, Sydney: ACCAN.

Australian Interactive Media Industry Association (AIMIA) 2009, *Australian mobile phone lifestyle index*, Sydney: AIMIA, http://www.aimia.com.au/enews/mobile/090929% 20AIMIA_Report_FINAL.pdf (accessed 26 May 2010).

Babe, R.E. (1995) *Communication and the Transformation of Economics: essays in information, public policy, and political economy*, Boulder, CO: Westview Press.

——(2009) *Cultural Studies and Political Economy: toward a new integration*, Lanham, MD: Lexington Books.

Baek, J., Jang, I.-J., Park, K., Kang, H.-S. and Yun, B.-J. (2006) 'Human computer interaction for the accelerometer-based mobile game', in E. Sha et al. (eds) *Proceedings of Embedded and Ubiquitous Computing 2006*, Seoul, 1–4 August, 509–18.

Balbi, G. and Prario, B. (2009) 'Back to the future: the past and present of mobile TV', in G. Goggin and L. Hjorth (eds) *Mobile Technologies: from telecommunications to media*, New York: Routledge, 161–73.

Ballon, P. and Delaere, S. (2009) 'Flexible spectrum and future business models for the mobile industry', *Telematics and Informatics*, 26: 249–58.

Ballon, P., Van Audenhove, L., Poel, M. and Staelens, T. (2009) 'Business models for wireless city networks in the EU and the US: public inputs and public leverage', in P. Curwen, J. Haucap and B. Preissl (eds), *Telecommunications Markets: drivers and impedi- ments*, Berlin: Springer, 325–40.

Balnaves, M., Donald, J. and Donald, S. H. (2001) *The Global Media Atlas*, London: British Film Institute.

Bardhan, P. and Ray, I. (eds) (2008) *The Contested Commons: conversations between economists and anthropologists*, Malden, MA, and Oxford: Blackwell.

Barkhuus, L., Chalmers, M., Tennent, P., Hall, M., Bell, M., Sherwood, S. and Brown, B. (2005) 'Picking pockets on the lawn: the development of tactics and strategies in a mobile game', in M. Beigl, S. Intille, J. Rekimoto and H. Tokuda (eds) *UbiComp 2005*, Berlin: Springer, 358–74.

Barking Robot (2006) 'Mobile social software, Gen Y & digital learning styles', *Barking Robot*, 15 June, http://www.debaird.net/blendededunet/2006/06/mobile_social_s.html (accessed 8 December 2009).

Barthold, J. (2009) '4G status report: making the 4G decision', *Fierce Wireless*, 11 March, http://www.fiercewireless.com/story/4g-status-report-making-4g-decision/2009-03-1(accessed 31 October 2009).

Bassett, C. (2008) 'New maps for old?: the cultural stakes of "2.0" ', *Fibreculture Journal* 13, http://journal.fibreculture.org/issue13/issue13_bassett.html

Bassoli, A., Moore, J. and Agamanolis, S. (2006) 'TunA: socialising music sharing on the move', in K. O'Hara and B. Brown (eds) *Consuming Music Together: social and collaborative aspects of music consumption technologies*, Berlin: Springer.

Battelle, J. (2005) *The Search: how Google and its rivals rewrote the rules of business and transformed our culture*, New York: Portfolio.

Bedia, A. (2005) 'Primera prueba piloto en España: Arranca la era de la TV en el móvil,' *Terra – Tecnología*, 26 October, http://www.terra.es/tecnologia/articulo/html/tec13422.htm (accessed 15 October 2007).

Bell, M., Chalmers, M., Barkhuus, L., Hall, M., Sherwood, S., Tennent, P., Brown, B., Rowland, D. and Benford, S. (2006) 'Interweaving mobile games with everyday life', *Proceeding of the SIGCHI conf. on Human Factors in computing systems*, New York: ACM Press, 417–26.

Bendas, D. and Myllyaho, M. (2002) 'Games as part of mobile entertainment', *Proceedings of the PROFES 2002 conference*, 9–11 December, Rovaniemi, Finland, Berlin: Springer.

Benkler, Y. (2006) *The Wealth of Networks: how social production transforms markets and freedom*, New Haven, CT and London: Yale University Press.

Benn, L. J. and Kachieng'a, M. O. (2005) 'Mobile data services in the South African wireless industry: a new value chain', *International Journal of Technology, Policy and Management*, 5: 121–31.

Bennett, T. and Carter, D. (eds) (2001) *Culture in Australia: policies, publics and programs*, Cambridge and New York: Cambridge University Press.

Bergman, M. (2008) 'The new wave of pragmatism in communication studies', *Nordicom Review*, 29: 135–53.

Berners-Lee, T. (2007) 'The mobile web', keynote address, 15 February, *3GSM World*, Barcelona, http://www.w3.org/2007/Talks/0222-23gsm-tbl/text.html (accessed 28 October 2009).

Berry, D. M. (2008) *Copy, Rip, Burn: the politics of copyleft and open source*, London: Pluto Press.

——(2009) 'A contribution towards a grammar of code', *Fibreculture Journal* 13, http://journal.fibreculture.org/issue13/issue13_mackenzie.html (accessed 13 May 2010).

Berry, D.M. and Moss, G. (2005) 'On the "Creative Commons": a critique of the commons without commonalty. Is the Creative Commons missing something?', *Free Software Magazine*, 5, June, 1–4.

Beschizza, R. (2007a) 'Eight great Linux smartphones' *Wired*, 2 March, http://www.wired.com/gadgetlab/2007/03/eight_great_lin/ (accessed 15 August 2009).

——(2007b) 'Speaking freely: unlocked, open source phones for weary iPhone hackers', 10 October, http://www.wired.com/gadgets/wireless/multimedia/2007/10/gallery_linux_phones (accessed 15 August 2009).

——(2008) 'Who dares call Garmin's Nuviphone an iPhone-killer?', *Wired.com*, 31 January, http://www.wired.com/gadgetlab/2008/01/who-dares-call/ (accessed 15 August 2009).

Best, J. and Paterson, M. (eds) (2009) *Cultural Political Economy*, London and New York: Routledge.

Bichard, J., Brunnberg, L., Combetto, M., Gustafsson, A. and Juhlin, O. (2006) 'Backseat playgrounds: pervasive storytelling in vast location based games' in R. Harper, M. Rauterberg and M. Combetto (eds) *Proceedings of 5th International Conference on Entertainment Computing*, ICEC 2006, 20–22 September, Cambridge, 117–22.

Bilandzic, M. and Foth, M. (2009) 'Social navigation and local folksonomies: technical and design considerations for a mobile information system', in S. Hatzipanagos and S. Warburton (eds) *Social Software and Developing Community Ontologies*, Hershey, PA: IGI Global, 52–66.

Bitzer, J. and Schröder, P. (eds) (2006) *The Economics of Open Software Development*, Amsterdam and Oxford: Elsevier.

Bloustien, G., Peters, M. and Luckman, S. (2008) *Sonic Synergies: music, technology, community, identity*, Burlington, VT and Aldershot: Ashgate.

Blum, J., Chipchase, J. and Lehikoinen, J. (2005) 'Contextual and cultural challenges for user mobility research', *Communications of the ACM*, 48: 37–41.

Boeder, P., Lovink, G., Niederer, S. and Struppek, M. (eds) (2006) 'Urban screens: discovering the potential of outdoor screens for urban society', *First Monday*, special issue 4, 11.2, http://www.firstmonday.org/issues/special11_2/index.html (accessed 13 May 2010).

Bogost, I. (2007) *Persuasive Games: the expressive power of videogames*, Cambridge, MA: MIT Press.

Bohlin, E., Burgelman, J.-C. and Casal, R. C. (2007) 'Special issue on mobile communications: from cellular to ad-hoc and beyond', *Telematics and Informatics*, 24: 161–63.

Bohman, J. (2004) 'Expanding dialogue: the Internet, the public sphere and the prospects for transnational democracy' in N. Crossley and J. M. Roberts (eds) *After Habermas: new perspectives on the public sphere*, London: Blackwell, 131–55.

Boler, M. (ed.) (2008) *Digital Media and Democracy: tactics in hard times*, Cambridge MA: MIT Press.

Bolle, N. (2000) 'Most everywhere – musical ringtones', *Guardian*, 14 July, 9.

Borrás, S. (2003) *The Innovation Policy of the European Union: from government to governance*, London: Edward Elgar.

Bouwman, H., Carlsson, C., Walden, P., and Molina-Castillo, F. J. (2008) 'Trends in mobile services in Finland 2004–6: from ringtones to mobile internet', *info*, 10: 75–93.

——(2009) 'Reconsidering the actual and future use of mobile services', *Information Systems and e-Business Management*, 7: 301–17.

Boyd, D. (2004) 'Friendster and publicly articulated social networking', in *Proceedings of the ACM CHI Conference on Human Factors in Computing Systems*, Vienna, Austria: ACM Press, 1279–82.

——(2007) 'Why youth (heart) social network sites: the role of networked publics in teenage social life', in D. Buckingham (ed.), *Youth, Identity, and Digital Media*, Cambridge, MA: MIT Press, 119–42.

——(2008) 'Facebook's privacy trainwreck: exposure, invasion, and social convergence', *Convergence*, 14: 13–20.

Boyd, D. and Ellison, N. (2007) 'Social network sites: definition, history, and scholarship', *Journal of Computer-Mediated Communication*, 13.1, article 11, http://jcmc.indiana.edu/vol13/issue1/boyd.ellison.html (accessed 13 May 2010).

Boyera, S. (2006) 'The mobile web in developing countries: the next steps', http://www.w3.org/2006/12/digital_divide/public.html (accessed 28 October 2009).

——(2009) 'Mobile Web for Social Development Roadmap', 17 November, http://www.w3.org/TR/2009/NOTE-mw4d-roadmap-20091117/ (accessed 8 December 2009).

Braet, O. and Ballon, P. (2008) 'Cooperation models for mobile television in Europe', *Telematics and Informatics*, 25: 216–36.

Breuer, H. (2009) 'Ubiquitous society: cultural factors driving mobile innovations and adoptions in Japan', in Nuray Aykin (ed.) *Proceedings of the Third International Conference on Internationalization, Design and Global Development*, San Diego, 19–24 July, Berlin: Springer, 328–36.

Brewer, J. and Dourish, P. (2008) 'Storied spaces: cultural accounts of mobility, technology, and environmental knowing', *International Journal of Human Computer Studies*, 66: 963–76.

Bria, A., Kärrberg, P. and Andersson, P. (2007) 'TV in the mobile or TV for the mobile: challenges and changing value chains', *Proceedings of 18th annual IEEE International Symposium on Personal, Indoor and Mobile Radio Communications*, 3–7 September, Athens.

Brightkite (2009a) 'All about Brightkite', http://brightkite.com/pages/bk_about.html (accessed 7 December 2009).

——(2009b) 'Raising the Kite-up in Kansas and Tokyo' 8 November, http://blog.brightkite.com/2009/07/13/how-to-organize-a-kiteup/ (accessed 7 December 2009).

Broll, G. and Benford, S. (2005) 'Seamful design for location-based mobile games' in F. Kishino, Y. Kitamura, H. Kato and N. Nagata (eds) *Proceedings of 4th International Conference on Entertainment Computing*, 19–21 September, Sanda, Japan and Berlin: Springer, 155–66.

Brown, M. B. (2009) *Science in Democracy: expertise, institutions, and representation*, Cambridge, MA: MIT Press.

Brown-Humes, C. (2001) 'Survey – Finland – Behemoth maintains growth prospects while rivals begin to feel the chill', *Financial Times*, 5 July, 10.

——(2002) 'Sony Ericsson in mobile games trial', *Financial Times*, 22 December, 16.

Bruno, A. (2007) 'Mobile milestones', *Billboard*, 22 December, 28.

——(2008a) 'Big stars – small screens', *Billboard*, 5 April, 30.

——(2008b) 'Create and innovate: music, mobile sectors must continue to work together', *Billboard*, 5 April, 14.

——(2008c) 'Handset heat', *Billboard*, 5 April, 32–34.

——(2008d) 'Tero Ojanpera & Dave Stewart', *Billboard*, 5 April, 25.

Bruns, A. (2008) *Blogs, Wikipedia, Second Life, and beyond: from production to produsage*, New York: Peter Lang.

Buck, S. (2002) 'Replacing spectrum auctions with a spectrum commons', *Stanford Technology Law Review*, 2, http://stlr.stanford.edu/STLR/Articles/02_STLR_2 (accessed 10 December 2009).

Buellingen, F. and Woerter, M. (2004) 'Development perspectives, firm strategies and applications in mobile commerce', *Journal of Business Research*, 57: 1402–8.

Bull, M. (2007) *Sound Moves: iPod culture and urban experience*, London: Routledge.

Burger, R. A., Jacovoni, G., Reader, C., Fu, X., Yang, X. and Hui, W. (2007) 'A survey of digital TV standards in China', *Proceedings of the Second International Conference on Communications and Networking in China*, 22–24 August, Shanghai, 687–96.

Burgess, J. and Green, J. (2009) *The Uses of YouTube: online video and the politics of participatory culture*, Cambridge: Polity.

Burke, B. E. (2001) 'Hardin revisited: a critical look at perception and the logic of the commons', *Human Ecology*, 29: 449–76.

Butler, S. (2006) 'Putting mobile digital markets first: Sony/ATV, Jamster sign ringtone co-publishing deal in Germany', *Billboard*, 19 August, 16.

Callois, R. (2001) *Man, Play and Games*, trans. M. Barash, Urbana, IL: University of Illinois Press.

Canberra Times (1933) 'Morning alarm: new phone service', *Canberra Times*, 24 March, 1.

Carlsson, C. and Walden, P. (2007) 'Mobile TV — to live or die by content', Proceedings of the 40th Hawaii International Conference on System Sciences, http://doi.ieee-computersociety.org/10.1109/HICSS.2007.382 (accessed 26 May 2010).

Carpentier, N. and De Cleen, B. (eds) (2008) *Participation and Media Production: critical reflections on content creation*, Newcastle: Cambridge Scholars.

Castells, M. (2009).*Communication Power*, Oxford and New York: Oxford University Press.

Castells, M., Fernández-Ardèvol, M., Qui, J. L. and Sey, A. (2007) *Mobile Communication and Society: a global perspective*, Cambridge, MA: MIT Press.

Castronova, E. (2006) *Synthetic Worlds: the business and culture of online games*, Chicago, IL: The University of Chicago Press.

Chabossou, A., Stork, C., Stork, M. and Zahonogo, P. (2008) 'Mobile telephony access and usage in Africa', *South African Journal of Information and Communication*, 9, http://www.sajic.org.za/index.php/SAJIC/article/view/191 (accessed 13 May 2010).

Chakravartty, P. and Zhao, Y. (eds) (2007) *Global Communications: Toward a transcultural political economy*, Lanham, MD: Rowman & Littlefield.

Chan, A. B. (2008) 'Creating wealth in twenty-first century China: Li Ka-shing and his progenies', *Asian Affairs: An American Review*, 34: 193–210.

Chan-Olmsted, S. M. (2006) 'Content development for the third screen: the business and strategy of mobile content and applications in the United States', *International Journal on Media Management*, 8: 51–59.

Chan-Olmsted, S.M. and Jamison, M.A. (2001) 'Rivalry through alliances: Competitive strategy in the global telecommunications market', *European Management Journal*, 19: 317–31.

Chehimi, F., Coulton, P. and Edwards, R. (2008) 'Evolution of 3D mobile games development', *Personal and Ubiquitous Computing*, 12: 19–25.

Cheok, A. D., Yang, X., Ying, Z. Z., Billinghurst, M. and Kato, H. (2002) 'Touch-space: mixed reality game space based on ubiquitous, tangible, and social computing', *Personal and Ubiquitous Computing*, 6: 430–42.

Chicago Daily Tribune (1962) 'Better dial ahead on phone plans', *Chicago Daily Tribune*, 12 May, N17.

Chigona, A. and Chigona, W. (2009) 'MXit up in the media: media discourse analysis on a mobile instant messaging system', *Southern African Journal of Information and Communication*, 9: 42–57.

Choi, J. H.-j. (2010) 'The city, self, and connections: "transyouth" and urban social networking in Seoul', in S. H. Donald, T. D. Anderson and D. Spry (eds) *Youth, Society and Mobile Media in Asia*, London and New York: Routledge, 88–107.

Choi, J. Y., Koh, D. and Lee, J. (2008) 'Ex-ante simulation of mobile TV market based on consumers' preference data', *Technological Forecasting & Social Change*, 75: 1043–53.

Chopra, S. and Dexter, S. (2008) *Decoding Liberation: the promise of free and open source software*, Oxford: Routledge.

Christ, P. and Pogrzeba, P. (1999) 'Introducing mobile multimedia broadcasting services', in H. Leopold and N. Garcia (eds), *Proceedings of 4th European Conference on Multimedia Applications, Services and Techniques 1999*, Madrid, May, Berlin: Springer, 564–72.

Clapperton, D. and Corones, S. (2007) 'Technological tying of the Apple iPhone: unlawful in Australia?', *QUT Law & Justice Journal*, 21, http://www.austlii.edu.au/au/journals/QUTLJJ/2007/21.html (accessed 1 September 2009).

Cohen, M. G. and Brodie, J. (eds) (2007) *Remapping Gender in the New Global Order*, London and New York: Routledge.

Coiana, M., Conconi, A., Nigay, L. and Ortega, M. (2008) 'Test-bed for multimodal games on mobile devices', in P. Markopoulos et al. (eds) *Fun and Games 2008*, Berlin: Springer, 75–87.

Collins, B. (2002) 'Multifaceted mobile', *Sunday Times*, 24 March, 55.

Collins, K. (2008) *Game Sound: an introduction to the history, theory and practice of video game music and sound design*, Cambridge, MA: MIT Press.

Consalvo, M. (2006) 'Console video games and global corporations: creating a hybrid culture', *New Media & Society*, 8: 117–37.

——(2009) 'There is no magic circle', *Games and Culture*, 4: 408–17.

Consentino, G. (2006) '"Hacking" the iPod: a look inside Apple's portable music player', in Michael D. Ayers (ed.) *Cybersounds: essays on virtual music culture*, New York: Peter Lang, 185–207.

Corneliussen, H. G. and Rettberg, J. W. (eds) (2008) *Digital Culture, Play and Identity: a World of Warcraft® reader*, Cambridge, MA: MIT Press.

Cowhey, P. F. & Aronson, J.D. (2009) *Transforming Global Information and Communication Markets: the political economy of innovation*, Cambridge, MA: MIT Press.

Crabtree, A., Benford, S., Capra, M., Flintham, M., Drozd, A., Tandavanitj, N., Adams, M. and Farr, J. R. (2007) 'The cooperative work of gaming: orchestrating a mobile SMS game', *Computer Supported Cooperative Work*, 16: 167–98.

Crack, A. (2008) *Global Communication and Transnational Public Spheres*, New York: Palgrave Macmillan.

Crawford, A. (2008) 'Taking social software to the streets: mobile cocooning and the (an-)erotic city', *Journal of Urban Technology*, 15: 79–97.

Crawford, K. (2009a) 'Following you: disciplines of listening in social media', *Continuum*, 23: 523–35.

——(2009b) 'These foolish things: on intimacy and insignificance in mobile media', in G. Goggin and L. Hjorth (eds) *Mobile Technologies: from telecommunications to media*, New York: Routledge, 250–63.

Creative Commons (2009) 'About history', http://creativecommons.org/about/history (accessed 26 May 2010).

Crow, B. and Sawchuk, K. (2006) 'Letter from the editors', *Wi: Journal of Mobile Media*, http://wi.hexagram.ca/?p=3 (accessed 9 December 2009).

Crow, B., Longford, M., Sawchuk, K. and Zeffiro, Z. (2009) 'Voices from beyond: ephemeral histories, locative media and the volatile interface', in M. Foth (ed.) *Handbook of Research on Urban Informatics: the practice and promise of the real-time city*, Hershey, PA: Information Science Reference, 158–78.

Crowley, D. (2008) 'The Dodgeball shut-down party', http://www.flickr.com/photos/dpstyles/3294855253/ (accessed 26 May 2010).

Cui, Y., Chipchase, J. and Jung, Y. (2006) 'Personal TV: a qualitative study of mobile TV users', http://www.janchipchase.com/blog/presentations/MobileTVPersonalTV_vFinal_External.pdf (accessed 3 December 2009).

Cunningham. S. (2008) *In the Vernacular: a generation of Australian culture and controversy*, Brisbane: University of Queensland Press.

Cunningham, S. and Potts, J. (2009) 'New economics for the new media', in G. Goggin and L. Hjorth (eds) *Mobile Technologies: from telecommunications to media*, New York: Routledge, 131–42.

Cunningham, S. and Sinclair, J. (eds) (1994) 'Global Media Games', special issue of *Media International Australia*, 71.

Curtin, M. and Shah, H. (eds) (2010) *Reorienting Global Communication: Indian and Chinese media beyond borders*, Urbana, IL: University of Illinois Press.

Curwen, P. (1997) *Restructuring Telecommunications: a study of Europe in a global context*, London: Macmillan.

——(2002) *The Future of Mobile Communications: awaiting the third generation*, Houndsmill, Basingstone: Palgrave Macmillan.

Curwen, P. and Whalley, J. (2004) *Telecommunications Strategy: cases, theory and applications*, London: Routledge.

——(2005) 'Structural change in African mobile telecommunications', *Communications and Strategies* Special Issue, WSIS 2005: 55–63.

——(2008a) *The Internationalisation of Mobile Telecommunications: strategic challenges in a global market*, Northampton, MA and Cheltenham: Edward Elgar.

——(2008b) 'Structural adjustment in the Latin American and African mobile sectors', *Telecommunications Policy*, 32: 349–63.

——(2008c) 'Mobile television: technological and regulatory issues', *info*, 10.1: 40–64.

——(2009) 'Can competition be introduced via the issue of new mobile telephony licences: the experience of 3G licensing in Europe', in P. Curwen, J. Haucap and B. Preissl (eds) *Telecommunications Markets: drivers and impediments*, Berlin: Springer, 265–82.

Damsgaard, J., Parikh, M. A. and Bharat, R. (2006) 'Wireless commons perils in the common good', *Communications of the ACM*, 49: 105–9.

Danet, B. and Herring, S. C. (eds) (2007) *The Multilingual Internet: language, culture, and communication online*, New York: Oxford University Press.

Dasgupta, P., Mäler, K.-G. and Vercelli, A. (eds) (1997) *The Economics of Transnational Commons*, Oxford and New York: Oxford University Press.

Davidsson, O., Peitz, J. and Björk, S. (2004) *Game Design Patterns for Mobile Games*, project report, Nokia Research Centre, Finland, http://procyon.lunarpages.com/~gamed3/docs/Game_Design_Patterns_for_Mobile_Games.pdf (accessed 14 November 2009).

Deek, F. P. and McHugh, J. A. (2008) *Open Source: technology and policy*, Cambridge and New York: Cambridge University Press.

Defeo, M. (2008) 'Unlocking the iphone: how antitrust law can save consumers from the inadequacies of copyright law', *Boston Law Review*, 49: 1037–80.

Dena, C. (2009) 'Released: ARG around the world data', 30 March, http://www.christydena.com/2009/03/released-args-around-the-world-data/ (accessed 15 November 2009).

DeNardis, L. (2009) 'Open standards and global politics', *International Journal of Communications Law and Policy*, 13: 168–84.

Dennis, T. (2003) 'Botfighters – a new Russian addiction', 21 October, *Inquirer*, http://www.theinquirer.net/inquirer/news/1005392/botfighters (accessed 13 May 2010).

Dewey, J. (1927) *The Public and its Problems*, New York: H. Holt.

De Zwart, M., Lindsay, D. and Rodrick, S. (2007) 'Mobile Phones: copyright in content', in G. Goggin and L. Hjorth (eds) *Mobile Media*, Sydney: Department of Media and Communications, University of Sydney, 276–87.

Digital Multimedia Broadcasting (DMB) (2006) 'Dynamic market', http://eng.t-dmb.org/ (accessed 2 December 2009).

Dodgeball (2003) 'Dodgeball.com', http://web.archive.org/web/*/http://www.dodgeball. com (accessed 26 May 2010).

Dodson, S. (2002) 'Ready, aim, text', *Guardian*, 15 August, http://www.guardian.co.uk/ technology/2002/aug/15/electronicgoods.games (accessed 13 May 2010).

Dolan, D.P. (2000) 'The big bumpy shift: digital music via mobile Internet', *First Monday*, 5. 12, http://firstmonday.org/issues/issue5_12/dolan/index.html (accessed 13 May 2010).

Donner, J. (2007) 'The rules of beeping: exchanging messages via intentional-missed calls on mobile phones', *Journal of Computer-Mediated Communication*, 13.1, http://jcmc.indiana. edu/vol13/issue1/donner.html (accessed 13 May 2010).

——(2008) 'Research approaches to mobile use in the developing world: a review of the literature', *The Information Society*, 24: 140–59.

——(2009a) 'Blurring livelihoods and lives: the social uses of mobile phones and socioeconomic development', *Innovations: Technology, Governance, Globalization*, 4: 91–101.

——(2009b) 'Mobile media on low-cost handsets: The resiliency of text messaging among small enterprises in India (and beyond)', in G. Goggin and L. Hjorth (eds) *Mobile Technologies: from telecommunications to media*, New York: Routledge, 93–104.

Dovey, J. and Kennedy, H. W. (2003) *Game Cultures: computer games as new media*, New York and Maidenhead: Open University Press.

Drescher, P. (2008) 'Ringtones and mobile phones: could ringtones be more annoying?' in K. Collins (ed.) *From Pac-Man to Pop Music: interactive audio in games and new media*, Burlington, VT and Aldershot: Ashgate, 47–54.

Dryer, D.C., Eisbach, C. and Ark, W.S. (1999) 'At what cost pervasive? A social computing view of mobile computing systems', *IBM Systems Journal*, 38: 652.

Ducheneaut, N., Oehlberg, L., Moore, R.J., Thornton, J.D. and Nickell, E. (2008) 'Social TV: designing for distributed, sociable television viewing', *International Journal of Human-Computer Interaction*, 24: 136–54.

Duckworth, W. (2005) *Virtual Music: how the web got wired for sound*, London and New York: Routledge.

Du Gay, P. and Pryke, M. (eds) (2002) *Cultural Economy*, Thousand Oaks, CA: Sage.

Du Gay, P., Hall, S., Janes, L., Mackay, H. and Negus, K. (1997) *Doing Cultural Studies: the story of the Sony Walkman*, Milton Keynes: Open University; Thousand Oaks, CA: Sage.

Duh, H. B.-L., Chen, V. H. H. and Tan, C. B. (2008) 'Playing different games on different phones: an empirical study on mobile gaming', *Proceedings of the 10th international conference on human computer interaction with mobile devices and services*, Amsterdam, 2–5 September, New York: ACM, 391–94.

Dyer, K. (2009) 'Operators offer unity on DVB-H handset demands', *Mobile Europe*, 1 December, http://www.mobileeurope.co.uk/news_analysis/115280/Operators_offer_ unity_on_DVB-H_handset_demands.html (accessed 2 December 2009).

Eagle, N. (2004) 'Can serendipity be planned?', *MIT Sloan Management Review*, 46: 9–14.

Eagle, N. and Pentland, A. (2005) 'Social serendipity: mobilizing social software' *IEEE Pervasive Computing*, 2: 28–34.

Engstörm, A., Norlin, C., Esbjörnsson, M. and Juhlin, O. (2007) 'More TV! support for local and collaborative production and consumption of Mobile TV', in *Interactive TV: A Shared Experience TICSP Adjunct Proceedings of EuroITV 2007*, Amsterdam, Netherlands, 24–25 May, 173–77.

Epps, S. R. (2009a) *Forrester's eReader Holiday Outlook 2009*, Cambridge, MA: Forrester Research.

——(2009b) 'EA flips for Nintendo DS: reader apps tested for portable gaming devices', *Forrester Blog*, 29 October, http://blogs.forrester.com/consumer_product_strategy/games/ (accessed 23 November 2009).

Ermi, L. and Mäyrä, F. (2005a) 'Challenges for pervasive mobile game design: examining players' emotional responses', *Proceedings of the 2005 ACM SIGCHI International Conference on Advances in Computer Entertainment Technology*, Valencia, 371–72.

——(2005b) 'Player-centred game design: Experiences in using scenario study to inform mobile game design', *Game Studies*, 5.1, http://gamestudies.org/0501/ermi_mayra/

Ernst, D. (2009) 'China's stimulus package: a catalyst for recovery?', *Asia Pacific Bulletin*, 35, 3 June.

Essl, G., Wang, G. and Rohs, M. (2008) 'Developments and challenges turning mobile phones into generic music performance platforms', *Proceedings of 5th Mobile Music Workshop '08*, 13–15 May, Vienna, Austria, 11–14.

EurActiv (2008) 'Reding to rescue mobile TV in Europe', *EurActiv*, 6 November, http://www.euractiv.com/en/infosociety/reding-rescue-mobile-tv-europe/article-177002 (accessed 2 December 2009).

European Commission (EC) (2007a) 'Antitrust: Commission initiates formal proceedings against Qualcomm', MEMO/07/389, 1 October, http://europa.eu/press_room/index_en.htm (accessed 2 December 2009).

——(2007b) 'Commission opens Europe's single market for mobile TV services', http://europa.eu/press_room/index_en.htm (accessed 2 December 2009).

——(2007c) *Strengthening the Internal Market for Mobile TV*, Communication, COM(2007) 409 final, http://eur-lex.europa.eu/en/index.htm (accessed 2 December 2009).

——(2008) *Mobile TV across Europe: Commission endorses addition of DVB-H to EU list of official standards*, 17 March, http://europa.eu/press_room/index_en.htm (accessed 2 December 2009).

——(2009) 'European Commission welcomes European Parliament approval of sweeping reforms to strengthen competition and consumer rights on Europe's telecoms markets', IP/09/1812, 24 November, http://europa.eu/press_room/index_en.htm (accessed 2 December 2009).

Evans, D.S., Hagiu, A. and Schmalensee, R. (2006) 'Software platforms', in G. Illing and M. Peitz (eds) *Industrial Organization and the Digital Economy*, Cambridge, MA: MIT Press, 31–70.

Facebook (2007) 'Announcement: Facebook platform for mobiles', press release, 24 October, http://www.facebook.com/press.php#/press/releases.php?p=8041 (accessed 8 December 2009).

FanBox (2009a) 'About us', http://corp.fanbox.com/aboutus.php (accessed 8 December 2009).

——(2009b) 'Company culture', http://corp.fanbox.com/companyculture.php (accessed 8 December 2009).

——(2009c) 'Fanbox', http://www.fanbox.com/socnet/ (accessed 8 December 2009).

Federal Communications Commission (FCC) (1968) 'In the matter of the use of the Carterfone device in message toll telephone service', Docket No. 16942 and 17073 13, *FCC* 2d 420, 26 June.

Feeny, D., Berkes, F., McCay, B. J. and Acheson, J. M. (1990) 'The tragedy of the commons: twenty-two years later', *Human Ecology*, 18: 1–19.

Feijóo, C., Gómez-Barroso, J. L. and Marín, A.-Á. (2007) 'Why YouTube cannot exist on a European mobile: the European regulatory strategy on mobile content access', in G. Goggin and L. Hjorth (eds) *Mobile Media*, Sydney: Department of Media and Communications, The University of Sydney, 253–62.

Feijóo, C., Maghiros, I., Abadie, F. and Gómez-Barroso, J.-L. (2009) 'Exploring a heterogeneous and fragmented digital ecosystem: mobile content', *Telematics and Informatics*, 26: 282–92.

Feldmann, V. (2005) *Leveraging Mobile Media: cross-media strategy and innovation for mobile media communication*, New York: Physica-Verlag.

Feller, J., Fitzgerald, B., Hissam, S. A. and Lakhani, K. R. (eds) (2005) *Perspectives on Free and Open Source Software*, Cambridge, MA: MIT Press.

Fischer, C. (1992) *America Calling: a social history of the telephone to 1940*, Berkeley: University of California Press.

Fitchard, K. (2007a) 'Mobile cinema debuts', *Telephony Online*, 19 February, http://telephonyonline.com/wireless/marketing/telecom_mobile_cinema_debuts/ (accessed 13 May 2010).

——(2007b) 'mSpot cuts the cord on music synch', *Telephony*, 248, 26 March, 3.

Fletcher, O. (2009a) 'China mobile to run e-book service like Amazon', *IDG news*, http://www.thestandard.com/news/2009/09/18/china-mobile-run-e-book-service-amazon (accessed 23 November 2009).

——(2009b) 'E-readers with China's 3G standard on the way', *IDG news*, http://www.thestandard.com/news/2009/08/21/e-readers-chinas-3g-standard-way (accessed 23 November 2009).

Flew, T. (2007) *Understanding Global Media*, Houndsmill, Basingstoke, and New York: Palgrave Macmillan.

——(2008) *New Media: an introduction*, Melbourne: Oxford University Press.

——(2009) 'The cultural economy moment?', *Cultural Science*, 2.1, http://cultural-science.org/journal/index.php/culturalscience/article/view/23/79 (accessed 13 May 2010).

——(2010a) *Creative Industries, Culture and Policy*. London: Sage.

——(2010b) 'Creative industries ten years on', *The Information Society*, in press.

Flichy, P. (2007a) *The Internet imaginaire*, Cambridge, MA: MIT Press.

——(2007b) *Understanding Technological Innovation: a socio-technical approach*, Northampton, MA and Cheltenham: Edward Elgar.

Flintham, M., Giannachi, G., Benford, S. and Adams, M. (2007) 'Day of the figurines: a slow narrative-driven game for mobile phones using text messaging', in M. Cavazza and S. Donikian (eds) *Virtual Storytelling: using virtual reality technologies for storytelling*, Berlin: Springer, 167–75.

FLO Technologies (2009a) 'Deliver compelling mobile multimedia', http://www.mediaflo.com/mediaflo/index.html (accessed 2 December 2009).

——(2009b) 'FLO technology overview', http://www.mediaflo.com/news/pdf/tech_overview.pdf (accessed 2 December 2009).

——(2009c) 'More Mobile. More Media. More You.', http://www.mediaflo.com/ (accessed 2 December 2009).

Fortunati, L. (2006) 'User design and the democratization of the mobile phone' *First Monday*, 7, http://www.uic.edu/htbin/cgiwrap/bin/ojs/index.php/fm/article/view/1615/1530 (accessed 13 May 2010).

Foursquare (2009) 'Foursquare', http://www.foursquare.com/ (accessed 7 December 2009).

Fox, M. A. (2004) 'E-commerce business models for the music industry,' *Popular Music and Society*, 27: 112–19.

——(2005) 'Technological and social drivers of change in the online music industry', *First Monday*, special issue 1, http://firstmonday.org/htbin/cgiwrap/bin/ojs/index.php/fm/article/viewArticle/1453/136 (accessed 13 May 2010).

Fox, M. A. and Wrenn, B. (2001) 'A broadcasting model for the music industry,' *JMM: The International Journal on Media Management*, 3: 112–19.

Fox, S., Zickuhr, K. and Smith, A. (2009) *Twitter and Status Updating, Fall 2009*, Washington, DC: Pew, http://pewinternet.org/ (accessed 13 December 2009).

Frere-Jones, S. (2005) 'Ring my bell: The expensive pleasures of the ringtone', *New Yorker*, 7 March, http://www.newyorker.com/archive/2005/03/07/050307crmu_music (accessed 23 November 2009).

Fritsch, T., Ritter, H. and Schiller, J. (2006a) 'Mobile phone gaming (a follow-up survey of the mobile phone gaming sector and its users)', in R. Harper, M. Rauterberg and M. Combetto (eds) *International Conference on Entertainment Computing 2006*, Berlin: Springer, 292–97.

——(2006b) 'User case study and network evolution in the mobile phone sector (a study on current mobile phone applications)', *Proceedings of the 2006 ACM SIGCHI international conference on advances in computer entertainment technology*, Hollywood CA.

Füller, J., Rieger, M. and Christoph, I. (2005) 'The Gamecreator: self-created mobile games on the internet', in *Changing Views: worlds in play*, proceedings of the 2005 DiGRA conference, Vancouver, June, http://www.digra.org/dl/db/06276.44285.pdf (accessed 13 November 2009).

Fung, A. (2004) 'Coping, cloning, and copying: Hong Kong in the global television format business', in A. Moran and M. Keane (eds), *Television across Asia: Television Industries, Programme Formats and Globalization*, London: RoutledgeCurzon, 74–87.

Funk, J. L. (2001) *The Mobile Internet: how Japan dialed up and the West disconnected*, Pembroke, Bermuda: ISI Publications.

——(2002) *Global Competition Between and Within Standards*, London: Palgrave.

——(2004) *Mobile Disruption: the technologies and applications driving the mobile internet*, Hoboken, NJ: Wiley-Interscience.

——(2009) 'The co-evolution of technology and methods of standard setting: the case of the mobile phone industry', *Journal of Evolutionary Economics*, 19: 73–93.

Gallagher, S. and Park, S. H. (2002) 'Innovation and competition in standard-based industries: ahistorical analysis of the US home video game market', *IEEE Transactions on Engineering Management*, 49: 67–82.

Galloway, A. R. (2004) *Protocol: how control exists after decentralization*, Cambridge, MA: MIT Press.

——(2007) *The Exploit: a theory of networks*, Minneapolis, MN: University of Minnesota Press.

Ganapati, P. (2008) 'Motorola bets big on Android', *Wired.com*, 29 October, http://www.wired.com/gadgetlab/2008/10/motorola-says-h/ (accessed 15 September 2009).

——(2009) 'Smartphone war heats up, Google phones still MIA', *Wired.com*, 8 April, http://www.wired.com/gadgetlab/2009/04/so-where-are-al/ (accessed 15 September 2009).

Gao, P. and Rafiq, A. (2009a) 'Analysing the mobile telecommunications market in a developing country: a socio-technical perspective on Pakistan', Working Paper 40, Manchester: Centre for Development Informatics, University of Manchester, http://www.sed.manchester.ac.uk/idpm/research/publications/wp/di/di_wp40.htm (accessed 13 December 2009).

——(2009b) 'The transformation of the mobile telecommunications industry in Pakistan: A developing country perspective', *Telecommunications Policy*, 33: 309–23.

García-Murilloa, M. and Rendón, J. (2009) 'A model of wireless broadband diffusion in Latin America', *Telematics and Informatics*, 26: 259–69.

Gardiner, B. (2007a) 'AT&T articulates its open handset alliance concerns', *Wired. com*, 20 November, http://www.wired.com/epicenter/2007/11/att-articulates/ (accessed 15 September 2009).

——(2007b) 'Nokia to Google: welcome to the mobile market (p.s. we're not afraid of you)', *Wired.com*, 5 November (accessed 15 September 2009).

——(2008) 'Google handset alliance to gain an ARM?', *Wired.com*, 7 February, http://www.wired.com/gadgetlab/2008/02/android-prototy/ (accessed 15 September 2009).

Garrett, R. and Astbrink, G. (2010) 'Are we there yet?: the struggle for phone accessibility information', *Telecommunications Journal of Australia*, 60.2: 22.1–22.9.

Gast, M. (2007) 'ETel coverage: OpenMoko', 2 March, http://www.oreillynet.com/etel/blog/2007/03/openmoko_1.html (accessed 1 May 2009).

Gaye, L., Mazé, R. and Holmquist, L. E. (2003) 'Sonic City: the urban environment as a musical interface', in *Proceedings of New Interfaces for Musical Expression (NIME03)*, 22–24 May, Montréal, 109–15.

Gayle, L., Holmquist, L. E., Behrendt, F. and Tanaka, A. (2006) 'Mobile music technology: report on an emerging community', *Proceedings of the 2006 conference on new interfaces for musical expression*, Paris, France, 4–8 June, 22–25.

Geekipedia (2007) 'iPhone', *Wired* magazine, 10 September, http://www.wired.com/culture/geekipedia/magazine/geekipedia/iphone (accessed 23 November 2009).

Geiger, C., Paelke, V. and Reimann, C. (2004) 'Mobile entertainment computing', S. Göbel et al. (eds) *Proceedings of Technologies for Interactive Digital Storytelling and Entertainment 2004*, Darmstadt, 22–24 June, Berlin: Springer, 142–47.

Gerbner, G., Mowlana, H. and Nordenstreng, K. (1993) *The Global Media Debate: its rise, fall, and renewal*, Norwood, NJ: Ablex.

Gibson, J.J. 1977) 'The theory of affordances,' in R. E. Shaw and J. Bransford (eds) *Perceiving, Acting, and Knowing: toward an ecological psychology*, Hillsdale, NJ: Lawrence Erlbaum Associates, 1977, 67–82.

——(1979) *The Ecological Approach to Visual Perception*, Hillsdale, NJ: Lawrence Erlbaum.

Gifford, G. (2009) 'MXit schoolgirl missing', *IOL: News for South African and the World*, http://www.iol.co.za/ (acccessed 26 May 2010).

Gillmor, D. (2006) *We the Media: grassroots journalism by the people, for the people*, Sebastopol, CA: O'Reilly Media.

Goff, P. M. (2007) *Limits to Liberalization: local culture in a global marketplace*, Ithaca, NY, and London: Cornell University Press.

Goggin, G. (1998) 'Universal service: voice telephony and beyond', in B. Langtry (ed) *All Connected?: universal service in telecommunications*, Melbourne: University of Melbourne Press, 78–105.

——(2006) *Cell Phone Culture: mobile technology in everyday life*, London: Routledge.

——(2007a) 'An Australian wireless commons?' *Media International Australia*, 125: 118–30.

——(2007b) 'Mobile digital television: *Dancing with the Stars*, or dancing in the dark?' in A. Kenyon (ed.) *TV Futures: digital television policy in Australia*, Melbourne: University of Melbourne, 27–53.

——(2008a) 'Innovation & Disability' 11.3, *M/C: Media and Culture* http://journal.media-culture.org.au/index.php/mcjournal/article/view/56 (accessed 13 May 2010).

——(2008b) 'Making the Australian mobile in the 1990s: creating markets, choosing technologies,' *Media International Australia* 129 (2008): 80–90

——(2008c) 'The mobile turn in universal service: prosaic lessons *and* new ideals', *info*, 10: 46–58.

——(2008d) 'New digital forms', in H. K. Anheier, Y. R. Isar, A. Paul, and S. Cunningham (eds) *The Cultural Economy*, Thousand Oaks, CA, and London: Sage, 241–52.

——(2008e) 'Regulating mobile content: convergences, commons, citizenship', *International Journal of Communications Law and Policy*, 12, http://www.ijclp.net/issue_12.html (accessed 26 May 2010).

Goggin, G. and Crawford, K. (2010) 'Generation disconnections: youth culture and mobile media', in R. Ling and S. Campbell (eds) *Mobile Communication: bringing us together or tearing us apart?*, New Brunswick, NJ: Transaction.

Goggin, G. and Gregg, M. (eds) (2007) 'Wireless cultures and technologies', special issue of *Media International Australia*, 125.

Goggin, G. and Hjorth, L. (eds) (2009) 'Waiting to participate: emerging modes of digital storytelling, engagement and online communities', *Communication, Politics and Culture*, 42.2.

Goggin, G. and McLelland, M. (2009) 'Introduction: internationalizing internet studies', in G. Goggin and M. McLelland (eds), *Internationalizing Internet Studies: beyond Anglophone paradigms*, New York: Routledge, 3–18.

Goggin, G. and Newell, C. (2003) *Digital Disability: the social construction of disability in new media*, Lanham, MD: Rowman & Littlefield.

——(2004) 'Disabled e-nation: telecommunications, disability and national policy', *Prometheus*, 22: 411–22.

——(2005) *Disability in Australia: exposing a social apartheid*, Sydney: University of New South Wales Press.

——(2006) 'Disabling cell phones: mobilizing and regulating the body' in A. P. Kavoori and N. Arceneaux (eds) *The Cell Phone Reader: essays in social transformation*, New York: Peter Lang, 155–72.

——(2007a) 'The business of digital disability', *The Information Society*, 24: 159–68.

——(2007b) 'Disability and online culture', in V. Nightingale and T. Dwyer (eds) *New Media Worlds*, Melbourne: Oxford University Press, 103–17.

Goggin, G. and Noonan, T. (2006) 'Blogging disability: the interface between new cultural movements and Internet technology' in A. Bruns and J. Jacobs (eds) *The Uses of Blogs*, New York: Peter Lang.

Goggin, G. and Spurgeon, C. (2005) 'Mobile message services and communications policy', *Prometheus*, 23: 181–93.

——(2007) 'Premium rate culture: the new business of mobile interactivity', *New Media & Society*, 9: 753–70.

——(2008) 'Mobile messaging and the crisis in participation television', in M. Hartmann, P. Rössler and J. Höflich (eds) *After the Mobile Phone? social changes and the development of mobile communication*, Berlin: Frank & Timme, 55–68.

Gopinath, S. (2005) 'Ringtones, or the auditory logic of globalization', *First Monday*, 10.12, http://firstmonday.org/issues/issue10_12/gopinath/index.html (accessed 1 October 2009).

Gordon, J (2007) 'The mobile phone and the public sphere: mobile phone usage in three critical situations', *Convergence*, 13.3: 307–19.

Gray, V. (2006) 'África, el continente móvil', *Economía Exterior*, 36; trans. As 'The un-wired continent: Africa's mobile success story', http://www.itu.int/ITU-D/ict/statistics/at_glance/Africa_EE2006_e.pdf

Green, N., Harper, R., Murtagh, G. and Cooper, G. (2001) 'Configuring the mobile user: sociological and industry views', *Personal and Ubiquitous Computing*, 5: 146–56.

Greenfield, A. and Shepard, M. (2007) *Urban Computing and its Discontents*, New York: The Architectural League of New York.

Groebel, J., Noam, E. M. and Feldmann, V. (eds) (2006) *Mobile Media*, Mahwah, NJ: Lawrence Erlbaum.

Grossman, L. (2007) 'Invention of the year: the iPhone', *Time*, http://www.time.com/time/specials/2007/article/0,28804,1677329_1678542,00.html (accessed 1 December 2008).

Gruber, H. (2005) *The Economics of Mobile Telecommunications*, Cambridge: Cambridge University Press.

Grüter, B. and Ok, M. (2007) 'Situated play and mobile gaming', Proceedings of DiGRA 2007, *Situated Play*, The University of Tokyo, September, 2007, 103–12.

GSM Association (2007) *MMT: Catalysing the Mobile Money Market*, London and Atlanta, GA: GSM Association, http://www.gsmworld.com/mmt/ (accessed 7 February 2008).

GSM World (2009) 'Mobile World Celebrates Four Billion Connections', 11 February, hwww.gsmworld.com/newsroom/press-releases/2009/2521.htm (accessed 8 December 2009).

Guardian (2002) 'Vizzavi contracts', 8 January, 19.

Guillén, M. F. (2005) *The Rise of Spanish Multinationals: European business in the global economy*, New York: Cambridge University Press.

Gundotra, V. (2009) 'Changes for Jaiku and farewell to Dodgeball and Mashup Editor', 14 January, *Google Code Blog*, http://googlecode.blogspot.com/2009/01/changes-for-jaiku-and-farewell-to.html (accessed 8 December 2009).

Hackett, R.A., and Zhao, Y. (eds) (2005) *Democratizing Global Media: one world, many struggles*, Lanham, MD: Rowman & Littlefield.

Haddon, L. (2007) 'Looking for diversity: children and mobile phones', in G. Goggin and L. Hjorth (eds) *Mobile Media*, Sydney: Department of Media and Communications, University of Sydney, 97–106.

Haddon, L. and Green, N. (2010) *Mobile Communications: an introduction to new media*, London: Berg.

Haddon, L., Mante, E., Sapio, B., Kommonen, K.-H., Fortunati, L. and Kant, A. (eds) (2005) *Everyday Innovators: researching the role of users in shaping ICTs*, London: Springer.

Hadenius, P. (2003) 'Multi-user adventures go mobile', *MIT Technology Review*, http://msnbc.msn.com/id/3226858/ (accessed 28 September 2009).

Hahn, H.P. and Kibora, L. (2008) 'The domestication of the mobile phone: oral society and new ICT in Burkina Faso', *Journal of Modern African Studies*, 46: 87–109.

Hardin, G. (1968) 'The tragedy of the commons', *Science*, 62 :1243–48.

Hardy, P. (2002) 'Winning the music game: music publishing is a growth business in an ailing sector', *Financial Times*, 18 June, 32.

Harmer, J. A. (2003) 'Mobile multimedia services', *BT Technology Journal*, 21.3: 169–80.

Hartford Courant (1899) 'That telephone bell – it never jangles in the telephone girl's ear', 31 January, 4.

Harvey, A. (2006) 'The liminal magic circle: boundaries, frames, and participation in pervasive mobile games', *Wi: Journal of the Mobile Digital Commons Network*, http://wi.hexagram.ca/?p=12 (accessed 13 May 2010).

Harvey, F. (2002) 'Noteworthy sounds a way off yet', *Financial Times*, 3 September, 11.

Hass, Michael (2006) *Management of Innovation in Network Industries: the mobile internet in Japan and Europe*, Wiesbaden: Deutscher Universtäts-Verlag.

Haubenreich, J. (2008) 'The iPhone and the DMCA: locking the hands of consumers', *Vanderbilt Law Review*, 61: 1507–53.

Heeks, R. (2009a) *The ICT4D 2.0 manifesto: where next for ICTs and international development?* Working Paper 41, Manchester: Centre for Development Informatics, University of Manchester, http://www.sed.manchester.ac.uk/idpm/research/publications/wp/di/di_wp42.htm (accessed 13 December 2009).

——(2009b) 'Mobile phone penetration: Google motion chart data visualisation', http://ict4dblog.wordpress.com/2009/11/30/mobile-phone-penetration-google-motion-chart-data-visualisation/ (accessed 13 December 2009).

Heitman, M., Prykop, C. and Aschomoneit, P. (2004) 'Using means–end chains to build mobile brand communities', *Proceedings of the 37th Hawaii International Conference on System Sciences*, 5–8 January, Big Island, HI.

Helft, M., and Markoff, J. (2007) 'Google enters the wireless world', *New York Times*, 5 November, http://www.nytimes.com/ (accessed 5 May 2009).

Henten, A. and Nicolajsen, H. W. (2009) 'Mobile and wireless communications: technologies, applications, business models and diffusion', *Telematics and Informatics*, 26: 223–26.

Herman, E.S. and McChesney, R.W. (1997) *The Global Media: the new missionaries of corporate capitalism*, London: Cassell.

Hills, J. (1986) *Deregulating Telecoms: competition and control in the United States, Japan, and Britain*, London: Pinter.

——(2002) *The Struggle for Control of Global Communication: the formative century*, Urbana, IL: University of Illinois Press.

——(2007) *Telecommunications and Empire*, Urbana, IL: University of Illinois Press.

Hjorth, L. (2005) 'Odours of mobility: Japanese cute customization in the Asia-Pacific region', *Journal of Intercultural Studies* 26: 39–55.

——(2006a) 'Playing at being mobile: gaming and cute culture in South Korea', *Fibreculture Journal*, 8, http://journal.fibreculture.org/issue8/issue8_hjorth.html

——(2006b) 'Postal presence: A case study of mobile customisation and gender in Melbourne', *Knowledge, Technology & Policy*, 19: 29–40.

——(2007) 'The place of mobile gaming: one history in locating mobility in the Asia-Pacific region', *Proceedings of DiGRA 2007*, University of Tokyo, 24–28 September, 789–95.

——(2009a) 'Gifts of presence: a case study of a South Korean virtual community, Cyworld's mini-hompy', in G. Goggin and M. McLelland (eds), *Internationalizing Internet Studies: beyond Anglophone paradigms*, Routledge, New York, 237–51.

——(2009b) *Mobile Media in the Asia Pacific: gender and the art of being mobile*, London and New York: Routledge.

——(2010) 'The price of being mobile: youth, gender and mobile media' in S. H. Donald, T. D. Anderson and D. Spry (eds) *Youth, Society and Mobile Media in Asia*, London and New York: Routledge, 74–87.

Hjorth, L. and Chan, D. (eds) (2009) *Gaming Cultures and Place in Asia-Pacific*, New York: Routledge.

Hongyan, Y. (2009) 'Hanwang eyes big e-reader market', *China Daily*, 18 November, http://www.chinadaily.com.cn/bizchina/2009-11/18/content_8997067.htm (accessed 23 November 2009).

Horrigan, J. (2009) *Wireless Internet Use*, Washington, DC: Pew Internet & American Life Project, http://pewinternet.org/ (accessed 13 December 2009).

Hounshell, D.A. (1975) 'Elisha Gray and the telephone: on the disadvantages of being an expert', *Technology and Culture*, 16: 133–61.

Howe, J. (2008) *Crowdsourcing: why the power of the crowds is driving the future of business*, New York: Crown Business.

Hu, K. (2008) 'Made in China: the cultural logic of OEMs and the manufacture of low-cost technology', *Inter-Asia Cultural Studies*, 9: 27–46.

Hudson, D. and Zimmermann, P.R. (2009) 'Taking things apart: locative media, migratory archives, and micropublics,' *Afterimage*, 36: 15–19.

Hughes, N. and Lonie S. (2007), 'M-PESA: mobile money for the "unbanked" turning cellphones into 24-hour tellers in Kenya', *Innovations*, vol. 2, no. 1–2, pp. 63–81.

Huizinga, J. (1949) *Homo Ludens: a study of the play-element in culture*, trans. R.F.C. Hull, London: Routledge & Kegan Paul.

Humphreys, L. (2007) 'Mobile social networks and social practice: a case study of Dodgeball', *Journal of Computer-Mediated Communication*, 13(1), article 17. http://jcmc.indiana.edu/vol13/issue1/humphreys.html (accessed 13 May 2010).

——(2008) 'Mobile devices and social networking', in M. Hartmann, P. Rössler and J. Höflich (eds) *After the Mobile Phone? social changes and the development of mobile communication*, Berlin: Frank & Timme, 115–30.

Humphreys, L. and Barker, T. (2007) 'Modernity and the mobile phone: exploring tensions about dating and sex in Indonesia,' *M/C Journal*, 10.1, http://journal.media-culture.org.au/0703/06-humphreys-barker.php (accessed 13 May 2010).

Hurd, A. and Schlatter, B. (2005) 'Geocaching: 21st century hide-and-seek', *Journal of Physical Education, Recreation, and Dance*, 76: 28–33.

Hutchison Whampoa Ltd (2003) 'H3G – Our mission – pathfinders for a new medium', http://www.hutchison-whampoa.com/eng/telecom/h3g/mission.htm (accessed 19 November 2009).

Hwang, J. and Yoon, H. (2009) 'A mixed spectrum management framework for the future wireless service based on techno-economic analysis: the Korean spectrum policy study', *Telecommunications Policy*, 33: 407–21.

IDC (2009a) 'Mobile phone market turns corner in third quarter, more gains expected in Q4', 29 October, *IDC Worldwide Quarterly Mobile Phone Tracker*, http://www.idc.com/getdoc.jsp?sessionId=&containerId=prUS22063909 (accessed 14 December 2009).

——(2009b) 'Worldwide converged mobile device (smartphone) market continues to grow despite economic malaise', 9 November, *IDC Worldwide Quarterly Mobile Phone Tracker*, http://www.idc.com/getdoc.jsp?sessionId=&containerId=prUS22070109 (accessed 14 December 2009).

Independent Committee for the Supervision of Standards of Telephone Information Services (ICSTIS) (2005) '£40,000 fine for misleading "Crazy Frog" service', 20 December, London: ICSTIS.

India Telecom (2005) 'Samsung launches new mobile phone', *India Telecom*, 11.1, 5.

Intel (2007) *Mobile WiMAX Technology for Fixed Broadband Developments*, Intel Corporation, http://www.intel.com/technology/wimax (accessed 31 October 2009).

Interfax China (2007) *China Online and Mobile Gaming Industry, 2008–2010: Summary*, http://www.mobilemondayshanghai.net/ (accessed 6 December 2009).

International Game Developers Association (IGDA) (2005) *Mobile Games White Paper*, http://www.igda.org/sites/default/files/IGDA_Mobile_Whitepaper_2005.pdf (accessed 14 November 2009).

International Telecommunications Union (ITU) (2004) 'Mobile cellular operators', http://www.itu.int/ITU-D/ict/statistics/at_glance/topptoc_2004.html (accessed 26 May 2010).

——(1998) 'Top 20 fixed line operators 1998', http://www.itu.int/ITU-D/ict/statistics/at_glance/ptof98.html (accessed 14 December 2009).

——(2007a) *Market Mechanisms for Spectrum Management*, Geneva: ITU, http://www.itu.int/osg/spu/stn/spectrum/workshop_proceedings/STN.MMSM-2007-PDF-E.pdf (accessed 13 May 2010).

——(2007b) *Telecommunications/ICT Markets and Trends in Africa*, Geneva: ITU, http://www.itu.int/ITU-D/ict/statistics/material/af_report07.pdf (accessed 13 December 2009).

——(2008) *World Information Society 2007: Beyond WSIS*, Geneva: ITU, http://www.itu.int/osg/spu/publications/worldinformationsociety/2007/report.html (accessed 13 December 2009).

——(2009a) *Confronting the Crisis: its impact on the ICT industry*, February, http://www.itu.int/osg/csd/emerging_trends/crisis/fc18.html (accessed 10 December 2009).

——(2009b) 'Mobile cellular, subscriptions per 100 people', http://www.itu.int/ITU-D/icteye/Indicators/Indicators.aspx# (accessed 13 December 2009).

——(2009c) *Information Society Statistical Profiles 2009: Africa*, Geneva: ITU, http://www.itu.int/dms_pub/itu-d/opb/ind/D-IND-RPM.AF-2009-PDF-E.pdf (accessed 13 December 2009).

——(2009d) *Information Society Statistical Profiles 2009: Americas*, Geneva: ITU, http://www.itu.int/dms_pub/itu-d/opb/ind/D-IND-RPM.AM-2009-E09-PDF-E.pdf (accessed 23 November 2009).

Invest in Sweden Agency (ISA) (2004) *Invest in Sweden: Game Development*, http://www.isa-northamerica.org/literature/isa_gamedevelopment.pdf (accessed 14 November 2009).

Ip, B. (2008) 'Technological, content, and market convergence in the games industry', *Games and Culture*, 3: 199–224.

Ito, M. (2008) 'Introduction', in K. Varnelis et al. (eds) *Networked Publics*, Cambridge, MA: MIT Press, 1–14.

Ito, M., Okabe, D. and Matsuda, M. (eds) (2005) *Personal, Portable, Pedestrian: mobile phones in Japanese life*, Cambridge, MA: MIT Press.

Iveson, K. (2007) *Publics and the City*, Malden, MA: Blackwell.

Iwatani, Y. (1998) 'Love: Japanese style', *Wired*, 6 November, http://www.wired.com/culture/lifestyle/news/1998/06/12899 (accessed 14 December 2009).

Jacobsson, M., Rost, M., Håkansson, M. and Holmquist, L. E. (2005) 'Push!Music: intelligent music sharing on mobile devices', *Adjunct Proceedings of 7th international conference on Ubiquitous Computing*, Tokyo, 11–14 September.

James, J. and Versteeg, M. (2007) 'Mobile phones in Africa: How much do we really know?' *Social Indicators Research* 84: 117–26.

Jamster (2009) 'Facts', http://www.jamster.com.au/jcw/press/factsPage.do (accessed 12 December 2009).

Jaokar, A. and Fish, T. (2006) *Mobile web 2.0*, London: Futuretext.

Java (2007) 'phoneME project vision', *Java.net*, https://phoneme.dev.java.net/phoneme_vision.html (accessed 15 November 2009).

Jenkins, H. (2006) *Convergence Culture: where new and old media collide*, New York: New York University Press.

Jian, M. and Liu, C. (2009) ' "Democratic entertainment" commodity and unpaid labor of reality TV: a preliminary analysis of China's Supergirl', *Inter-Asia Cultural Studies*, 10: 524–43.

Joffe, B. (2008) 'Mogi: location-based services – a community game in Japan', in F. von Borries, S.P. Walz and M. Böttger (eds) *Space Time Play: computer games, architecture and urbanism: the next level*, Basel: Birkhäuser, 224–5.

Johnson, B. (2009) 'Facebook now reaches 300 million users – and makes money', Technology Blog, *Guardian*, 15 September, http://www.guardian.co.uk/technology/blog/2009/sep/15/facebook-300-million (accessed 25 October 2009).

Johnson, J. (2008) 'Is the iPhone the next Wii?' *WiiNintendo*, 7 March, http://www.wiinintendo.net/2008/03/07/is-the-iphone-the-next-wii/ (accessed 1 May 2009).

Jung, J.-Y. (2009) 'Where do you go online? A comparison of internet connectedness via personal computers and mobile phones in Japan', *International Journal of Mobile Communications*, 7: 21–35.

Kahney, L. (2007) 'The perils of taking the iPhone mainstream' 19 September, http://www.wired.com/gadgets/mac/commentary/cultofmac/2007/09/cultofmac_0919 (accessed 31 March 2009).

Kam, M., Rudraraju, V., Tewari, A. and Canny, J. (2007) 'Mobile gaming with children in rural India: contextual factors in the use of game design patterns', *Situated Play, proceedings of DiGRA 2007 conference*, Tokyo, 24–28 September, 292–301.

Van de Kar, E. and den Hengst, M. (2009) 'Involving users early on in the design process: closing the gap between mobile information services and their users', *Electronic Markets*, 19: 31–42.

Kärrberg, P. and Liebenau, J. (2007) 'Mobile service delivery business models in Europe and Japan: the shift from "wherever and whenever" to "right here and now" ', *Proceedings of the 18th Annual IEEE International Symposium on Personal, Indoor and Mobile Radio Communications* (PIMRC'07), 3–7 September, Athens.

Katz, J.E. and Aakhus, M. (eds) (2002) *Perpetual Contact: mobile communication, private talk, public performance*, Cambridge: Cambridge University Press.

Katz, E. and Scannell, P. (eds) (2009) 'The End of Television? its impact on the world (so far)', *Annals of the American Academy of Political and Social Science*, 625, September.

Keane, M. (2007) *Created in China: the great new leap forward*, London and New York: Routledge.

Keegan, V. (2002) 'Ringing the changes – One of the biggest mobile earners is not really there', *Guardian*, 10 January, 6.

Kelty, C.M. (2008) *Two Bits: the cultural significance of free software*, Durham, NC: Duke University Press.

Kim, Y.J., Jeon, S.J. and Kim, M.J. (2009) 'User needs of mobile phone wireless search: focusing on search result pages', in M. Kurosu (ed.) *Human Centered Design, HCII 2009*, Berlin: Springer, 446–51.

Kim, C.-Su, Oh, E.-H., Yang, K.H. and Kim, J.K. (2009) 'The appealing characteristics of download type mobile games', *Service Business*, published online 27 November: DOI 10.1007/s11628-009-0088-0

Kimball, L. (2002) 'Feedback – personal tone', *Guardian*, 17 January, 2.

King, L. (ed.) (2008) *Game On: the history and culture of videogames*, London: Laurence King.

Kini, R. and Thanarithiporn, S. (2004) 'Mobile commerce and electronic commerce in Thailand: a value space analysis', *International Journal of Mobile Communications*, 2: 22–37.

Klopfer, E. (2008) *Augmented Learning: research and design of mobile educational games*, Cambridge, MA: MIT Press.

Kolko, Beth E. (ed.) (2003) *Virtual Publics: policy and community in an electronic age*, New York: Columbia University Press.

Konig, A., Enders, A., Hungenberg, H. and Rohrig, M. (2006) 'How can music majors increase their success in the market for over-the-air downloads? – the case of Germany', *International Journal on Media Management*, 8: 4: 182–92.

Kontio, P. (2004) 'Mobile gaming business', http://www.tml.tkk.fi/Opinnot/T-109.551/2004/reports/mobile_gaming.pdf (accessed 13 November 2009).

Korhonen, H., Saarenpää, H. and Paavilainen, J. (2008) 'Pervasive mobile games: a new mindset for players and developers', in P. Markopoulos et al. (eds) *Fun and Games 2008*, Berlin: Springer, 21–32, 2008.

Koskela, T. and Väänänen-Vainio-Mattila, K. (2004) 'Evolution towards smart home environments: empirical evaluation of three user interfaces', *Personal and Ubiquitous Computing*, 8.3–4, 234–40.

Koski, H., and Tobias, K. (2007) 'Catching up? differences in 2G mobile diffusion in industrialized and developing countries' *Journal of Scientific and Industrial Research* 66: 305–11.

Koskinen, I.K. (2007) *Mobile Multimedia in Action*, New Brunswick, NJ: Transaction.

Krikke, J. (2003) 'Samurai Romanesque, J2ME, and the battle for mobile cyberspace,' *IEEE Computer Graphics and Applications*, 23: 16–23.

Lance, G. D. (2008) 'Forget the iPhone: accessibility trumps trendiness', *Computing Unplugged Magazine*, http://www.computingunplugged.com/issues/issue200803/00002063001.html (accessed 15 July 2009).

Latour, B. (1996) *Aramis, or the Love of Technology*, trans. Catherine Porter, Cambridge, MA: Harvard University Press.

——(2005a) 'From Realpolitik to Dingpolitik, or how to make things public', in Bruno Latour and Peter Weibel (eds) *Making Things Public: atmospheres of democracy*, Karlsruhe: ZKM; Cambridge, MA: MIT Press, 14–41.

——(2005b) *Reassembling the Social: an introduction to actor-network-theory*, Oxford: Clarendon Press.

Laughey, D. (2006) *Music and Youth Culture*, Edinburgh: Edinburgh University Press.

Law, P.-L., Fortunati, L. and Yang, S. (eds) (2006) *New Technologies in Global Societies*, Singapore: World Scientific.

Leavitt, N. (2003) 'Will wireless gaming be a winner?', *Computer*, January, 24–27.

Le Borgne-Bachschmidt, F., Girieud, S. and Leiba, M. (2008) *User-Created-Content: supporting a participative Information Society*, final report, IDATE Consulting & Research, http://ec.europa.eu/information_society/eeurope/i2010/docs/studies/ucc-final_report.pdf (accessed 6 November 2009).

Lee, S. and Kwak, D. (2005) 'TV in your cell phone: the introduction of Digital Multimedia Broadcasting (DMB) in Korea', paper presented at the annual Telecommunications Policy Research Conference, Arlington, VA, 24 September 2005.

Lee, H., and Oh, S. (2006) 'A standards war waged by a developing country: understanding international standard setting from the actor-network perspective', *Journal of Strategic Information Systems*, 15: 177–96.

Lee, S., Chan-Olmsted, S.M. and Kim, H. (2008) 'The deployment of third-generation mobile services: a multinational analysis of contributing factors', http://warrington.ufl. edu/purcdocs/papers/0918_Lee_The_Deployment_of.pdf (accessed 13 December 2009).

Lee, S., Chan-Olmsted, S.M. and Ho, H.-Hui (2008) 'The emergence of Mobile Virtual Network Operators (MVNOs): an examination of the business strategy in the global MVNO Market', *International Journal on Media Management*, 10: 10–21.

Lemstra, W. and Hayes, V. (2009) 'License-exempt: Wi-Fi complement to 3G', *Telematics and Informatics*, 26: 227–39.

Lessig, L. (2000) *Code and other laws of cyberspace*, New York: Basic Books.

——(2001) *The Future of Ideas: the fate of the commons in a connected world*, New York: Random House.

——(2004) *Free Culture: how big media uses technology and the law to lock down culture and control creativity*, New York: Penguin.

——(2008) *Remix: making art and commerce thrive in the hybrid economy*, New York: Penguin.

Leung, J. (2006) 'Learning from commercial mobile games', *Wi: Journal of Mobile Media*, http://wi.hexagram.ca/?p=9 (accessed 13 May 2010).

Li, F. and Whalley, J. (2002) 'Deconstruction of the telecommunications industry: from value chains to value networks', *Telecommunications Policy*, 26: 451–72.

Liarokapis, F. (2006) 'An exploration from virtual to augmented reality gaming', *Simulation & Gaming*, 37: 507–33.

Licoppe, C. and Guillot, R. (2006) 'ICTs and the engineering of encounters. A case study of the development of a mobile game based on the geolocation of terminals,' in J. Urry and M. Sheller (eds) *Mobile Technologies of the City*. New York: Routledge, 152–76.

Licoppe, C. and Inada, Y. (2006) 'Emergent uses of a multiplayer location-aware mobile game: The interactional consequences of mediated encounters,' *Mobilities*, 1: 39–61.

——(2008) 'Geolocalized technologies, location-aware communities, and personal territories: the Mogi case,' *Journal of Urban Technology*, 15: 5–24.

——(2009) 'Mediated co-proximity and its dangers in a location-aware community: a case of stalking,' in A. de Souza e Silva & D. M. Stuko (eds) *Digital Cityscapes: merging digital and urban playspaces*. New York: Peter Lang; 100–128.

Lindvall, H. (2009) 'Behind the music: the real reason why the major labels love Spotify', 17 August, Music Blog, *Guardian.co.uk*, http://www.guardian.co.uk/music/musicblog/2009/aug/17/major-labels-spotify (accessed 13 May 2010).

Ling, R. (2005) *The Mobile Connection: the cell phone's impact on society*, San Francisco, CA: Morgan Kaufmann.

——(2008) *New Tech, New Ties: How mobile communication is reshaping social cohesion*. Cambridge, MA: MIT Press.

——(2009) 'Mobile adoption by GDP', 8 December, http://mobilesociety.ning.com/profiles/blogs/mobile-adoption-by-gdp (accessed 26 May 2010).

Ling, R. and Donner, J. (2009) *Mobile Phones and Mobile Communication*, Cambridge: Polity.

Lippmann, W. (1925) *The Phantom Public*, New York: Harcourt, Brace.

Livingstone, S. (ed.) (2005) *Audiences and Publics: when cultural engagement matters for the public sphere*, Portland, OR and Bristol: Intellect.

Loftus, P. (2002) 'Wireless gaming is a hit on the streets of Sweden', *Wall Street Journal*, 12 June, D5.

Longford, M. (2006) 'Mapping the mobile digital commons network', *Wi: Journal of Mobile Media*, http://wi.hexagram.ca/?p=4 (accessed 9 December 2009).

——(2007) 'Territory as interface: design for mobile experiences', *Wi: Journal of Mobile Media*, Winter/Spring, http://wi.hexagram.ca/?p=16 (accessed 9 December 2009).

Loopt (2009) 'About Loopt', http://www.loopt.com/about (accessed 7 December 2009).

Lovink, G. (2008) *Zero Comments: blogging and critical internet culture*, New York: Routledge.

Lugano, G. (2008) 'Mobile social networking in theory and practice', *First Monday*, 13.11, 3 November, http://firstmonday.org/htbin/cgiwrap/bin/ojs/index.php/fm/article/viewArticle/2232/2050 (accessed 13 May 2010).

Lull, J. (1990) *Inside Family Viewing: ethnographic research on television's audiences*, London: Routledge.

Mackenzie, A. (2005) 'Untangling the unwired: Wi-Fi and the cultural inversion of infrastructure', *Space and Culture*, 8: 269–85.

——(2006) *Cutting Code: software and sociality*, Oxford: Peter Lang.

——(2009) *Wirelessness: radical network empiricism*, Cambridge, MA: MIT Press

Mahan, A. (2003) 'Regulatory peripheries: using prepaid to extend the network', *Info*, 5: 37–44.

Maitland, C.F., Bauer, J. M. and Westerveld, R. (2002) 'The European market for mobile data: evolving value chains and industry structures,' *Telecommunications Policy*, 26: 485–504.

Maitland, C.F., Van De Kar, E.A.M., De Montalvo, U.W. and Bouwman, H. (2005) 'Mobile information and entertainment services: business models and service networks', *International Journal of Management and Decision Making*, 6: 47–64.

Malkani, G. (2002) 'Sony Europe warns on piracy', *Financial Times*, 11 November, 18.

Manabe, N. (2008) 'New-technologies, industrial structure, and the consumption of music in Japan', *Asian Music*, 39: 81–107.

——(2009) 'Going mobile: the mobile internet, ringtones, and the music market in Japan', in G. Goggin and L. Hjorth (eds) *Mobile Technologies: from telecommunications to media*, New York: Routledge, 317–32.

Manovich, L. (2008) *Software Takes Command*, 20 November, http://lab.softwarestudies.com/2008/11/softbook.html (accessed 15 June 2009).

Mansell, R. (1993) *The New Telecommunications: a political economy of network evolution*, London: Sage.

Marisca, J. and Rivera, E. (2005) 'New trends in the Latin American telecommunications market: Telefonica and Telmex', *Telecommunications Policy*, 29, 757–77.

——(2006) 'Mobile communications in Mexico in the Latin American context', *Information Technologies and International Development*, 3: 41–55.

Marketing Week (2005) 'Samsung prepares to engage gaming market', *Marketing Week*, May, 25.

Martínez, G. (2008) *Latin American Telecommunications: Telefónica's conquest*, Lanham, MD: Lexington Books.

Martini, R. (2007) *Nokia and mobile gaming*, MBA thesis, Simon Fraser University, Vancouver.

Marvin, C. (1988) *When Old Technologies Were New: thinking about electric communication in the late nineteenth century*, New York: Oxford University Press.

Matsuda, M. (2010) 'Japanese mobile youth in the 2000s', in S.H. Donald, T.D. Anderson and D. Spry (eds) *Youth, Society and Mobile Media in Asia*, London and New York: Routledge, 31–42.

Mäyrä, F. (2007) *An Introduction to Game Studies: games in culture*, London: Sage.

McGinn, R.E. (1983) 'Stokowski and the Bell Telephone laboratories: collaboration in the development of high-fidelity sound reproduction', *Technology and Culture*, 24: 38–75.

McGonigal, J. (2003) 'A real little game: The Pinocchio effect in pervasive play', in *Level Up*, proceedings of the 2003 DiGRA conference, University of Utrecht, Utrecht, November, http://www.digra.org/dl/db/05097.11067.pdf (accessed 13 November 2009).

McPhail, T. (2010) *Global Communication: theories, stakeholders, and trends*, Malden, MA: Wiley-Blackwell.

Meikle, G. and Young, S. (eds) (2008) 'Beyond broadcasting?: television for the twenty-first century', *Media International Australia*, 128: 67–70.

Meng, B. (2009) 'Who needs democracy if we can pick our favorite girl? *Super Girl* as media spectacle', *Chinese Journal of Communication*, 2: 257–72.

Mezrich, B. (2009) *The Accidental Billionaires: the founding of Facebook. A tale of sex, money, genius and betrayal*, New York: Doubleday.

Miller, T. (2002) 'A view from a fossil: the new economy, creativity and consumption – two or three things I don't believe in', *International Journal of Cultural Studies* 7: 55–65.

Miller, T., Govil, N., McMurria, J., Maxwell, R. and Wang, T. W. (2005) *Global Hollywood 2*, London: British Film Institute.

Milne, C. (2006), *Telecoms Demand: measures for improving affordability in developing countries: a toolkit for action*, Main report, discussion paper WDR0603, World Dialogue on Regulation for Network Economics, *Regulateonline.org*, http://www.regulateonline.org/content/view/619/71/ (accessed 20 May 2008).

Minges, M. (1999) 'Mobile cellular communications in the southern African region', *Telecommunications Policy*, 23: 585–93.

MOBILE 3.0 (2008) 'Mobile Television', http://mobiledreinull.tv/index.php?id=19 (accessed 31 July 2009)

MobileActive (2009) 'Our vision', http://mobileactive.org/vision (accessed 15 December 2009).

Mobile Interactive Group (MIG) (2009) 'MIG companies', http://www.migcan.com/ (accessed 12 December 2009).

Mobile Monday (2003) 'B'ngo to compete with Nokia's N-Gage', 18 February, http://www.mobilemonday.net/news/bngo-to-compete-nokias-n-gage (accessed 6 December 2009).

Moran, A. and Keane, M. (eds) (2010) *Cultural Adaptation*, London and New York: Routledge.

Morley, D. (1980) *The Nationwide Audience: structure and decoding*, London: British Film Institute.

Mosen, J. (2009) email post, Accessible Phones discussion list, 9 June, http://www.mosenexplosion.com (accessed 15 July 2009).

Mosco, V. (1982) *Pushbutton Fantasies: critical perspectives on videotext and information technology*, Norwood, NJ: Ablex.

——(2004) *The Digital Sublime: myth, power and cyberspace*, Cambridge, MA: MIT Press

——(2009) *The political economy of communication*, 2nd edition, London: Sage.

Mosco, V. and McKercher, C. (eds.) (2007) *Knowledge Workers in the Information Society*, Lanham, MD: Lexington Books.

——(2008) *The Laboring of Communication: will knowledge workers of the world unite?*, Lanham: MD, Lexington Books.

Moss, T. (2003) 'Play time', *Mobile Communications*, June, 1.

Mudhai, O. F. (2006) 'Exploring the potential for more strategic use of mobile phones', in J. Anderson, J. Dean and G. Lovink (eds) *Reformatting Politics: information networks and global civil society*, London: Routledge, 107–20.

Mueller, M. (1989) 'The switchboard problem: scale, signaling, and organization in manual telephone switching, 1877–97', *Technology and Culture*, 30: 534–60.

——(1997) *Universal Service: competition, interconnection, and monopoly in the making of the American telephone system*, Cambridge, MA: MIT Press, Washington, DC: AEI Press.

Murphy, P.D. and Kraidy, M.M. (eds.) (2003) *Global Media Studies: ethnographic perspectives*, New York and London: Routledge.

Nairn, G. (2001) 'Revenue sharing will demand extra smart systems', *Financial Times*, 19 September.

Nam, C., Kim, S. and Lee, H. (2008) 'The role of WiBro: filling the gaps in mobile broadband technologies', *Technological Forecasting & Social Change*, 75: 438–48.

National Council on Disability (NCD) (2004) *Design for Inclusion: creating a new marketplace*, Washington, DC: NCD.

Natsuno, T. (2003a) *i-Mode Strategy*, Chichester, England: John Wiley.

——(2003b) *The i-Mode Wireless Ecosystem*, trans. R. S. McCreery, Chichester: John Wiley.

Netanel, N.W. (2007) 'Digital rights management: temptations of the walled garden: digital rights management and mobile phone carriers', *Journal on Telecommunications & High Technology*, 6

N-Gage News (2005) 'Snakes invades game decks worldwide', 25 January, *N-Gage Gaming*, http://www.ngagegaming.com/ (accessed 13 May 2010).

Ng Choon Sim, C. and Mitter, S. (eds) (2005) *Gender and the Digital Economy: perspectives from the developing world*, Thousand Oaks, CA and New Delhi: Sage.

Nightingale, V. and Dwyer, T. (2006) 'The audience politics of "enhanced" TV formats', *International Journal of Media and Cultural Politics*, 2: 25–42.

Nokia (1997) 'Nokia announces an agreement to sell its audio electronics business', 23 December, http://www.nokia.com/press/press-releases/archive/archiveshowpressrelease?newsid=774947 (accessed 14 November 2009).

——(2001a) 'Nokia and Loki Software in agreement to distribute Linux games with Nokia Media Terminal', 16 May, http://www.nokia.com/press/press-releases/archive/archiveshowpressrelease?newsid=821338 (accessed 13 November 2009).

——(2001b) 'Nokia and RealNetworks to deploy RealPlayer on Media Terminal', 16 May, http://www.nokia.com/press/press-releases/archive/archiveshowpressrelease?newsid=821372 (accessed 13 November 2009).

——(2001c) 'Nokia Music Player secure music downloads and great sounds for mobile music fans', 21 March, http://www.nokia.com/press/press-releases/archive/archiveshowpressrelease?newsid=813141 (accessed 14 November 2009).

——(2001d) 'Sanrio's Hello Kitty makes her way to Nokia phones in industry's first Hello Kitty downloadable game packs, amongst other exclusive services', 1 December, http://www.nokia-asia.com/about-nokia/press/press-releases/archive/archiveshowpress release?newsid=-2948 (accessed 13 November 2009).

——(2002a) 'Nokia brings mobility to the Games industry by making Rich Games mobile', 4 November, http://www.nokia.com/press/press-releases/archive/ archiveshowpressrelease?newsid=880085 (accessed 13 November 2009).

——(2002b) 'Sony Ericcson introduces mobile gaming phone with colour screen', *Nordic Business Report*, 1.

——(2003a) 'Electronic Arts to develop titles for Nokia N-Gage™ mobile game deck' 27 August, http://www.nokia.com/press/press-releases/archive/archiveshowpressrelease? newsid=915366 (accessed 13 November 2009).

——(2003b) 'Nokia N-GageTM game deck expands its game portfolio with new interactive titles', 14 May, http://www.nokia.com/press/press-releases/archive/ archiveshowpressrelease?newsid=903666 (accessed 13 November 2009).

——(2003c) 'Play, share and compete via the N-Gage™ Arena', 20 August, http://www. nokia.com/press/press-releases/archive/archiveshowpressrelease?newsid=914572 (accessed 13 November 2009).

——(2003d) 'Take the challenge: Nokia Game 2003 goes mobile!', 12 September, http://www.nokia-asia.com/about-nokia/press/press-releases/archive/ archiveshowpressrelease?newsid=-3058 (accessed 13 November 2009).

——(2005a) 'Nokia fosters mobile innovation through open source development'. 2 November, http://press.nokia.com/PR/200511/1019240_5.html (accessed 14 November 2009).

——(2005b) 'Nokia introduces the Nokia N91 for a true mobile music experience', 27 April, http://www.nokia.com/press/press-releases/archive/archiveshowpressrelease? newsid=991481 (accessed 14 November 2009).

——(2006) 'Memorable music makes us want to pick up the phone', 14 December, http://www.nokia.com/press/press-releases/showpressrelease?newsid=1093291 (accessed 14 May 2010).

——(2007a) 'Meet Ovi, the door to Nokia's Internet services', 29 August, http:// www.nokia.com/press/press-releases/showpressrelease?newsid=1149749   (accessed 14 May 2010).

——(2007b) 'Nokia and EMI Music announce global marketing and content agreement', 28 March, http://www.nokia.com/press/press-releases/showpressrelease?newsid=1115262 (accessed 14 November 2009).

——(2008a) 'Nokia launches new digital music store in Sweden', 20 May, http:// www.nokia.com/press/press-releases/showpressrelease?newsid=1220925 (accessed 14 November 2009).

——(2008b) 'Nokia to launch "Comes with Music" first in the United Kingdom', 1 September, http://www.nokia.com/press/press-releases/showpressrelease?newsid= 1247823 (accessed 14 November 2009).

——(2008c) 'Nokia Music Store opens in Singapore with millions of songs', 29 April, http://www.nokia.com/press/press-releases/showpressrelease?newsid=1214438 (accessed 14 November 2009).

——(2008d) 'Nokia welcomes Warner Music Group to Comes with Music', 1 July, http://www.nokia.com/press/press-releases/showpressrelease?newsid=1232568 (accessed 14 May 2010).

——(2009a) 'Snake is born: a mobile gaming classic', http://www.nokia.com/about-nokia/ company/story-of-nokia/mobile-revolution/snake-game (accessed 14 November 2009).

——(2009b) 'Starting today, Nokia 5800 Comes With Music is available in the Brazilian market', 29 April, http://www.nokia.com/press/press-releases/showpressrelease?newsid=1309455 (accessed 14 November 2009).

——(2009c) 'N-Gage', *Nokia Conversations*, 26 April, http://conversations.nokia.com/almanac/introducing-nokia-n-gage/ (accessed 14 November 2009).

Nordic Business Report (2002a) 'Sony Ericcson forms mobile gaming partnerships', *Nordic Business Report*, 14 March, 1.

Nova, N. and Girardin, F. (2009) 'Framing issues for the design of location-based games,' in A. de Souza e Silva and D.M. Sutko (eds) *Digital Cityscapes: merging digital and urban playspaces*, New York: Peter Lang, 168–86.

NTT DoCoMo (2009) 'One Seg', http://www.nttdocomo.co.jp/english/service/function/1seg/index.html (accessed 2 December 2009).

Nyre, L. (2008) *Sound Media: from live journalism to music recording*, London and New York: Routledge.

Obadare, E. (2006) 'Playing politics with the mobile phone in Nigeria: civil society, big business and the state', *Review of African Political Economy* 33: 93–111.

Ofcom (2009a) *The Consumer Experience 2009: research report*, London: Ofcom, http://www.ofcom.org.uk/research/tce/ce09/ (accessed 13 December 2009).

——(2009b) *Ofcom Technology Tracker, Q1 2009*, http://www.ofcom.org.uk/research/stats/ (accessed 13 December 2009).

O'Hara, K. (2008) 'Understanding geocaching practices and motivations', *Proceeding of the twenty-sixth annual SIGCHI conference on Human factors in computing systems*, Florence, 1177–86.

O'Hara, K. and Brown, B. (eds) (2006) *Consuming Music Together: social and collaborative aspects of music consumption technologies*, Berlin: Springer.

Oksman, V. (2009) 'Media contents in mobiles: comparing video, audio and text', in G. Goggin and L. Hjorth (eds) *Mobile Technologies: From Telecommunications to Media*, Routledge, New York, 118–30.

Oksman, V., Ollikainen, V., Noppari, E., Herrero, C. and Tammela, A. (2008) '"Podracing": experimenting with mobile TV content consumption and delivery methods', *Multimedia Systems Journal*, 14: 105–14.

Oksman, V., Noppari, E., Tammela, A., Mäkinen, M., and Ollikainen, V. (2007) 'Mobile TV in everyday life contexts – individual entertainment or shared experiences?', in P. Cesar et al., *EuroITV 2007*, Berlin: Springer-Verlag, 215–25.

Olla, P. and Patel, N.V. (2002) 'A value chain model for mobile data service providers', *Telecommunications Policy* 26: 551–71.

One Seg (2009) 'One Seg digital TV on iPhone', http://mb.softbank.jp/mb/iphone_en/oneseg/ (accessed 2 December 2009).

Open Handset Alliance (OHA) (2009a) 'Open Handset Alliance', http://www.openhandsetalliance.com/ (accessed 28 August 2009).

——(2009b) 'Overview', http://www.openhandsetalliance.com/oha_overview.html (accessed 28 August 2009).

Open Mobile Alliance (OMA) (2004) 'Open Mobile Alliance Takes Critical Next Step In Delivering Premium Content to Consumers Via Wireless Media Devices'. Media release, February 2, 2004, http://www.openmobilealliance.org/docs/DRMPressReleaseFinal020104.doc (accessed 25 May 2007).

Openmoko (2008) 'Neo Freerunner', http://wiki.openmoko.org/wiki/Neo_FreeRunner, 26 September (accessed 1 July 2009).

Organization for Economic Co-operation and Development (OECD) (1991) *Universal Service and Rate Restructuring in Telecommunications*, Paris: OECD.

——(2005) *Digital Broadband Content. Mobile Content: new content for new platforms*, Working Party on the Information Economy, Paris: OECD, http://www.oecd.org/dataoecd/19/7/34884388.pdf (accessed 12 December 2009).

——(2006) *Mobile Multiple Play: new service pricing and policy implications*, Paris: OECD, http://www.oecd.org/dataoecd/6/52/37917740.pdf (accessed 14 May 2010).

——(2007) *Participative Web: user-generated content*, Paris: OECD, http://www.oecd.org/dataoecd/57/14/38393115.pdf (accessed 14 May 2010).

——(2008a) *Global Opportunities For Internet Access Developments*, Paris: OECD, http://www.oecd.org/dataoecd/17/53/40596368.pdf (accessed 14 May 2010).

——(2008b) *Information Technology Outlook*, Paris: OECD.

——(2009) *Communications Outlook*, Paris: OECD.

O'Rorke, I. (2000) 'Media 2000 New Media', *Guardian*, 18 December, 26.

Paavilanen, J. (2003) *Mobile Games: creating business with Nokia's N-Gage*, Berkeley, CA: New Rider Games.

Paavilanen, J., and Lamble, S. (2002) *Mobile Business Strategies: understanding the technologies and opportunities*, Boston, MA: Addison-Wesley Longman.

Pagani, M. (2009) 'Roadmapping 3G mobile TV: strategic thinking and scenario planning through repeated cross-impact handling', *Technological Forecasting & Social Change*, 76: 382–95.

Papakonstantinou, S. and Brujic-Okretic, V. (2009) 'Framework for context-aware smartphone applications', *Visual Computer*, 25: 1121–32.

Parikka, J., and Suominen, J. (2006) 'Victorian snakes? towards a cultural history of mobile games and the experience of movement', *Game Studies*, 6.1, http://gamestudies.org/0601/articles/parikka_suominen (accessed 14 May 2010).

Parsons, G. (2006) 'PCAG: London', *ARGNet*, 28 February, http://www.argn.com/2006/02/pcag_london/ (accessed 15 November 2009).

Peitz, M. and Waelbroeck (2006) 'Digital music', in G. Illing and M. Peitz (eds) *Industrial Organization and the Digital Economy*, Cambridge, MA: MIT Press, 71–144.

Pelago (2009a) 'About Pelago', http://www.pelago.com/about/ (accessed 7 December 2009).

——(2009b) 'Our products', http://www.pelago.com/products/ (accessed 7 December 2009).

Pelkonen, T. (2006) 'Mobile games: an emerging content business area', in P.A. Bruck, Z. Karssen, A. Buchholz and A. Zerfass (eds), *E-Content: technologies and perspectives for the European market*, Berlin: Springer,

Perez, B. (2001) 'Swedish giant looks to drive newly formed alliance beyond mobile handset manufacture', *South China Morning Post*, 22 June, 11.

Pertierra, R. (ed.) (2007) *The Social Construction and Usage of Communication Technologies: Asian and European experiences*, Manila: University of the Philippines Press.

Pertierra, R., Ugarte, E.F., Pingol, A., Hernandez, J. and Dacanay, N.L. (2002) *Txt-ing Selves: cellphones and Philippine modernity*, Manila: De La Salle University Press, <http://www.finlandembassy.ph/texting1.htm> (accessed 22 July 2005).

Peters, J.W. (2008) 'Geocaching: the combination of technology and the outdoors', in F. von Borries, S.P. Walz and M. Böttger (eds) *Space Time Play: computer games, architecture and urbanism: the next level*, Basel: Birkhäuser, 222–23.

Peters, S. (2009) 'Perplex City: an alternate reality treasure hunt', in F. von Borries, S. P. Walz and M. Böttger (eds) *Space Time Play: computer games, architecture and urbanism: the next level*, Basel: Birkhäuser, 244–45.

Pirita, I. and Pauliina, T. (2009) 'Understanding 21st century's mobile device-based games within boundaries', in *Breaking New Ground: innovation in games, play, practice and theory*, proceedings of 2009 DiGRA conference, London, Brunel University, September.

Prario, B. (2007) 'Mobile Television in Italy: value chains and business models of telecommunications operators,' *Journal of Media Business Studies*, 4: 1–19.

Pringle, D. (2002) 'Mobile firms tout games – wireless industry pins hopes on improved action graphics to push handset arcades', *Asian Wall Street Journal*, 20 September, A4.

Pupillo, L. M. and Noam, E.M. (2008) *Peer-to-Peer Video: the economics, policy, and culture of today's new mass medium*, Berlin: Springer.

Qiu, J. L. (2009) *Working-Class Network Society: communication technology and the information have-less in urban China*, Cambridge, MA: MIT Press.

Qualcomm (2004) 'QUALCOMM Announces MediaFLO Content Distribution System for Network-Scheduled Delivery of High-Quality Wireless Content Via 3G Networks', media release, 22 March, 2004, http://www.qualcomm.com/press/releases/2004/040322_mediaflo_announce.html (accessed 1 July 2008).

Quico, C. (2003) 'Are communication services the killer applications for Interactive TV? or "I left my wife because I am in love with the TV set"', *Proceedings of European conference on Interactive Television: from viewers to actors?*, Berlin: Springer, 99–107.

Quinn, S. (2009) *Mojo: mobile journalism in the Asian region*, Singapore: Konrad-Adenauer-Stiftung.

Rafael, V. L. (2003) 'The Cell Phone and the Crowd: messianic politics in the contemporary Philippines', *Public Culture*, 15: 399–425.

Rajala, R., Rossi, M., Tuunainen, V. and Vihinen, J. (2005) 'Channel choices and revenue logics of software companies developing mobile games', in T. Saarinen, M. Tinnilä, and A. Tseng (eds), *Managing Business in a Multi-Channel World: success factors for e-business*, Hershey, PA: Ideas Group, 220–34.

Ramnarayan, A. (2009) 'Nokia fights back for share of smartphone market', *Guardian.co.uk*, 2 September, http://www.guardian.co.uk/business/2009/sep/02/nokia-smartphones-apple-iphone-music-mobiles (accessed 4 September 2009).

Rangaswamy, N., Nair, S. and Toyama, K.o (2008) ' "My TV is the family oven/toaster/grill": personalizing TV for the Indian audience', *Proceedings of the 1st international conference on Designing interactive user experiences for TV and video*, Silicon Valley, CA, 19–22.

Rantanen, M. (2007) 'Case geocaching: networks in a mobile content community', in M. Turpeinen and K. Kuikkaniemi (eds) *Mobile Content Communities*, Helsinki: HIIT, 124–36, http://pong.hiit.fi/dcc/publications.html (accessed 11 November 2009).

Ray, B. (2008) 'Reding still pushing Mob-TV', 10 December, http://www.theregister.co.uk/2008/12/10/mob_tv_guidelines/ (accessed 2 December 2009).

Redding V. (2006) 'Television is going mobile – and needs a pan European policy approach', Speech of the European Commissioner for Information Society and Media at the International CeBIT Summit, Hannover, Germany, 8 March 2006, http://europa.eu/press_room/index_en.htm (accessed 14 December 2009).

Research in Motion (RIM) (2007) 'RIM introduces Facebook for Blackberry Smart-phones', 24 October, http://press.rim.com/release.jsp?id=1354 (accessed 14 May 2010).

De Reuvera, M., and Haakerb, T. (2009) 'Designing viable business models for context-aware mobile services', *Telematics and Informatics*, 26: 240–48.

Rheingold, H. (2002) *Smart Mobs: the next social revolution*, Cambridge, MA: Perseus.

Rhodes, S. (2006) *Social Movements and Free-Market Capitalism in Latin America: telecommunications privatization and the rise of consumer protest*, Albany, NY: State University of New York Press.

Robbins, B. (ed.) (1993) *The Phantom Public Sphere*, Minneapolis, MI: University of Minnesota Press.

Rose, F. (2005) 'Battle for the soul of the MP3 Phone', *Wired magazine*, 13.11, November, http://www.wired.com/wired/archive/13.11/phone.html (accessed 14 May 2010).

Rosen, J. (1999) *What are Journalists For?*, New Haven, CT: Yale University Press.

Rosling, T. (2006) 'Debunking myths about the "Third World"', presentation to TED, 22–25 February, Monterey, CA: http://www.gapminder.org/videos/ted-talks/hans-rosling-ted-2006-debunking-myths-about-the-third-world/ (accessed 13 December 2009).

Rugman, A.M. (2005) *The Regional Multinationals: MNEs and 'global' strategic management*, Cambridge: Cambridge University Press.

Rugman, A.M. and Verbeke, A. (2004) 'A perspective on regional and global strategies of multinational enterprises', *Journal of International Business Studies*, 35: 3–18.

Russill, C. (2005) ' "Now back to pragmatism ... ": thinking about publics with Bruno Latour', *The Communication Review* 8, 265–76.

——(2006) 'For a pragmatist perspective on publics: advancing Carey's cultural studies through John Dewey – and Michel Foucault?', in J. Packer and Robertson, C. (eds) *Thinking with James Carey: essays on communication, transportation, history*, New York: Peter Lang.

Salvador, T., Bell, G. and Anderson, K. (1999) 'Design ethnography', *Design Management Journal*, 10: 35–41.

Sandvig, C. (2004) 'An initial assessment of cooperative action in Wi-Fi networking', *Telecommunications Policy*, 28: 579–602.

——(2006) 'Access to the electromagnetic spectrum is a foundation for development', in M. Harvey (ed.) *Media Matters: perspectives on advancing governance and development from the global forum on media development*, Paris: Internews Europe, 50–54.

Satchell, C. (2009) 'From social butterfly to urban citizen: the evolution of mobile phone practice', in M. Foth (ed.) *Handbook of Research on Urban Informatics: the practice and promise of the real-time city*, Hershey, PA: Information Science Reference, 353–65.

Sawhney, H. (1994) 'Universal service: prosaic motives and great ideals', *Journal of Broadcasting & Electronic Media*, 38.4: 375–95.

——(2005) 'Wi-Fi Networks and the re-organization of wireline-wireless relationship', in R. Ling and P.E. Pedersen (eds.), *Mobile Communications: re-negotiation of the social sphere*, London: Springer-Verlag, 2005, 45–61.

——(2009) 'Innovations at the edge: the impact of mobile technologies on the character of the internet', in G. Goggin and L. Hjorth (eds) *Mobile Technologies: from telecommunications to media*, New York: Routledge, 105–17.

Sawhney, H. and Lee, S. (2005) 'Arenas of innovation: understanding new configurational potentialities of communication technologies', *Media, Culture & Society*, 27: 391–414.

Scelsi, C. (2007) 'The iPhone: hacking and cracking and copyright,' *The Entertainment and Sports Lawyer*, 25.3.

Scharl, A. and Tochtermann, K. (eds) (2007) *The Geospatial Web: how geobrowsers, social software and the Web 2.0 are shaping the network society*, London: Springer.

Schatz, R., Jordan, N. and Wagner, S. (2007) 'Beyond broadcast: a hybrid testbed for mobile TV 2.0 services', *Proceedings of ICN '07, Sixth International Conference on Networking*, 22–28 April, Sainte-Luce, Martinique.

Schatz, R., Wagner, S., Egger, S. and Jordan, N. (2007) 'Mobile TV becomes social – integrating content with communications', in *Proceedings of the ITI 2007 Conference*, 25–28 June, Croatia.

Schiffer, M.B. (1991) *The Portable Radio in American Life*, Tucson, AZ: University of Arizona Press.

Schiller, D. (1999) *Digital Capitalism: networking the global market system*, Cambridge, MA: MIT Press.

——(2007) *How to Think about Information*, Urbana, IL: University of Illinois Press.

Schroeder, F. (2008) 'Caressing the skin: mobile devices and bodily engagement', Proceedings of 5th *Mobile Music Workshop '08*, 13–15 May, Vienna, Austria, 26–30.

Schroeder, F. and Rebelo, P. (2006) 'Wearable music in engaging technologies' *AI & Society*, 22: 85–91.

Schuurman, D., De Mareza, L. Veevaetea, P. and Evensa, T. (2009) 'Content and context for mobile television: integrating trial, expert and user findings', *Telematics and Informatics*, 26: 293–305.

Schwankert, S. (2008) 'Softbank eyes world's top mobile internet company', *IDG News Service*, 2 August, http://www.networkworld.com/news/2008/080208-softbank-eyes-worlds-top-mobile.html (accessed 14 May 2010).

Seijdel, J. and Melis, L. (eds) (2008) *The Rise of the Informal Media, Open 13*, Rotterdam: NAI.

Sengupta, S. (2006) 'A letter to the Commons: from the participants of the "Shades of the Commons Workshop"', in L. Bansal, P. Keller and G. Lovink (eds) *In the Shade of the Commons: towards a culture of open networks*, Amsterdam: Waag Society, 19–21.

Shanker, B., Brown, A., MacMillan, D., O'Donovan, P. and Wood, B. (2002) *Games and Entertainment within the Mobile Industry*, Gartner, http://www4.gartner.com/resources/105600/105694/105694.pdf (accessed 26 May 2010).

Shannon, V. (2006) 'The end user: noticing a red flag', *New York Times*, 22 February, http://www.nytimes.com/2006/02/22/technology/22iht-ptend23.html?_r=1 (accessed 14 May 2010).

Sheller, M. (2004) 'Mobile publics: beyond the network perspective.' *Environment and Planning D-Society & Space*, 22: 39–52.

Sheller, M. and Urry, J. (2003) 'Mobile transformations of "public" and "private" life', *Theory, Culture & Society*, 20: 107–25.

Shannon, V. (2001) 'Mobile games mobility', *International Herald Tribune*, 4 July, 11.

Shazam (2009) 'Discover new music on your mobile with Shazam', http://www.shazam.com/music/web/home.html (accessed 15 December 2009).

Shim, J.P., Shin, S. and Weiss, Martin B. H. (2006) 'Digital Multimedia Broadcasting (DMB): Standards, Competition, and Regulation in South Korea,' *Journal of Information Technology Theory and Application*, 8: 69–81.

Shin, D. H. and Bartolacci, M. (2007) 'A study of MVNO diffusion and market structure in the EU, US, Hongkong and Singapore', *Telematics and Informatics*, 24: 86–100.

Shin, D.H., Kim, W.-Y. and Lee, D.-H. (2006) 'A web of stakeholders and strategies in the development of Digital Multimedia Broadcasting (DMB): why and how has DMB been developed in Korea?', *International Journal on Media Management*, 8: 70–83.

Sicker, D.C., Grunwald, D., Anderson, E., Doerr, C., Munsinger, B. and Sheth, A. (2006) 'Examining the wireless commons', paper presented to the 34th Telecommunications Policy Research Conference, George Mason University School of Law, Arlington, VA,

29 September–1 October, http://web.si.umich.edu/tprc/papers/2006/576/proposal. pdf (accessed 10 December 2009).

Sieber, A. and Weck, C. (2004) 'What's the difference between DVB-H and DAB – in the mobile environment', *EBU Technical Review*, 299, http://www.ebu.ch/en/technical/trev/trev_299-weck.pdf (accessed 10 December 2009)

Siegler, M.G. (2009) 'Aiming to "make meaning," Jaiku co-founder leaves Google', 12 October, http://www.techcrunch.com/2009/10/12/aiming-to-make-meaning-jaiku-co-founder-leaves-google/ (accessed 8 December 2009).

Siitonen, Marko (2003) 'Building and experiencing community in internet-based multi-player computer games', paper given at the National Communication Association, Miami Beach, http://www.cc.jyu.fi/~marsiit/BuildingandExperiencingCommunity.pdf (accessed 13 November 2009).

Skiöld, D. (2006) 'An economic analysis of DAB and DVB-H', *EBU Technical Review*, 305, http://www.ebu.ch/fr/technical/trev/trev_305-skiold.pdf (accessed 14 December 2009).

SMS Sugarman (2008) 'SMS Sugarman', http://www.smssugarman.com/home_page. html (accessed 30 June 2008).

Södergard, C. (2003) *Mobile Television — Technology and User Experiences: Report on the Mobile-TV project*, VTT Technical Research Centre of Finland, Vuorimiehentie, http://www. vtt.fi/inf/pdf/publications/2003/P506.pdf (accessed 25 May 2010)

Sorrel, C. (2009) 'Cellphone makers bet big on apps stores', *wired.com*, http://www.wired. com/gadgetlab/2009/02/does-everybody/ (accessed 14 May 2010).

Sotamaa, O. (2002) 'All the world's a botfighter stage: notes on location-based multi-user gaming', in F. Mäyrä (ed.) *Proceedings of Computer Games and Digital Cultures Conference*, Tampere: Tampere University Press, 35–44.

De Souza e Silva, A. (2006) 'From cyber to hybrid: mobile technologies as interfaces of hybrid spaces', *Space & Culture*, 9: 261–78.

——(2009) 'Hybrid reality and location-based gaming: redefining mobility and game spaces in urban environments', *Simulation & Gaming*, 40.3: 404–24.

De Souza e Silva, A. and Hjorth, L. (2009) 'Playful urban spaces', *Simulation & Gaming*, 40: 602–25.

Spigel, L. (2001) 'Media homes', *International Journal of Cultural Studies*, 4: 385–411.

Spring, M., Brown, D. and Marko, P. (1993) 'Telephone ring mute with auto re-enable', *Motorola Technical Developments*, 19 June, 117.

Spurgeon, C. and Goggin, G. (2007) 'Mobiles into media: premium rate SMS and the adaptation of television to interactive communication cultures', *Continuum*, 21: 317–29.

Stafford, G. (2002) 'Feedback – MIDI tones', *Guardian*, 17 January, 2.

Steen, H.U. (2009) 'Technology convergence, market divergence: fragmentation of standards in mobile digital broadcasting carriers', *Information Systems and e-Business Management*, 7: 319–45.

Steinbock, D. (2003) *Wireless Horizon: strategy and competition in the worldwide mobile marketplace*, New York: American Management Association.

——(2005) *Mobile Marketing: the making of mobile services worldwide*, London: Kogan Page.

Stenbacka, B. (2008) 'The impact of the brand in the success of a mobile game: comparative analysis of three mobile J2ME racing games', *Computers in Entertainment*, 5.4, article no. 6.

Stites, T. (2006) 'Someone to watch over me (on a Google map)', *New York Times*, 9 July, http://www.nytimes.com/2006/07/09/fashion/sundaystyles/09love.html (accessed 26 May 2010).

Stross, R. (2007) 'Want an iPhone?: beware the handcuffs', *New York Times*, 14 January, http://www.nytimes.com/2007/01/14/business/yourmoney/14digi.html (accessed 14 May 2010).

Struppek, M. and Willis, K.S. (2008) 'Botfighters: a game that surrounds you', in F. von Borries, S.P. Walz and M. Böttger (eds) *Space Time Play: computer games, architecture and urbanism: the next level*, Basel: Birkhäuser, 226–27.

Stuart, K. (2009) 'Rockstar smashes iPhone: GTA and Beaterator to arrive on App Store … ', Games Blog, 1 September,http://www.guardian.co.uk/technology/gamesblog/2009/sep/01/games-iphone (accessed 4 September 2009).

Sullivan, J. (2008) 'Why free software and Apple's iPhone don't mix', 30 July, http://www.fsf.org/blogs/community/why-free-software-and-apples-iphone-dont-mix (accessed 31 August 2009).

Sullivan, N.P. (2007), *Can You Hear Me Now? how microloans and cell phones are connecting the world's poor to the global economy*, San Francisco, CA: Jossey-Bass.

Suominen, J. (2008) 'The past as the future? Nostalgia and retrogaming in digital culture', *Fibreculture Journal*, 11, http://journal.fibreculture.org/issue11/issue11_suominen.html (accessed 14 May 2010).

Sutherland, E. (2008) 'Counting mobile phones, SIM cards & customers', Link Centre, http://www.itu.int/ITU-D/ict/statistics/material/sutherland-mobile-numbers.pdf (accessed 14 May 2010).

Tacchi, J. and Grubb, B. (2007) 'The case of the e-tuktuk', *Media International Australia*, 125: 71–82.

Takeishi, A and Lee, K.J. (2005) 'Mobile music business in Japan and Korea: copyright management institutions as a reverse', *Journal of Strategic Information Systems*, 14: 291–306.

Tanaka, A. (2003) 'Composing as a function of infrastructure', in K. Ehrlich and B. LaBelle (eds) *Surface Tension: problematics of site*, Los Angeles, CA: Errant Bodies Press.

——(2006) 'Interaction, agency, experience, and the future of music', in K. O'Hara and B. Brown (eds) *Consuming Music Together: social and collaborative aspects of music consumption technologies*, Dordrecht: Springer, 267–88.

Tanaka, A. and Gemeinboeck, P. (2009) 'Net_ Dérive: conceiving and producing a locative media artwork', in G. Goggin and L. Hjorth (eds) *Mobile Technologies: From Telecommunications to Media*, New York: Routledge, 174–86.

Tanaka, A., Valadon, G. and Berger, C. (2007) 'Social music navigation using the compass', *Proceedings of 4th International Mobile Music Workshop*, May 6–8, 2007, Amsterdam, The Netherlands.

Tanaka, Y. (2009) 'Japan's mixi has launched its OpenSocial Container for all users!', *Open Social Blog*, 17 September, http://blog.opensocial.org/2009/09/japans-mixi-has-launched-its-opensocial.html (accessed 8 December 2009).

Taylor, C. (2004) *Modern social imaginaries*, Durham, NC: Duke University Press.

Telmex (2009) *Informe Annual*, http://www.telmex.com/ (accessed 15 July 2010).

Terdiman, D. (2005) 'MoSoSos not so so-so', *Wired News*, 8 March, http://www.wired.com/culture/lifestyle/news/2005/03/66813 (accessed 8 December 2009).

The Australian (2008) 'Extras in iPhone queue', *The Australian*, 26 August, 37.

Thomas, S. (2006) 'Pervasive learning games: exploration of hybrid educational gamescapes', *Simulation & Gaming*, 37: 41–55.

Thom-Santelli, J. (2007) 'Mobile social software: Facilitating serendipity or encouraging homogeneity?,' *IEEE Pervasive Computing* 6: 46–51.

Tilson, D., Lyytinen, K.J., Sørensen, C. and Liebenau, J. (2006) 'Coordination of technology and diverse organizational actors during service innovation – the case of wireless data services in the United Kingdom', paper presented to *Helsinki Mobility Roundtable*, 1–2 Jun 2006, Helsinki, Finland, http://project.hkkk.fi/helsinkimobility/submissions.htm (accessed 3 December 2009).

Ting, C., Wildman, S.S. and Bauer, J.M. (2005) 'Comparing welfare for spectrum property and spectrum commons governance regimes', *Telecommunications Policy*, 29: 711–30.

Townsend, A. (2000) 'Life in the real-time city: mobile telephones and urban metabolism', *Journal of Urban Technology*, 7: 85–104.

——(2006) 'Locative-media artists in the contested-aware city,' *Leonardo Electronic Almanac* 39(4): 345–47.

Trueman, P. (2001) 'Confound fellow commuters with an offbeat ring tone', *Guardian*, 1 March, 4.

Turner, V. (1982) *From Ritual to Theatre: the human seriousness of play*, New York: Performing Arts Journal Publications.

Tuters, M. (2004) 'The locative commons: situating location-based media in urban public space,' *Futuresonic 2004*, http://www.futuresonic.com/futuresonic/pdf/Locative_Commons.pdf (accessed 28 November 2009).

Tuters, M. and Varnelis, K. (2006) 'Beyond locative media: Giving shape to the internet of things' *Leonardo Electronic Almanac* 39: 357–63.

Tuulos, V.H., Scheible, J. and Nyholm, H. (2007) 'Combining web, mobile phones and public displays in large-scale: Manhattan story mashup' in A. LaMarca, M. Langheinrich and K.N. Trong (eds) *Proceedings of Pervasive 2007: 5th International Conference on Pervasive Computing*, 13–16 May, Toronto, 37–54, Berlin: Springer.

Twitter (2009) 'About Twitter', http://twitter.com/about#about (accessed 15 January 2009).

Tyler, M.F. (1884) 'The legal history of the telephone', *Journal of Social Science*, 18, May, 163–77.

Tyler, T. (2008) 'A procrustean probe', *Game Studies*, 8.2, http://gamestudies.org/0802/articles/tyler (accessed 14 May 2010).

Urban, A. (2008) 'Mobile television: is it just a hype or a real consumer need?', in J. Pierson, E. Mante-Meijer, E. Loos & B. Sapio (eds) *Innovating for and by Users*, Brussels: COST Action 298, pp. 27–38.

Urry, J. (2007) *Mobilities*, Cambridge: Polity.

Vangenck M., Jacobs A., Lievens B., Vanhengel E. and Pierson J. (2008) 'Does mobile television challenge the dimension of viewing television? An explorative research on time, place and social context of the use of mobile television content', paper presented to the EuroITV 2008 Conference, July 3–4, Salzburg, Austria.

Varnelis, K. et al. (eds) (2008) *Networked Publics*, Cambridge, MA: MIT Press.

Vincent, J. (2004) 'Incorporating social shaping into technology planning for 3G/UMTS 2004', *Proceedings of IEE Fifth International Conference on Mobile Communication Technologies*.

Vedder, K. (2001) 'The Subscriber Identity Module: past, present, and future', in F. Hillebrand (ed.) *GSM and UMTS: the creation of global mobile communication*, New York: John Wiley, 341–370.

Vlachos, P., Vrechopoulos, A.P. and Doukidis, G. (2003) 'Exploring consumer attitudes towards mobile music services', *International Journal on Media Management*, 5: 138–48.

Vlachos, P., Vrechopoulos, A.P. and Patelli, A. (2006) 'Drawing emerging business models for the mobile music industry', *Electronic Markets*, 16: 154–68.

Vogelstein, F. (2008) 'The untold story: how the iPhone blew up the wireless industry', *Wired magazine*, 16 February, http://www.wired.com/gadgets/wireless/magazine/16–02/ff_iphone (accessed 1 December 2008).

Vogiazou, Y., Raijmakers, B., Geelhoed, E., Reid, J. and Eisenstadt, M. (2006) 'Design for emergence: experiments with a mixed reality urban playground game,' *Personal and Ubiquitous Computing* 11: 45–58.

Walton, M. and Donner, J. (2009) 'Read-write-erase: mobile mediated publics in South African's 2009 elections', paper given to *Mobiles and Social Policy* conference, Center for Mobile Communication Studies, Rutgers University, New Brunswick, NJ, 9–11 October.

Wang, G., Essl, G. and Penttinen, H. (2008) 'Do mobile phones dream of electric orchestras?', *International Computer Music Conference (ICMC) 2008*, 24–29 August, Belfast, http://mopho.stanford.edu/publish/mopho_icmc2008.pdf (accessed 28 November 2009).

Wang, J. (2005) 'Youth culture, music, and cell phone branding in China', *Global Media and Communication*, 1: 185–201.

——(2008) *Brand New China: advertising, media, and commercial culture*, Cambridge, MA: Harvard University Press.

Ward, M. (2007) 'Mobile TV warned to standardise', *BBC News*, 16 March, http://news.bbc.co.uk/2/hi/technology/6459161.stm (accessed 2 December 2009).

Warner, M. (2005) *Publics and Counterpublics*, New York: Zone Books; London: MIT Press.

Watkins, J. and Tacchi, J. (eds) (2008) *Participatory Content Creation for Development: principles and practices*. New Delhi: UNESCO New Delhi.

Weber, I. and Jia, L. (2007) 'Internet and self-regulation in China: the cultural logic of controlled commodification', *Media, Culture & Society*, 29: 772–89.

Weck, C. and Wilson, E. (2006) 'Broadcasting to handhelds: An overview of systems and services' *EBU Technological Review*, 305, http://www.ebu.ch/en/technical/trev/trev_305-wilson.pdf (accessed 13 December 2009).

Wei, R., Xiaoming, H. and Pan, J. (2006) 'Lifestyles and new media: Adoption and use of wireless communication technologies in China', *New Media and Society*, 8: 991–1008.

——(2010) 'Examining user behavioral response to SMS ads: implications for the evolution of the mobile phone as a bona-fide medium', *Telematics and Informatics*, 27: 32–41.

Werbach, K. (2004) 'Supercommons: towards a unified theory of wireless communication', *Texas Law Review*, 82: 863–972.

Wetzel, R., Waern, A., Jonsson, S., Lindt, I., Ljungstrand, P. and Åkesson, K.-P. (2009) 'Boxed pervasive games: an experience with user-created pervasive games', in H. Tokuda et al. (eds) *Pervasive 2009*, Berlin: Springer, 220–37.

Whalley, J. and Curwen, P. (2006) 'Third generation new entrants in the European mobile telecommunications industry', *Telecommunications Policy*, 30: 622–32.

Wikipedia (2009) 'Ringtones', 2 September, http://en.wikipedia.org/w/index.php?title=Ringtone&oldid=311381785 (accessed 4 December 2009).

——'Snake (video game)', *Wikipedia*, 12 November, http://en.wikipedia.org/w/index.php?title=Snake_(video_game)&oldid=325460089 (accessed 4 December 2009).

——'SMS.ac', *Wikipedia*, http://en.wikipedia.org/w/index.php?title=SMS.ac,_Inc.&oldid=309254563 (accessed 8 December 2009).

——(2009) 'Spaceball (game)', *Wikipedia*, 3 November, http://en.wikipedia.org/w/index.php?title=SpaceBall_(game)&oldid=323668697 (accessed 1 December 2009)

Wilken, R. and Sinclair, J. (2009a) 'Contests of power and place in mobile media advertising', *Australian Journal of Communication*, 36: 85–109.

——(2009b) ' "Waiting for the kiss of life": mobile media and advertising', *Convergence*, 15: 427–45.

Williams, D. (2002) 'Structure and competition in the U.S. home video game industry', *International Journal on Media Management*, 4: 41–54.

Williams, D.M.L. (2006) 'Co-design, China, and the commercialization of the mobile user interface', *Interactions*, 13: 36–41.

Willis, K., Roussos, G., Chorianopoulos, K. and Struppek, M. (eds) (2010) *Shared Encounters*, Berlin: Springer.

Winseck, D. (1998) *Reconvergence: a political economy of telecommunications in Canada*, Creskill, NJ: Hampton Press.

Wirzenius, A. (2008) 'Telecommunications universal service in Finland', *info*, 10: 107–20.

Wolf, M.J.P. (ed.) (2007) *The Video Game Explosion: a history from PONG to playStation and beyond*, Westport, CT: Greenwood.

World Web Web Consortium (W3C) (2005) 'W3C launches "mobile web initiative" ', http://www.w3.org/2005/05/mwi-pressrelease (accessed 28 October 2009).

Wu, X. and Zhang, W. (2009) 'Business model innovations in China: from a value network perspective', paper given to *US/China Business Cooperation in the 21st Century: Opportunities and Challenges for Enterpreneurs*, Indiana University, Indiana, 15–17 April, 2009, http://www.indiana.edu/~rccpb/uschinacooperation/papers/P8%20Wu %20Xiaobo.pdf (accessed 12 December 2009).

Xing, W. (2009) ' "Shanzhai" culture now in crosshairs', *China Daily*, 18 May, http://www. chinadaily.com.cn/bw/2009–05/18/content_7785393.htm (accessed 12 December 2009).

Xu, X., MaWill, W.K. and See-To, E.W.K. (2008) 'Will mobile video become the killer application for 3G mobile internet? a model of media convergence acceptance', *Information Systems Frontiers*, DOI: 10.1007/s10796-008-9139-7.

Yamakami, T. (2006) 'Lessons in business model development from early mobile internet services in Japan', *Mobile Business 2006*, 26–27 June 2006.

——(2009) 'Sub-culture-driven Mobile Internet Business Models,' *Proceedings of 2009 8th International Conference on Mobile Business*, 27–28 June, Dalian, China, 76–81.

Yu, H. (2004) 'The power of thumbs: the politics of SMS in urban China', *Graduate journal of Asia-Pacific studies*, 2: 30–43.

Yu, J. and Tan, K.H. (2005) 'The evolution of China's mobile telecommunications industry: past, present and future', *International Journal of Mobile Communications*, 3: 114–26.

——(2006) 'Attempts for radical innovation in the big emerging countries: the case of China', *International Journal of Technology, Policy, and Management*, 6: 183–89.

Yuan, L. and Buckman, R. (2006) 'Social networking goes mobile: MySpace, Facebook strike deals with cell companies', *Wall Street Journal*, 4 April, D1

Zdziarski, J.A. (2008) *iPhone: open application development*, 2nd ed. Sebastopol, CA: O'Reilly.

Zhao, Y. (2007) 'After mobile phones, what? Re-embedding the social in China's "Digital Revolution"', *International Journal of Communication*, 1: 92–120.

——(2008) *Communication in China: political economy, power, and conflict*, Lanham, MD: Rowman & Littlefield.

Zhipei, J. et al. (2009) 'Forum on trends: jurisprudential and sociological review of copycat culture', *China Law*, 76: 94–98.

Zittrain, J. (2008) *The Future of the Internet – and how to stop it*, New Haven, CT: Yale University Press.

Ziv, N. D. (2005) 'Toward a new paradigm of innovation on the mobile platform: redefining the roles of content providers, technology companies, and users', Paper given to the *Mobile Business Management* conference, http://web2.poly.edu/management/_doc/nina/zivn_paradigm2.pdf (accessed 14 May 2010).

——(2008) 'Exploring convergence and innovation on the mobile platform: mobile social media services as a case in point,' *Proceedings of 7th International Conference on Mobile Business*, 126–33.

Zuckerberg, M. (2009) '300 million and on', 16 September, *Facebook, blog*, http://blog.facebook.com/blog.php?post=136782277130 (accessed 14 May 2010).

Index